MOMENT *of* GLORY

THE YEAR UNDERDOGS RULED GOLF

JOHN FEINSTEIN

BACK BAY BOOKS

Little, Brown and Company

New York Boston London

Back Bay Books / Little, Brown and Company
Hachette Book Group
237 Park Avenue, New York, NY 10017
www.hachettebookgroup.com

Originally published in hardcover by Little, Brown and Company, May 2010
First Back Bay paperback edition, May 2011

Back Bay Books is an imprint of Little, Brown and Company. The Back Bay Books name and logo are trademarks of Hachette Book Group, Inc.

The publisher is not responsible for websites (or their content) that are not owned by the publisher.

Library of Congress Cataloging-in-Publication Data
Feinstein, John.
   Moment of glory : the year underdogs ruled golf / John Feinstein.
       p. cm.
   Includes index.
   ISBN 978-0-316-02531-7(hc) / 978-0-316-02532-4 (pb)
   1. Golf.   2. Golfers.   I. Title.
   GV965.F43 2010
   796.352 — dc22   2010007069

10 9 8 7 6 5 4 3 2 1

RRD-C

Printed in the United States of America

Praise for John Feinstein's
MOMENT *of* GLORY

"John Feinstein's golf books have succeeded in giving equal billing to headliners and journeymen....Feinstein's genius is his ability to peel back several layers on the personalities involved, reminding you in the process that even the most obscure players have a story worth telling."
— Sam Weinman, *Golf Digest*

"With unprecedented access, Feinstein provides readers with a true behind-the-scenes look at the 2003 major championships....A quite enjoyable book. If you're a true fan of the game—young or old—*Moment of Glory* is a book that's certainly worth reading."
— Michael Fitzpatrick, CBSSports.com

"It may seem odd that a bestselling writer would write a golf book about four players, none of them Tiger Woods. If anybody can do it and move a lot of product, John Feinstein is the guy....Because the author has been close to the tour players for years, he had excellent access to all of the winners about whom he wrote, and, in some cases, access to their families as well....Feinstein certainly knows his territory, and he's adept at making us feel sorry for a guy who scales the heights of his profession, only to drop down to number 125 on the tour."
— Bill Littlefield, National Public Radio's *Only a Game*

"*Moment of Glory* tells the story of those victories and the aftermath for the winners and the losers."   — Reid Cherner, *USA Today*

"John Feinstein assays the burdensome weights on and off the course that attend both winning and...just falling short."
— Jeff Silverman, Golf.com

"Fascinating....Feinstein's work, like that of the best American sportswriters, is richly detailed and emotionally articulate."
— David Goldblatt, *Guardian*

"It's a compelling story, very well researched....Feinstein paints a very personal picture of the obstacles players on the tour have to overcome....Feinstein has crafted a great page-turner."
— Steve Leventhal, *Chicago Now*

"With *Moment of Glory*, Feinstein has added another top-notch work to his oeuvre."   — GolfBlogger.com

ALSO BY JOHN FEINSTEIN

To the memory of Patty Conway,
who was loved by many but none more than Brigid,
who will always think of her when she hits
it past the big kids

Contents

MOMENT
of GLORY

Introduction

Early in the evening of June 15, 2002, Butch Harmon stood on the driving range at Bethpage State Park waiting for his star pupil to arrive. It was already 7:30 and there was barely an hour of daylight left, but Harmon knew his day wasn't close to being over.

This "range" wasn't actually a range. It was part of Bethpage's Green Course—one of the five golf courses that make up the massive park—but for the week of the 2002 United States Open, which was being conducted on the park's famed Black Course, it was serving as the driving range. The real driving range, located on the other side of the parking lot, was being used to house structures like the media tent, and, given that it was normally covered by mats for players to hit off of, it hardly would have been suitable for the world's best—and most pampered—golfers.

There was no doubt that Harmon's pupil, one Eldrick Tiger Woods, would be more than happy to be hitting golf balls a parking lot away from where the media worked rather than right next to them. At that moment, though, where the range was located wasn't Harmon's concern.

He knew that once Woods finished his obligations in the media tent, he would cross the parking lot and walk onto the range in a sour mood.

"When he starts to get the club inside a little too much, he sometimes gets caught coming down," he said, the techno-talk of a swing coach coming to him easily after a lifetime of teaching. "When that happens, it's fairly simple to get him out of it, but that's not always good enough. One of the things that makes him great is that fixing a mistake isn't good enough. He wants to fix it *and* improve on what he's been doing, often all at the same time. Even for him that's not easy. But it's what he expects of himself and what he always wanted from me."

Woods had just completed his third round of the Open. He had shot an even-par 70, not a spectacular round but a solid one on a brutally tough golf course. He had started the day with a three-shot lead on Padraig Harrington and had ended it with a four-shot lead on Sergio Garcia. A four-shot lead with 18 holes to play in a major championship would send most players home with a smile on their face and a dream of kissing the trophy the next day.

If anyone should have felt good about a four-shot lead—or any lead—with one day left in a major, it was Woods. At the age of twenty-six, he had already won seven major titles, including an extraordinary stretch during which he had won four in a row. Seven times he had led a major after 54 holes, and seven times he had been the winner a day later. There was absolutely no reason to believe that his eighth such lead would be unlucky.

Woods didn't see it quite that way. All he knew as he and his omnipresent caddy, Steve Williams, walked onto the empty range that evening was that he wasn't comfortable with his swing, and he had less than an hour of daylight to figure out exactly what the problem might be. He and Harmon had worked together since Woods's days as a teenage phenom, so Harmon knew exactly what he was dealing with when the grim-faced Woods strode onto the range to the cheers of several hundred people who had packed the grandstand once they spotted Harmon. Golf fans knew that if Butch was on the range, Tiger was likely to be there shortly.

"I'm getting stuck again," Woods said as he walked up to Harmon.

Woods isn't one for small talk, especially during a major. There was no chatting about how the day had gone or any discussion of the lead or about playing the next day with Garcia. The two men were focused on one thing: Woods's golf swing.

"I know you are," Harmon said. "Let's get it fixed."

They went to work, Woods hitting shots, Harmon, arms folded, standing opposite him, watching. Every once in a while, Harmon would stand next to Woods and show him the kind of motion he wanted him to make. Woods would nod and hit more balls.

Even though the sun wouldn't set until 8:30, Woods and Harmon knew they were rapidly running out of time. The sun dropped in the western sky, and the air began to cool. Woods kept hitting ball after ball; Harmon kept watching and talking.

It was dark when they finally stopped. Harmon liked what he was seeing. "By the time we finished, he had it exactly where we wanted it to be," Harmon said. "Even so, I could tell he wasn't happy."

It is that perfectionist nature that is part of Woods's greatness. Every time he wins a major title, he celebrates for about fifteen minutes and then turns his mind to the next one. At that moment, he wasn't just thinking about winning the U.S. Open the next day, he was thinking about winning all four majors in the same year.

He had already won the Masters in April, and he was now 18 holes away from winning the Open for the second time in three years. But he wasn't especially happy with his golf swing. Harmon knew that.

"He always wants to tinker," he said. "If I say to him, 'I like what I'm seeing; that's fine,' that's not what he really wants to hear. He wants me to tell him something—anything—that's going to make him feel better about his swing.

"That day at Bethpage, I knew what was going on. It wasn't just that his swing hadn't been great that day. It wasn't bad, just not great. But he had been talking to [Mark] O'Meara and Hank [Haney] about Hank's swing theories. I got that. I know how close he and Mark are and how much he respects Mark. But I could tell he wanted to make some swing changes. I wasn't going to give him some kind of new move just to tell him something. His golf swing was good — hell, he was about to win his eighth major title and his second in a row. Why would I tell him to change *that?*"

As Woods walked to his car, followed by Williams and his security retinue, Harmon watched him. It occurred to him at that moment that he might not be Woods's teacher for very much longer.

WOODS WON THE OPEN the next day by three shots over Phil Mickelson. The only thing that could have stopped him was darkness. A rain delay kept him on the golf course until dusk, and it looked as if he might not finish until Monday morning. But, with a comfortable three-shot lead, he eagerly played the 18th hole, even in terrible light, so he could take the trophy home with him that night.

Four weeks later, Woods arrived at Muirfield, which is located outside Edinburgh in Scotland, to begin preparing for the British Open. As always, Harmon was waiting for him, ready to go through their normal premajor ritual: spend some time on the range, then walk with Woods around the golf course as he played his practice rounds. This is standard procedure for most teachers and their pupils.

When Woods spotted Harmon waiting for him on the range at Muirfield, he walked over, and the two men shook hands.

"Look, Butch. I'm okay this week," Woods said quietly. "I've got it."

Harmon understood exactly what Woods was saying, but he wanted to be sure.

"You don't need me out here," he said, making it more a statement than a question.

"No, I don't. Thanks."

"Good luck, Tiger."

"Thanks."

That was it. Eight years after they first began working together—eight major championship victories later—Woods, in a matter of about thirty seconds, had fired Harmon. Woods walked to a spot on the range that had been cleared for him to start hitting balls—without Harmon watching him.

Within forty-eight hours, the story was out that Woods and Harmon had split. That Saturday, playing in gale-like conditions, Woods shot 81 and blew himself out of contention. Within months, he would turn to Hank Haney as his new teacher and make over his golf swing.

Prior to splitting with Harmon, Woods had won seven of the previous eleven majors in which he had played. He would not win any of the next ten and would be a nonfactor in most of them. His absence at the top of the leaderboards in the majors changed the lives of many golfers because it gave them a chance—in many cases, a once-in-a-lifetime chance—to win a major championship.

During that ten-tournament stretch, seven players won their first major title. Since Woods began winning majors again at the start of 2005 when he won the Masters for the fourth time in his career, he has won six more of the golf tournaments that matter most. Of the seven players who won a first major during his "slump," only one—Phil Mickelson—has won another. Mickelson has now won three.

It was Mickelson who best described what the absence of Woods on a major leaderboard means to other players. Tied for the lead after 54 holes at the Masters in 2004, he was asked how he felt knowing that Woods was nine shots behind and, realistically, not in contention. Usually players answer such a question by saying something like, "You aren't just playing one player, you're playing the whole field. Your real competition is always the golf course."

Mickelson did none of that. Instead he shook his head, smiled, and said, "It doesn't suck."

Woods seriously contended twice during his drought. At the 2002 PGA Championship, before the remaking of his swing had really started, he chased Rich Beem to the finish line, making birdies on the final four holes on Sunday, only to fall two shots short and finish second. At the 2003 British Open he was one of a number of big names, including Vijay Singh and Davis Love III, who had a chance to win coming down the stretch. All of the big names came undone over the last few holes, opening the door for Ben Curtis to win the championship.

Yes, *that* Ben Curtis.

When he arrived at the British Open that year, Ben Curtis was a rookie on the PGA Tour and had played in a total of thirteen tournaments. He had qualified for the British Open because the Royal and Ancient Golf Club, which administers the Open, had agreed to exempt the top eight finishers at the Western Open who weren't already qualified for the championship. The Open did this to get more players from the PGA Tour to make the trip; few American golfers were willing to fly over the Atlantic Ocean, stay in a tiny bed-and-breakfast, play a 36-hole qualifier, fail, and then fly home if they didn't make the field.

Curtis had shot a four-under-par 68 on the last day of the Western to finish tied for 13th—his best finish on tour up until that point—to become one of the eight to make the British Open field. He was thrilled, and he and his fiancée, Candace Beatty, flew to England four days later. On the night before the championship began, Ben and Candace were eating dinner at a house rented for the week by the International Management Group (IMG), the management company that represented Curtis.

Curtis looked up from his food and saw Mike Weir, who had won the Masters a few months earlier, sitting down across from him with a plate of food. He introduced himself to Weir, introduced Candace, and congratulated Weir on his remarkable win at Augusta.

"Oh, thanks very much," Weir said. "So, what brings you guys over here? Did you come for the tournament?"

Curtis smiled sheepishly. "Well, actually, I'm playing in it," he said.

Weir was embarrassed. "Oh God, I'm so sorry," he said. "I didn't know…"

"Don't be sorry," Curtis answered. "I'm just a rookie. Why should you know?"

Later, Weir would laugh when he retold the story. "I had no idea who he was," he said. "Four days later, he was the British Open champion."

Four days later, Curtis's life changed forever, just as Weir's had — even though most golfers already knew Weir was a golfer — when he won the Masters.

The same thing would happen to Shaun Micheel when he won the PGA Championship in August, the first victory of his career, almost ten years after he had first qualified to play on tour. Even Jim Furyk, that year's U.S. Open champion, established as one of the best players on tour, admits that his life was different after winning the Open.

"Most of it was good," he said. "Certainly it was good financially. But I've always liked the fact that most of the time I can fly under the radar and let guys like Tiger and Phil and Vijay and Sergio be the stars. You become a U.S. Open champion, you become the number two player in the world, you can't really do that anymore."

The four major champions in 2003 were Weir at the Masters, Furyk at the U.S. Open, Curtis at the British Open, and Micheel at the PGA Championship. None of them had ever won a major before, and in fact only Furyk had finished in the *top 10* in a major. Curtis and Micheel had never won on tour prior to their victories. On the same July weekend in 2002, Curtis had been playing on the Hooters Tour, which isn't just one level below the PGA Tour but two.

Perhaps just as startling, none of the four has won another major title since his breakthrough moment. Furyk has contended on several occasions — missing playoffs at the U.S. Open by one shot in both 2006 and 2007 — and Curtis made a run at the PGA Championship in 2008. Weir finished in a tie for third behind Furyk at Olympia Fields and was three shots behind Micheel and Chad Campbell after 54 holes at that year's PGA. Micheel finished second to Woods in the 2006 PGA but was five shots behind him as Woods cruised to an easy win. Micheel hasn't been in the top 20 in any of the other majors he has played in since his victory at Oak Hill.

Life doesn't just change when you win a major; it also changes when you come agonizingly close and don't win. Len Mattiace, who lost the 2003 Masters to Weir in a playoff, tore up both his knees on a skiing trip later that year and has not been the same player since. He is no longer a fully exempt player on tour and ended 2008 playing in South Africa, searching for his game. He played all of 2009 on the Nationwide Tour, hoping that would be his ticket back to fully exempt status on the PGA Tour. When the 2003 Masters comes up, he admits that, even now, it is difficult to talk about. "It's still raw," he said five years later. "There's a lot inside me I still haven't purged."

Furyk beat Stephen Leaney, a young Australian who had been trying to play his way onto the PGA Tour for several years, for his big win at Olympia Fields Country Club. Leaney's life also changed as a result of his runner-up finish, because it allowed him to move to the United States and play on the world's most lucrative golf tour. He played well enough to remain exempt through 2008 but never finished as high as second again. In 2008 he struggled with what doctors finally became convinced was vertigo due to an inner ear infection, and began 2009 with a partial exemption because he had been sick with that long-undiagnosed case of vertigo the previous year.

Thomas Bjorn was the runner-up when Curtis won. Bjorn had been one of the most successful players on the European Tour heading into that year's Open Championship (as the British Open is called everywhere in the world except the United States), and it seemed to be only a matter of time before he won a major.

But after taking three shots to get out of a bunker on the par-three 16th hole on Sunday to lose the lead, Bjorn finished second to Curtis. He did contend again at the 2005 PGA, but his career has not been the same since the near miss at Royal St. George's. Six years later, he still couldn't bring himself to talk about what had happened in that bunker. He wouldn't even answer questions by e-mail. Other players on the European Tour told stories about Bjorn "seeing demons" whenever he walked into a bunker.

Among the 2003 runners-up, the one who has been the most successful is Chad Campbell, who finished second to Micheel at the PGA. He still hasn't won a major, but he's won four times on tour, been on three Ryder Cup teams, and finished 24th on the 2008 money list. Just prior to the PGA in 2003, Campbell was chosen by his fellow pros as the next player likely to win his first major in a survey done by *Sports Illustrated*.

He came agonizingly close again at the Masters in April 2009, losing in a three-way playoff that included Kenny Perry and Angel Cabrera, the eventual winner. Still only thirty-four, he remains convinced his time to win a major will come. And yet, it is worth noting that Arnold Palmer and Tom Watson won their *last* majors at age thirty-four.

"It's one of those things where you have to play well *and* get a little bit lucky," he said. "I've been close a couple times but haven't quite gotten there yet. I still believe I will."

Of course, there's no way to know if it will ever happen for Campbell. It never did for Colin Montgomerie, Europe's best player for more than a decade but never a major champion, although he came up just short several times, twice losing play-offs, and finishing second on two other occasions. Perry has now lost two majors—the 1996 PGA and the 2009 Masters—when a par on the final hole would have made him a winner.

I FIRST THOUGHT ABOUT writing a book like this one in 1990, as I watched Mike Donald and Hale Irwin play off for the U.S. Open title at Medinah. Irwin was already a two-time Open champion, a future Hall of Famer who would end up winning twenty times on the PGA Tour and another forty-five times on the Champions Senior Tour. Winning was important to him, but it wasn't going to be life-changing.

Donald was having the week of his life. He was the quintessential "journeyman" pro, really a misnomer if you think about it, since *journeyman* implies "mediocre," and anyone who stays on the PGA Tour for almost twenty years (Donald played in 548 tournaments) has to be an excellent player. Donald won once on tour during his career. Winning the Open would have left him set for life financially and in the golf world. Once the words "U.S. Open champion" come before your name, there's no door that isn't open to you in golf and, for the most part, in the world.

Irwin ended up winning the playoff in sudden death, after Donald, who had led by a shot going to the 18th, made bogey and gave Irwin the chance to birdie the first hole of sudden death and win.

Two years later, Irwin was voted into the World Golf Hall of Fame. Two years after that, Donald finished out of the top 125 on the money list and was reduced to partial status on tour, forced to scramble for sponsor exemptions and to get into weaker fields later in the year when the stars went home. Donald turned fifty in 2005, making him eligible for the Champions Tour. As a past Open champion, he would have been able to play wherever and whenever he wanted to play. As a near Open champion, he has to scramble each year to get into tournaments.

Unlike a lot of players, Donald has talked candidly through the years about how different his life might have been if he had made a par putt on 18 on that Sunday or Monday in 1990.

Donald flashed through my mind in 1998 at Royal Birkdale as I watched Mark O'Meara and Brian Watts play off for that year's British Open title. O'Meara had been a star for years but had solidified his place in golf history that April by winning the Masters for his first major title. Watts was an Oklahoman who had spent most of his career playing in Japan because he hadn't been able to secure a spot for himself on the PGA Tour.

My sense was that this was Watts's moment the same way Medinah had been Donald's moment. He lost the playoff, but the money he made allowed him to come home and play the U.S. Tour. Watts had some success but never won a tournament, never contended again in a major, and was eventually knocked off the tour by a series of injuries.

But the moment when I truly knew this was a book that needed to be written came during the Weir-Mattiace playoff at Augusta. By then I had been around golf long enough that I knew and liked both men. Each had pieced together solid careers. Both were very comfortable financially by that point in their lives.

Even so, there was no doubt in my mind as they walked down the 10th fairway on that gorgeous late afternoon/early evening that their lives were about to go in entirely different directions.

One would always be a Masters champion no matter what happened the rest of his life. The other would always wonder what might have been if one more putt had gone in the hole over the course of four days.

Nerves affected them both on the playoff hole, and Weir ended up winning by making a bogey.

My thought as I watched the two of them shake hands was that the book I would write would be about guys who got into contention at a major knowing this was a chance that might not come again—and how winning or losing changed their lives. At that moment, I had just agreed to do a book on my friend Bruce Edwards (*Caddy for Life*), so I tucked the idea into a corner of my brain knowing I wanted to come back to it.

As the rest of 2003 unfolded, I knew I had been handed the keys to the book I wanted to write. Jim Furyk was hardly an unknown or a one-time wonder when he won the Open that year, but the other winners and runners-up were players who had never before contended in a major. Or, in the case of Ben Curtis, had never *played* in a major. Only time would tell if they were one-win wonders.

In a very real sense this book began on the range at Bethpage on that Saturday evening in 2002 when it occurred to Butch Harmon that Tiger Woods was getting ready to fire him. The Woods-Harmon split led to the longest drought of Woods's career and opened the door for the events that unfolded in 2003.

Six years later, none of the winners or contenders in '03 has won another major—unless you want to count Vijay Singh and Woods, who finished tied for second and fourth, respectively, behind Curtis at the British Open.

What is clear after spending time with all these men is this: their lives were never the same after their Moment in 2003. And the difference between first and second is a lot wider than the gulf between first-place money and second-place money.

On the Tuesday before the 2004 Masters, Weir hosted the annual Champions Dinner in the second-floor dining room of the Augusta National clubhouse. He sat between Byron Nelson and Arnold Palmer and listened to the two of them—and the other champions—tell stories all night.

Len Mattiace was at the Masters that year, but he was nowhere near the Champions Dinner. He was in the process of trying to come back from surgery on both knees only four months earlier.

The Masters was Mattiace's fourth tournament back after the surgery. He had rehabbed for three months—five months less than Tiger Woods would take after his knee surgery in 2008—before returning to the tour. One reason he had pushed to come back so soon was that he wanted to be ready to play at Augusta.

As it turned out, he came back too quickly. Not only did he miss the cut at the Masters, he went on to a disastrous year, playing in twenty-five tournaments but only earning $213,707, more than $1 million less than he had earned a year earlier, prior to the injury. Because he had won twice in 2002, he was still a fully exempt player in 2005, but he played even worse that year: thirty-four starts, earnings of $209,638. That sent him plummeting to 191st on the money list, which meant he was exempt in 2006 only as a past champion. In other words, he only got into tournaments *after* the top 125 on the money list from 2005, after all those who came through Qualifying School and the Nationwide Tour, even after those who finished between 126th and 150th on the money list.

Because he had a reputation as a good guy, Mattiace received a number of sponsor exemptions that year from tournament directors who liked him and remembered his close call at the Masters. On tour, players often refer to this as a one-year "good guy" extension. The good-guy extension got Mattiace into twenty-two events, but his golf got worse. He earned $66,540, making just four cuts. A year later, without the extension, he played only ten events, making zero cuts and zero dollars.

By 2008 he was playing almost as much on the Nationwide Tour as on the PGA Tour, still searching for his swing, his game, and his career.

Mike Weir also missed the cut at the 2004 Masters, which was a disappointment but nothing more. Weir knew his spot in the Masters field and in the champions locker room was secure—for life.

Mattiace has not been back to the Masters since 2004. In fact, he has not played in any of the major championships since the 2005 U.S. Open. The case can be made that the best day of his life playing golf produced the biggest disappointment, a memory he can't shake even though he played brilliantly for 17 holes.

Four days can change your life forever. And at the end, in the white-hot crucible of those final moments, one swing, one putt, one lucky or unlucky break, is often the difference between a lifetime of happy memories and telling and retelling a story that makes you smile, and a lifetime of wondering, years later, if you'll ever be able to shake that memory.

Sudden fame can mean radical life changes—for good and for bad. Seven years after fulfilling their lifelong dreams, the four major winners of 2003 have taken very different roads: Jim Furyk is still one of the most successful players in the world but wonders, as he turns forty in 2010, if that Open will be his only major title. Mike Weir, who was born on the same day as Furyk (Furyk is a few hours older), is still very successful but has been through some serious valleys in recent years.

So has Ben Curtis, who struggled to deal with going from being a golfer other golfers didn't recognize to being a major champion. He struggled for two years, found his game again in 2006, almost won the PGA in 2008, and then struggled again in 2009.

At least the first three remain fully exempt players on the tour. Shaun Micheel ended 2009 at the PGA Tour's Qualifying School, trying to regain his status as a fully exempt player on tour but still battling to come back after having major shoulder surgery in June 2008. He came up short of the top 25, which would have made him fully exempt again, finishing in a tie for 64th place in the 170-player field.

"There are times I tell myself I should just walk away and do something else," he said one night late in 2009. "I'm forty, I'm in good shape financially, so why not give it a shot?"

He shook his head. "But then I remember how much I love golf, how much I love to compete. I've loved it since I was ten years old. I want to win again. I want something close to the feeling I had that day at Oak Hill."

He paused. "Then again, maybe that was a once-in-a-lifetime experience. If it was, well, I guess I should consider myself lucky that it happened once."

They all feel that way. All four want to win again, but they know how privileged they were to win once. And if they ever forget that, they might want to spend a few moments with Len Mattiace, Stephen Leaney, Thomas Bjorn, or Chad Campbell, in whose shoes they almost stood.

1

One Moment in Time

IT WAS ONE OF those perfect early-spring Sunday evenings that are as traditional at the Masters as the azaleas, the magnolias, and the green jackets. It was shortly past 7 o'clock on April 13, 2003, and the sun was beginning to slide into the western sky, causing just a hint of coolness in the air as dusk slowly began to close in.

Two men walked off the 10th tee of the Augusta National Golf Club, hearing the cheers and shouts of the thousands who lined each side of the fairway, all of them pressing forward to get as close a look as possible at the next Masters champion.

Mike Weir was a month shy of his thirty-third birthday. He was Canadian, and even though, like most Canadian kids, he had grown up as a huge hockey fan, his hometown of Sarnia, Ontario, is less than an hour from Detroit, and his team was the Red Wings, not the Montreal Canadiens or the Toronto Maple Leafs.

He was in his seventh full year on the PGA Tour and had carved out a solid, lucrative living. He had opened the 2003 season by winning the Bob Hope Chrysler Classic, the fourth win of his career, and had followed it up a few weeks later with a victory at the Nissan Open in Los Angeles.

Len Mattiace was thirty-five and had been on tour two years longer than Weir. He was coming off what had been by far the best year of his professional career. In 2002, he had won in Los Angeles and in Memphis, his first two victories on tour, and had made well over $2 million in prize money.

This, though, was a moment unlike any other in the lives of Weir and Mattiace. They had started out playing golf because they loved the game, and they had kept playing it because they had talent. Golf had been responsible for Weir's scholarship to Brigham Young and Mattiace's scholarship to Wake Forest. Each had been good enough in college to think that it was possible to make a living playing golf and had successfully pursued that dream.

Having played golf for money throughout their adult lives, they were now playing for far more than that. They were playing for history, and they were playing for a legacy.

"It's the first line of any story that's written about you for the rest of your life," Weir would say years later. "'Masters champion' becomes part of your name."

For all the success they'd had, both knew that there was no guarantee they would ever be this close to a major championship again. This had been one of those weeks when Tiger Woods was a factor only briefly, and they knew that was more exception than rule. Woods was such an intimidating figure in the game that after he had gotten up and down from a bunker on the final hole of his second round to make the 36-hole cut right on the cut number, Mark Chaney, who caddied for Jeff Sluman, put his arm around Brennan Little, Weir's longtime friend and caddy, and said, "Too bad, Butchie [Little's nickname], you almost had him."

At that moment, Woods trailed Weir by 11 shots.

But Woods was long gone, having finished in a tie for 15th place, when Weir rolled in a six-foot par putt on the 18th green to force a sudden-death playoff with Mattiace. Forty minutes earlier, Mattiace had stood on the 18th tee with a two-shot lead, having pieced together a remarkable eight-under-par final round until that moment. Whether it was nerves or just turning human at the wrong time, Mattiace had pushed his drive on 18 into trees and pine straw to the right of the fairway and had made bogey from there to shoot 65.

Three holes behind Mattiace, playing in the last group with third-round leader Jeff Maggert, Weir knew he had to birdie the par-five 15th hole and then not make any mistakes on the last three holes to at least force a playoff. He did exactly that, slamming his par putt into the back of the hole on 18, while Mattiace stood a few yards away on the putting green, warming up for the playoff he thought was likely to come.

And so, once Weir had signed his scorecard to make it official that he and Mattiace had both finished four rounds at seven-under-par 281 (two shots clear of Phil Mickelson and three shots ahead of fourth-place finisher Jim Furyk), the two men headed to the 10th tee.

The Masters is the only major championship that breaks a tie with a sudden-death playoff. Both the British Open and the PGA Championship use aggregate-score playoffs — the British is four holes, the PGA three — so the championship can be decided on Sunday but not in sudden death, the notion being that three or four holes is a fairer test than a single hole, where one break, good or bad, can decide the winner. The United States Open still holds an 18-hole Monday playoff, which was the norm for all majors until the Masters went to sudden death in 1979.

The five previous sudden-death playoffs at the Masters had all been decided on the 11th hole. In 1979, Fuzzy Zoeller, Tom Watson, and Ed Sneed all parred the 10th hole before Zoeller birdied the 11th hole to win. Three years later, Craig Stadler beat Dan Pohl to win his only major title. In 1987, Seve Ballesteros was eliminated when he bogeyed the 10th. Larry Mize then beat Greg Norman on the 11th when he chipped in from 112 feet away, arguably the most dramatic shot in golf history. In 1989, after

Scott Hoch had missed a three-foot par putt that would have clinched the win on the 10th hole, Nick Faldo birdied the 11th to beat him. And a year later, Faldo beat Raymond Floyd when Floyd's second shot found Rae's Creek, which runs down the left side of number 11.

Weir versus Mattiace was the first playoff at Augusta since Faldo's victory over Floyd. If either man had thought about it standing on the 10th tee, he might have realized that each playoff in the five sudden-death affairs at the Masters had been a seminal moment in the life of almost every man who had taken part.

Zoeller's victory had launched him into stardom and made him a wealthy man. Five years later, he added a U.S. Open title to his résumé, and even thirty years later—despite an embarrassing misstep involving Tiger Woods in 1997—he remained one of the most popular players on the Champions Tour, as the PGA Tour now euphemistically calls its senior tour for players over fifty.

Ed Sneed, who bogeyed the last three holes to blow a three-shot lead and allow Zoeller and Watson to tie him, won only once more on the PGA Tour and never again came close to contending in a major championship. The only member of the trio whose life wasn't altered dramatically was Watson, who had already won three majors, including the 1977 Masters, and went on to win five more.

Stadler's 1982 win was the signature moment in an otherwise solid career, an event that distinguished him from men like Hoch and, for that matter, Pohl, who finished third in two other majors and won the Vardon Trophy in 1987 for the lowest stroke average on tour but is considered merely a good player, not a major champion.

Ballesteros was the Watson of the 1987 playoff. He had already won four majors, including two Masters, and he bounced back from the disappointment of not winning a third green jacket to win the British Open for a third time in 1988.

Mize and Norman remain linked forever in golfing lore, thanks to Mize's chip-in. Norman is the only man in history to have lost playoffs in all four major championships. He had lost to Zoeller in 1984 at Winged Foot in the U.S. Open, and would lose to Mark Calcavecchia in the 1989 British Open and to Paul Azinger in 1993 at the PGA.

But no defeat in his life was more stunning than this one. He was safely on the 11th green in two, about 25 feet below the hole, when Mize lined up his chip from the right side of the green. From where Mize stood, getting up and down for par would clearly be a challenge. If he failed to do that, a two putt by Norman would make him the Masters champion.

Instead, Mize, who was twenty-eight at the time with one PGA Tour victory to his name, chipped in, leading to a dance that has been replayed over and over through the years. Shocked, Norman missed his lengthy birdie putt to give Mize the victory.

Norman never won the Masters—he famously blew a six-shot lead on the final day in 1996—and his 2009 appearance at age fifty-four was probably his last, barring some sort of miracle. Mize plays every year as a past champion and has a secure spot in the upstairs champions locker room in the clubhouse, his green jacket hanging in his locker every April when he arrives. He never won another playoff—losing three times in three attempts—but it hardly mattered.

To this day, when someone in golf misses a critical short putt, people invoke the name Scott Hoch. Not only did he miss from a little more than three feet with the Masters title at stake in his 1989 playoff with Nick Faldo, he missed by a *lot*. The putt was a dead pull the instant it left his putter. It never touched the hole, and his putt coming back for bogey—which he made—was at least as long. To this day, if you miss a short putt, someone will say you "Hoched it."

Faldo, who won with a long birdie putt one hole later for his first Masters, went on to win three times at Augusta and won six major championships before he retired to the TV booth. Hoch won eleven PGA Tour titles and is still a very successful Champions Tour player, but he is remembered most for one missed putt, not for any of the ones he made to win in places like Las Vegas and Greensboro.

The playoff a year later involved two Hall of Famers, Faldo and Floyd. Floyd had already won four majors and at age forty-seven was trying to become the second-oldest player in history to win a major title. After Floyd's second shot at the 11th went into the water, giving Faldo the win, he actually had another chance to win two years later, but he came up two shots short of Fred Couples.

In 2003, Weir was playing in his fourth Masters, and although he had made the cut in each of the previous three, he had never finished higher than a tie for 24th place. He had played in fifteen majors during his career, contending once at the 1999 PGA Championship when he played with Woods in the last group on Sunday and shot 80 to finish in a tie for 10th place.

"My game just wasn't ready for everything I had to deal with that day," he said. "Playing in the last group, playing with Tiger — all of it. I learned from it, but it certainly wasn't a fun way to learn."

Now, four years later, he felt ready. He had felt that way all week, even when he had fallen out of the lead after a 75 on Saturday; even when Mattiace had gone past him on Sunday afternoon.

Mattiace had less experience than Weir on the four Sundays that matter most in golf. He had played in the Masters as an amateur in 1988, qualifying because he was a member of the U.S. Walker Cup team that year, and in those days the entire ten-man squad was invited to play in the Masters. He had not made it back to Augusta as a pro until his 18th-place finish on the 2002 tour money list qualified him for the 2003 tournament. In all, he had played in ten previous majors, his best finish, also a tie for 24th, in 1997 at the U.S. Open.

"I guess it would be fair to say I came out of nowhere," he said, laughing, a few years later. "But I had been playing the best golf of my life."

Weir actually had an off year in 2002, dropping to 78th on the money list — after finishing 23rd, 6th, and 11th the three previous years — while failing to win a tournament for the first time since 1998. But, after reworking his game during the off-season, he had come out flying at the start of 2003, winning twice and contending, it seemed, on an almost weekly basis.

Now, though, he and Mattiace had reached a moment every golfer dreams about but can't possibly imagine until it actually arrives. One of them was about to add two words to his name: "Masters champion." The other was going to be left to wonder if he would ever have another chance like this one, if he would ever play this well at the right moment and not just come close but win.

That evening, one of them was going to walk away with a green jacket, an endless string of new endorsement opportunities, and a piece of history. The other would receive a hefty check ($648,000), congratulations for his play, and condolences for the missed opportunity.

Both men hit good drives on the 10th, not showing any of the nerves that might be expected given what was at stake. The 10th hole is not one of Augusta National's more famous holes. It has none of the romance of "Amen Corner," so dubbed by the great Herbert Warren Wind because players pray that they can get through that three-hole stretch — 11, 12, 13 — without seeing their hopes of winning the tournament drown in Rae's Creek. It isn't as memorable as the par-five 15th, the classic risk-reward hole: short enough to reach in two but eminently dangerous because of water in front and in back of the green. It isn't as slick as the uphill ninth hole, with its treacherous tilted back-to-front green; or as pretty as the par-three 16th, where both Woods and Jack Nicklaus have had, arguably, their most dramatic moments; or as memorable as the 18th, where so much history has occurred.

But less than an hour before sunset on a lovely spring evening, the 10th is a spectacular setting for the sort of drama that was about to unfold. The hole plays straight downhill, dropping almost 100 feet in elevation from tee to green, bending to the left just beyond the landing area, which leads to a tree-surrounded bowl at the green. There's a huge bunker in front of the green and another one to the right.

There are two things TV simply cannot do justice to at Augusta: the severe nature of the hills on the golf course, and the soaring trees that abound everywhere. Nowhere is this more true than on the 10th hole, with trees running all the way down the left, more trees behind the green, and trees pushed back from the fairway on the right that extend to the right side of the 18th fairway.

Weir and Mattiace marched down the hill to where their golf balls had come to rest on the fairway. It was 7:10 in the evening. Both men knew that the next few minutes would drastically alter the rest of their lives—one way or another.

2

Tiger versus the Field

As THE 2003 GOLF season began, there was one name that stood out above all others for serious golf fans, and only one name that mattered at all to casual golf fans: Tiger Woods.

Woods had burst onto the golf scene in August 1996 when he had turned pro shortly after winning his third straight U.S. Amateur title. He signed a number of lucrative endorsement contracts before he had ever hit a shot as a pro, and his debut in Milwaukee was so hyped that it seemed almost impossible that the kid who wouldn't turn twenty-one until late December could live up to what people were expecting of him.

Woods not only lived up to the hype, he surpassed it. He finished tied for 60th at Milwaukee, but that was the last time in eight appearances that year that he didn't finish in at least the top 25. He won two tournaments, finished third in two others, and won more than $790,000—good enough for 24th on the money list.

His play that fall was best described by tour veteran Paul Goydos, who for three days played in the group directly behind Woods at the Walt Disney Classic, one of the tournaments Woods won. Walking off the golf course one day, Goydos shook his head and said, "You guys [the media] are always asking who the best player in the world who hasn't won a major yet is. I can tell you who it is:

Tiger Woods. You want to know why? Because he's the best player in the world—*period*."

That might have sounded hyperbolic, just as Woods's father, Earl, sounded a little bit over the top when he compared his son to Gandhi. There was also *Sports Illustrated,* which named Woods Sportsman of the Year, causing *New York Daily News* columnist Mike Lupica to say, "It's the first time they've ever given that award on spec."

Woods turned all the hype and speculation into fact early in 1997 when he won the Masters—his first major as a pro—by *twelve* shots. "He's a boy among men, and he's teaching the men a lesson," eight-time major champion Tom Watson commented. A year later when the four-year-old son of a friend asked Watson if he was as good a golfer as Tiger Woods, Watson shook his head and said, "I'm not even close."

Woods's play and his stardom redefined the PGA Tour. As luck would have it, the tour's TV contracts were being renegotiated during his first full year as a pro. The tour's TV money went way up, and purses soared. So did corporate interest, especially for those tournaments in which Woods was guaranteed to play. As time went on and Woods settled into a predictable schedule each year, there were—unofficially—two tours: the Tiger tour and the non-Tiger tour.

If Woods was playing, everything doubled: ticket sales, corporate sales, TV ratings (especially if he contended, which he did more often than not), and media interest. This became a problem for the non-Tiger events, and, as the economy began to go south during the second Bush administration, Commissioner Tim Finchem began to have trouble keeping corporate sponsors involved at the non-Tiger events.

So when a non-Tiger event went under in Colorado in 2007, Finchem reinvented it in Washington with Tiger Woods as host.

Getting a title sponsor and corporate interest for the new tournament was not a problem.

After Woods's runaway Masters victory, he became *the* story at every golf tournament, and every major, that he entered. But he didn't win any of his next ten majors, in part because he had decided that the golf swing that had won the '97 Masters needed retooling. He wanted more consistency, especially off the tee.

Once the retooling was complete, Woods became as dominant as any player in the history of the game has ever been. He won the 1999 PGA Championship and then finished fifth at the 2000 Masters. His next four starts in majors produced a *fifteen*-shot victory in the U.S. Open, an *eight*-shot win at the British Open, a playoff victory at the PGA (clearly he had an off week), and a two-shot win at the 2001 Masters.

It was, with all due respect to Bobby Jones, the most remarkable accomplishment in golf history. Jones had won the so-called Grand Slam in 1930, but that was when two of the four majors were strictly for amateurs, and long before golf became the ultra-competitive sport that it is today. To win four majors in a row was an unheard-of feat. The only comparable achievement was Ben Hogan's performance in 1953 when he won the Masters, the U.S. Open, and the British Open. He didn't compete in the PGA that year because it overlapped with the British Open.

That alone tells you how different golf was in those days. At the time, no one had even uttered the phrase "Grand Slam" in the modern game. In fact, it wasn't until 1960 when Arnold Palmer won the Masters and the U.S. Open to begin the year and then entered the British Open for the first time (he finished second) that Grand Slam was used to describe those three events and the PGA Championship.

It was Jack Nicklaus who really focused attention on the modern slam and on the importance of winning major championships.

From the moment he won the U.S. Open as a twenty-two-year-old in 1962—beating Arnold Palmer in a playoff at Oakmont Country Club—Nicklaus made it clear that his priority each year was to prepare for the four major championships. He built his schedule so his game would peak during those four weeks, and he was the first player to travel regularly to tournament sites in advance to survey and play the golf courses.

Nicklaus's relentless pursuit of major titles—he ended up winning eighteen as a pro, blowing away Walter Hagen's previous record of eleven (Jones won fourteen majors, but eight of them were U.S. and British Amateur titles)—focused attention on them like never before. That's why a young Tiger Woods became fixated on Nicklaus's eighteen major wins as his primary goal as a golfer.

Nicklaus had also talked openly about wanting to do what was generally considered to be impossible—win all four majors in the same year. This is a feat that has been accomplished in tennis on a number of occasions; Don Budge, Maureen Connolly, Rod Laver (twice), and Steffi Graf have all done it. In golf, Jones's 1930 "slam" came close, but it was in a different era with different tournaments serving as the majors, and Hogan was next closest when he went three-for-three in 1953.

Early in his career, Nicklaus had several remarkable years. In 1963, after winning his first Masters, he missed the cut at the U.S. Open. He then finished third at the British Open and won the PGA. In 1966, he won the Masters for the third time in four years, finished third in the U.S. Open, then won the British before a disappointing tie for 22nd at the PGA. A year later, after missing the cut at the Masters, he bounced back to finish 1–2–T3 in the last three majors of 1967.

The closest he ever came to a slam was in 1972 when he won the Masters and the U.S. Open before finishing second to Lee

Trevino in the British Open. The dream of the slam gone, he finished tied for 13th at the PGA.

Woods knew that one way to surpass Nicklaus on his way to the eighteen majors was to win all four majors in a year. He did — just not in the *same* year — starting what became known as the "Tiger Slam," with his remarkable victory at Pebble Beach in June 2000, then closing out his run at the Masters in April 2001.

He had a rare letdown after that victory at Augusta, failing to finish in the top 10 at any of the remaining majors in '01. But he came right back at the start of the next year with victories at the Masters and the U.S. Open, meaning he had won six of nine and seven of eleven. For comparison purposes, Nicklaus's best run came at the start of his career when he won seven of twenty-one.

After his 2002 win at Bethpage, Woods was asked how he felt being halfway to a Grand Slam. "I've already won a Grand Slam," he answered. "So this is no big deal."

His Tiger Slam wasn't a Grand Slam, which would have meant winning all four majors in the same year. But to be fair, Woods wasn't the first to try changing what constitutes a slam. During one stretch in her career, Martina Navratilova won *six* consecutive major tennis titles. Unfortunately, she won three to end one year and three to begin another year, but never four in one year. Navratilova insisted that winning four in a row at any point meant you had won a slam. According to that theory, she would have won *three* slams during a six-tournament stretch.

Not possible — even for Navratilova, even for Woods.

It was after Bethpage that Woods made the decision to fire Butch Harmon. He has never really explained his reasoning in any detail, but several factors appear to have been involved.

Clearly, one was the influence of Mark O'Meara, Woods's best friend on tour and a mentor to him in many ways. O'Meara had worked with Hank Haney for years, and Harmon now says he could see changes in Woods's swing that reflected the influence of O'Meara and Haney, even before that day in Scotland when Woods told him their teacher-pupil relationship was over.

"He kept wanting to try things that I knew came from Hank and Mark," Harmon said. "Did I think they were going to make his golf swing better? No. I thought he had a pretty good golf swing, and the record kind of spoke for itself on that subject.

"But one of Tiger's strengths is he's never satisfied. He could win *ten* majors in a row, and he'd still be searching for ways to get better. I would stand there with him on the range at times and say, 'I like what I see.' I mean, the swing he had in 2002 was good enough to win four straight majors and seven of eleven. I'm not going to mess with that just for the sake of sounding like I've got something for him I haven't got.

"He would say to me, 'I'm too steep.' I knew where that was coming from; I understood it. He thought what they were telling him could improve his swing. I didn't. Obviously, in the end, the final decision on what direction to go in was always going to be his."

Woods's swing transition didn't start right away. In fact, he didn't start working with Haney on a full-time basis until 2003. He worked by himself on the range at Muirfield. He contended for two days but shot 81 in the third round on a day when the golf course was buffeted by gale-force winds. The 65 he shot the next day—to finish tied for 28th—might have been one of the best rounds of his life, given that he had nothing to play for but still played as hard as he possibly could for all 18 holes. At the PGA a month later, he finished second to Rich Beem, still without a formal working relationship with any swing coach.

That fall he began working on the second major swing change of his career. It would take him a full two years to become comfortable with his golf swing again and to return to the dominance fans and sponsors had come to expect. But for the rest of the golf world, to paraphrase Phil Mickelson at his most directly eloquent, Woods going from dominant to almost dormant didn't suck.

3

The Little Lefty Who Could

MICHAEL RICHARD WEIR WAS born May 12, 1970, the third son of Richard and Rosalie Weir. He was ten years younger than Jim and seven years younger than Craig.

"I still tease my mom about being an accident," he likes to say. "She denies it, of course."

Richard Weir was a chemist working in the rubber division of a company called Polysar—later bought out by Bayer—in Sarnia, Ontario, a mostly blue-collar town of about seventy-five thousand people that sat right on Lake Ontario. He was a reasonably good golfer, and when he bought a house directly across the street from Huron Oaks Golf Club, all his sons became involved in the game. Mike was the most athletically gifted and the one with the most interest in sports. When he was nine, Mike began working in the Huron Bay pro shop for Steve Bennett, picking up the range and cleaning clubs for the members.

Like most Canadian kids, he had started playing hockey almost from the day he could walk—and skate—and, even though he wrote with his right hand, he picked up his first hockey stick with his left hand and began playing left-handed. Since it is generally considered an advantage to be a lefty in hockey (because a left-handed shot will in all likelihood go in the direction of a right-handed goalie's stick rather than his glove), Weir was encouraged to play that way.

Being left-handed is not an advantage in golf. Some buy the theory that a lefty playing the game right-handed is at an advantage because his front side is his left, and, thus, he has more strength with his lead hand and lead leg. But if that were really the case, why wouldn't lefties be taught to pitch right-handed?

Ben Hogan was left-handed and played the game right-handed with (to put it mildly) a good deal of success. Like a lot of people, Hogan learned the game right-handed because left-handed clubs were scarce when he was growing up. Weir was able to learn golf as a lefty because his godfather's son, Aldo Iacobelli, played left-handed and gave him a hand-me-down set that had three woods and the three-, five-, seven-, and nine-irons in the bag.

"I was lucky," Weir said. "He was only a couple years older than me, but he gave me the clubs because he wasn't into golf, and I guess he could tell that I was."

When he was eleven, Mike spotted a left-handed Gene Sarazen sand wedge in the pro shop and, with the money he made working in the shop, spent $50 to buy it. "I wore it down until it had no grip at all," he said. "I still have it in my house today."

Bennett could see early on that the youngest of the Weir boys had talent. When Mike was twelve, Bennett took him to a junior tournament, and when Mike won the tournament he handed him a card with a picture of a complete set of Wilson blade irons — two through nine plus a pitching wedge. The clubs were Weir's reward for the win. He tossed the hand-me-downs and added the new irons to his beloved Sarazen sand wedge.

"From that point on, I was pretty much hooked on golf," he said. "I loved all sports. I played baseball and, of course, hockey, and I pulled for all the Detroit teams: Red Wings, Tigers, Lions. I was never very big, but I was always a pretty good athlete."

Mike was a reasonably good pitcher, but he gave up baseball as a high-school freshman. It just took too much time away from the already short Canadian golf season. He did, however, keep playing hockey. As much as he enjoyed golf, in a perfect world he would have grown to be a 6-foot-3-inch center for the Red Wings. In real life he never got past 5 foot 9 or high-school hockey.

"Until I was about fourteen, I was one of the better players around," he said. "But after a while, size became a factor. Every year the guys were a little bit bigger, and I wasn't. I was still a reasonably good player, but by the time I was fifteen or sixteen I knew I wasn't going to be good enough to get drafted. If I'd been superfast at 5 foot 9, 150 pounds I might have been okay. But I was just fast, and at that size fast isn't quite good enough.

"I also knew by then that golf was my best sport."

By the time he was thirteen, Weir was a very good low-handicap player who did well in junior tournaments around Canada. But there was some feeling that he might be even better if he switched around and played right-handed.

This was 1984, and only one left-handed golfer in history had made a serious impact on the game: Bob Charles, who was right-handed but played lefty and won the British Open in 1963. Many, if not most, pros turned lefty players around in those days and taught them to play righty. When the subject came up, Weir decided to write to an expert looking for some guidance.

He had met Jack Nicklaus in 1981 when Nicklaus came to Huron Oaks and played an exhibition with Bennett. Because Weir was eleven and because he worked for Bennett, he got to watch the match from up close all day. He got Nicklaus's autograph that afternoon and a handshake and a smile from the great man.

So, when the question came up about switching from left to right, Weir decided to write Nicklaus a letter to ask him what he thought. He got an answer back quickly. "If you are a good player left-handed, don't change anything—especially if that feels natural to you," Nicklaus wrote.

That ended any thoughts of relearning the game right-handed. Weir still has Nicklaus's letter—framed—in his home.

By the time Weir wrote to Nicklaus, he was hooked on golf and beginning to understand that he was more than just a decent junior golfer. The idea that he might want to play the game for a living had first crossed his mind in the summer of 1983 when he and his dad had made the two-and-a-half-hour drive to Toronto to attend the Canadian Open.

"The first time I went, we were there on Tuesday, and Andy Bean and Tom Kite did a clinic," he said. "I remember being amazed by the fact that they were using new Titleists as *range* balls. I couldn't believe that. Then, at the end of the clinic, they rolled some of the balls over to us to keep. I was awed."

Weir went back to see the actual tournament a few days later, piling into a car, this time with some friends, one of whom was sixteen and able to drive. "Jack and Johnny Miller were paired together," he said. "We walked around with them for a while. I couldn't get over the whole thing—the way the golf course looked, the way they played, the crowds." He smiled. "And the Titleists on the range. I'm *still* a little bit in awe of that."

Weir kept playing hockey until he graduated from high school, but the last two years his focus was on golf, because he and his dad and Bennett all believed it was going to be his route to college. He wasn't an overwhelmingly good junior player—"I never won the Canadian Amateur; best I did was second," he said—but he was a very good player, good enough to make it to the round of 16 at the U.S. Junior championships when he was sixteen.

"If I'd won one more match, I'd have played Phil [Mickelson]," he said. "It would have been lefty versus lefty."

Mickelson is exactly five weeks younger than Weir. In an odd coincidence, both are right-handed and play golf left-handed.

Mickelson first learned the golf swing standing opposite his father and mirroring him. Thus, when he took his arms back in the same direction as his father, he did it left-handed.

Weir went to a qualifier for the U.S. Junior that year in Michigan with Brennan Little, one of his closest golfing buddies back then. There were two spots available at the Michigan qualifier, and the Canadian kids won both spots. Little has been Weir's caddy for most of his professional career and remains, to this day, one of his closest friends.

Playing well at the U.S. Junior brought Weir to the attention of a number of American colleges. Weir and his dad had written letters to several schools early in his junior year, with mixed results. "I think we wrote to about twenty-five schools," he said. "We probably got responses from about eight or nine. Then, when I did pretty well before my senior year, we started hearing from more schools."

He was allowed to make four official campus visits and opted to go see Marshall, Texas El Paso, Michigan State, and Brigham Young. None had elite golf programs, but all were solid Division 1 golf schools. Michigan State was also appealing because it was only a couple of hours from home. Weir had a friend, Bill Hutchinson, who was at Marshall. Texas El Paso was very eager to have him, and BYU's coach, Jim Tucker, had recruited a number of Canadians, including Jim Nelford, one of the most successful Canadian players in PGA Tour history.

"I just thought I'd stay focused at a school like [BYU]," Weir said. "The campus was nice, and everyone was friendly—*very* friendly. You walk around there, and it seems like everyone is smiling. There's a reason why they call the place Happy Valley.

"In the end, though, I made a golf decision. We played a very good schedule, a lot of tournaments, good ones, and that was important because I thought to get better I needed to play regularly against better players. I knew by then golf was going to be my focus in college, and I thought BYU was the best place for my golf game to improve."

Brigham Young is primarily a Mormon school, named after the founder of the Church of Latter-day Saints. Weir was raised as a Catholic, although he has never been terribly religious. Even so, he was aware of his surroundings from the day he stepped on campus.

"They don't put a lot of pressure on you or anything like that," he said. "But there are occasions where they'll try to recruit you. It helped when I got there that my roommate was also Catholic. I think we both felt a little bit out of place. When you first get there, they will ask you—very politely of course—every chance they get, if you'd like to know more about the Mormon religion.

"But they never tried to shove it down your throat. There were a lot of rules: no beards, no long hair, no caffeine." He smiled. "The good news was that Coach Tucker was a Mormon, but he wasn't militant. He would look the other way if any of us decided we wanted a Coke. He understood that he had recruited kids from different backgrounds, and he always respected that."

In fact, Weir's freshman roommate was from the Philippines. "I remember he had Mizuno blade irons with his name on them," Weir said. "Right away that told me he must be a pretty good player."

It took Weir a while to adjust to the new world he found himself in. It helped that Tucker had recruited two other Canadians—Jason Tomlinson and Jeff Kramer—that year, and Weir soon began to feel comfortable on campus. Even though golf was his number one priority, he did well academically, graduating in four years with a 3.0 GPA. He majored in recreation management.

"Huron Oaks has always had a rec center in addition to the golf course," he said. "I was thinking I might go back there someday and run it."

He fit in well socially once he got over his initial homesickness and began to get to know people. Ty Detmer, who would go on to win the Heisman Trophy, was BYU's quarterback when Weir arrived, and the Cougars were consistently ranked in the top 25.

"My sophomore year Miami came in to play, and they had won a bunch of games in a row over a couple of seasons," he said. "We beat them, and we all ran onto the field to tear down the goalposts and celebrate. I remember the grass was so long that it came up over my shoes. I remember thinking, 'So this is how we slowed them down.'"

The golf team he joined as a freshman was a good one. Tucker recruited worldwide, and there were players from the United States, Canada, the Philippines, Ecuador, and Colombia on the team.

"Coach believed in qualifying before every tournament," Weir said. "He thought the pressure was good for us—and it was. You had to go out and play for your spot every time. Most of my freshman year, I played somewhere between number four and number six—which I was happy about. A couple times I made it up to third. I actually won one tournament out in Monterey, so, in all, I had a very good freshman year."

Weir learned a great deal during that year. More than anything, he learned that he had a lot of work to do if he wanted to make his dream of playing golf professionally come true. Seeing good college players up close gave him a sense of how his game stacked up compared to those he had been watching on TV all his life.

"I wasn't, by any means, one of the better college players in the country, and most college players don't make it to the tour," he said. "I knew I had to get a lot better if I was going to have a chance when I graduated."

Freshman year was important for another reason: he met Bricia Rodriguez. She was a dark-haired beauty from Los Angeles whom Weir first met in the food court connected to his dorm. As luck would have it, when he moved off campus the next year, Bricia was living in the same apartment complex. She had grown up in a Spanish-speaking family but also spoke French and English fluently.

"Some guys joke about their wives being the smart ones in the family," he said. "With me, it's no joke."

Bricia remembers first spotting Weir at the food court. It was his looks that got her attention. "I thought he was Hispanic," she said, laughing. "He had dark hair and a little wispy mustache, and I knew there weren't a lot of Hispanic guys at BYU, so I thought I'd like to meet him. The minute he opened his mouth and started talking, I knew he wasn't Hispanic."

She liked him anyway, even though he didn't speak a word of Spanish. "I came from a chaotic family life," she said. "My family always reminded me of that movie *The War of the Roses*. Mike's family was so mellow. They lived in this cute town right by the lake, and there was a laid-back quality to their life I had never experienced. Plus, he was very sweet."

Bricia was at BYU on an academic scholarship, working toward a career in social work. Mike was working toward a career in golf. He improved steadily throughout his college years. By the time he graduated, he thought his game was good enough to at least merit a tryout.

"My freshman year, my scoring average was about 74–75," he said. "Obviously that wasn't good enough. By senior year [1993], I was a lot better. I was never a great ball striker; I pretty much just mucked it around. But I got a lot better at getting it up and down and scoring, with experience. I won a couple good tournaments as a senior and finished seventh at the NCAAs. [He was second team All American.] That told me I was good enough to at least give it a shot."

Weir's plan after graduation was to remain an amateur until he entered PGA Tour Qualifying School that fall. He had been

picked to represent Canada in the World Amateur Championships that would be played a few weeks before Q-School began.
Unfortunately, he never got to play.

"I filled out my Q-School application and sent it in," he said. "I
guess I didn't read it closely enough. A few weeks later someone
asked me what I was doing about my Q-School entry form. I said
I'd sent it in. They said 'Uh-oh.' It turned out, as soon as I sent the
form in I was a pro. So I couldn't play in the World Amateur."

That disappointment was mitigated when he breezed through
the first stage of Q-School. Second stage, he knew, was the key,
because making it through second stage to the finals meant he
would—at worst—have some status on what was then the Nike
Tour, which is golf's version of Triple-A baseball, one step down
from the big leagues.

He ended up in a playoff at second stage—eight players fighting for one last remaining spot. One player birdied the first hole.
That left Weir and six others playing on in the darkness for the
first alternate's spot, which seemed important since it had already
been decided that the first alternate from that site would be the
first alternate for the finals.

"I finally birdied a par-three in the dark to get it," he said.
"Everyone congratulated me because never in history had the first
alternate *not* gotten into the finals. Back then, 190 guys made the
finals. There was bound to be one who didn't get there for some
reason."

Weir flew to Palm Springs, where the finals were being played,
hired a caddy, and played several practice rounds to get ready.
Every evening he checked with the tour to see if anyone had withdrawn yet. On Wednesday morning, the first day of play, he
warmed up and then sat on the tee and watched as each of the
190 players teed off.

"Everyone showed; no one withdrew," he said, able to smile
now at the memory. "Everyone kept saying to me, 'This has *never*

happened before.' Well, now I can tell guys it's happened at least once."

He wrote a check for $1,500 to Jim Freedman, who had been scheduled to caddy for him, and made the ten-hour drive back to Provo to tell Bricia that they had to go to Plan B. "Felt more like one hundred hours," he said. "And the $1,500 felt more like $15,000."

Plan B was the Canadian Tour, which also had a Q-School, although it wasn't nearly as difficult as the one for the PGA Tour. Weir made it onto the Canadian Tour, and he and Bricia were married on April 30, 1994. She caddied for him part-time in Canada, and he played well, finishing in the top 10 on the money list. That qualified him to play that winter on the Australian Tour, which is where he went after again failing the second stage of Q-School.

"I wasn't an alternate this time," he said. "I figured I saved some time, some money, and some heartache that way."

That first winter in Australia wasn't easy. The tour was set up much the same way the PGA Tour had been set up until 1983: if you missed a cut in a tournament, you had to play the next Monday to qualify for the next tournament. If you made a cut, you were automatically in the next week.

"I had one six-week stretch where I made it through Monday every week and missed the cut every week," Weir said. "I was playing a lot of golf and making absolutely no money."

His caddy most of the time was Bricia. That wasn't easy on either one of them. "It was culture shock for me," she said. "I didn't know anything about golf. I remember one of the first tournaments I worked in, I walked onto a green and laid the bag down right in the middle of the green. Mike got this look in his eyes like, 'Oh no, this isn't going to work.'"

But when Mike began making cuts and making money, things got better. Bricia read books on Ben Hogan—Mike's hero because he was a little guy who became a superstar—and on sports psychology so she could better understand what her husband was trying to accomplish. That was all good. But Mike still couldn't get through what a lot of players call "the second-stage wall."

"Every year it was the same thing," he said. "I'd cruise through first stage, come into second stage convinced I was ready to get through. Then something would happen, and I would miss. In '96 it was by one shot."

Somehow, he managed not to get discouraged. Part of the reason was that he still believed there was great room for improvement in his game. He and Bricia had gotten into a pattern of living each year that wasn't awful: he would play Australia in the winter and Canada in the summer. Since there were no kids yet, they would load up their Toyota Camry after coming home from Australia, put everything else in storage, and head north.

"It was actually a fun time looking back at it," he said. "I guess you could say we were still young and carefree, and I was just trying to make myself a better ball striker. My swing was pretty much homemade, so I had to figure out a way to improve it to the point where I could compete with the top guys."

Bricia's confidence in Mike never really wavered during that period, and she still caddied for him often. "If anything, it was my confidence in me," she said. "I knew Mike well enough to know he was going to keep after it and keep getting better. I just wasn't sure how much longer I could keep doing it.

"Working with your husband isn't easy under any circumstances, I don't think. There were times when we'd *both* be uptight out there. He might say, 'Will you please give me the goddamn four-iron *now*,' and I would snap back, 'Get the damn four-iron yourself.' In the end, it probably made us closer, but there were some difficult moments."

Mike experienced two turning points along the way during his search for a better swing. The first, a wake-up call, came in 1995 when he got the chance to play in the Canadian Open—a spot he earned because of his ranking on the Canadian tour's Order of Merit.

"I went out to the range on one of the practice days, and it was packed," Weir said, smiling at the memory. "The only open spot I could find was next to Pricey [Nick Price], who was still the number one player in the world at the time. I was nervous just being *next* to him. I stood there and watched him for a while, and I was in complete awe.

"I thought I was making pretty good progress with my ball striking, but when I watched him for a while I realized I was *so* far away from where I needed to be it was almost a joke. I stood there and said to myself, 'Okay, what you've been doing isn't good enough—I have *got* to find a way to get better, a lot better.'"

The second turning point came that winter. Weir was getting ready to play a minitour event in Palm Springs, and he went to visit Brennan Little, who was working at a club there. Brennan was also taking some lessons from a pro named Mike Wilson, who had worked at the Leadbetter Academy. Weir had studied Price's swing on tape after the driving range revelation in Canada and had also studied Nick Faldo. Both were students of Leadbetter.

"I decided to tag along one day when Brennan was working with Mike to see what they were working on," Weir said. "I was impressed. I could see Brennan's swing getting more efficient. There was a real organization to what Mike was trying to do. I knew that the path I'd been going down wasn't getting me where I wanted to go. I needed a more reliable path. I decided to try to work with Mike for a while and see what happened.

"One thing about teaching me is that it's harder because I'm lefty. Mike actually started to hit some balls and play lefty a little bit to get a better feel for my swing. He even got pretty good playing lefty. All of that helped me a lot."

After working with Wilson, Weir went back to Q-School for his fifth try in the fall of 1997. His lifestyle was already changing. Bricia was due to give birth to their first child two weeks after the conclusion of the Q-School finals.

"It was pretty good motivation," Weir said. "But the fact was I was a better player and a more confident player by then. Mike and I had worked on my swing and on my short game. I got myself into good position at second stage and kind of hung on."

Bricia is a firm believer in both karma and mojo. "They say golfers with pregnant wives have good karma," she said. "I really think that was a factor that year at Q-School."

As is always the case at Q-School, Weir couldn't be absolutely sure how he stood on the final day of second stage. But he played solidly and walked off the 18th green thinking he was inside the number. He was — by three shots.

"It was a big relief," he said. "It meant I had a place to play over here regardless of what happened in the finals. I didn't have to go back to Australia right after we'd had our first child. I think I played the finals without really feeling any pressure as a result."

He played well the entire six days and erased any doubt about whether he was going to get his PGA Tour card during the sixth and final round when he holed a 40-foot birdie putt on 14, got up and down for par at 15, and almost holed a four-iron for a hole in one at 16, tapping in for another birdie.

"I had about a 15-footer for birdie at the 18th, and I wondered if I should go for it," he said. "I really thought I was in if I made a par, so I cozied it up there and then got a little bit nervous after I tapped in, thinking I might have needed a birdie. Fortunately, I was right. I made it with a shot to spare."

He had a solid though unspectacular rookie year on the tour, making a little less than half the cuts (thirteen) in twenty-seven tournaments. Still, he thought he had wrapped up his card with six weeks to play when he holed an eight-iron from 155 yards on the 18th hole at the B.C. Open to jump up to a tie for seventh place.

"I really thought I'd made enough at that point," he said. "But I struggled the last few weeks. Then I made a 10-footer at Disney [the last tournament of the year] to make the cut and thought I was absolutely locked. But a bunch of guys played really well on the weekend and passed me."

He ended up 131st on the money list, making a little more than $218,000 for the year. Going back to Q-School was a disappointment, but like a lot of players who have gone through the rigors of their rookie year on tour, he went back a much better and far more confident player. Players who go back to Q-School after a reasonably good, but not quite good enough first year on tour will almost unanimously tell you that they go back convinced they will mop up their Q-School competition.

"You know the guys at Q-School aren't as good as the guys you've been playing against all year on tour," Weir said. "If they were, they wouldn't be at Q-School. So you sort of go in with the attitude, 'I may not be as good as Nick Price or Nick Faldo or Fred Couples or Davis Love but I *am* better than you guys.'"

Since he had finished in the top 150 on the money list, he was exempt into the finals, meaning he had a five-week break after Disney. It also helped that he and Wilson had spent the time between Disney and the finals working on a new move on the range.

Wilson was concerned that Weir made a big swaying move on his way back, causing his swing to be inconsistent. Sometimes when he got to the top, he was able to get the club back into position on the way down, sometimes not. Wilson's idea was to get Weir to cut down on the motion in his wrists and to keep his right arm—the front arm in a left-handed swing—up against his chest. That would make it impossible for him to sway on the way up. In order to make sure his arm was in the proper place, Weir adopted a preswing waggle, taking the club back almost to the top to make sure he felt his arm against his chest, and then, instead of swinging, he would simply come down and reset his club behind the ball. Then he would swing.

The waggle was almost like a fake out to those watching. "There were a few times after I started using the waggle that I would make the move, and guys in my group would start walking off the tee expecting the ball to be in the air," he said. "Obviously I wasn't trying to fake anybody out, but a few times I did."

Armed with his new confidence and his new move, Weir headed for the finals in Palm Springs. "First day I hit the ball as well as I could hit it and couldn't make a putt," he said. "I shot 75. The good news was I knew I still had five rounds left, and I couldn't possibly putt that badly again."

He didn't. He shot 27 under par the last five days and finished first in the 169-man field, three shots ahead of runner-up Jonathan Kaye. That not only returned him to the tour, but, as the medalist at Q-School, he was high enough in the exempt pecking order that he would be able to play every week without worrying about how many players ranked ahead of him had decided to enter.

Right from the start, his second year on tour was entirely different from his first. He finished fifth in Atlanta, his best finish ever, but the real turning point may have come on a Monday playing with no official money at stake.

"There was a Skins Game up in Montreal," he said. "It was me, David Duval, and Freddie [Couples]. I just had one of those days where I made everything. I shot 63 and won all the skins. After that, I really felt I could compete with almost anyone."

Couples, who is now a close friend of Weir's, remembered that day vividly, even ten years later. "When you see Weirsy, at first you don't think there's that much there," he said, shaking his head. "He's a little guy, he's lefty, he's got that funny waggle and all. But he's become a solid ball striker, and around the greens he's got a magician's touch. That's what I remember about that Skins Game. And you could tell it wasn't just luck or a fluke. I mean he had real touch, a real feel for what he was doing. I remember thinking, 'This is a guy who's going to make some noise out here.'"

If Weir had any lingering doubts about his ability to hang in with the best players, they went away a week later when he was in the last group on Sunday for the first time in his two years on tour. The setting was the Western Open outside Chicago. The venue was Cog Hill, one of the tougher tests on tour at the time. The second player in the group was Eldrick T. Woods, also known as Tiger.

"I was three shots behind, and it was Tiger who never loses a lead," Weir said. "So, in a sense I had absolutely nothing to lose. I just told myself to go out and play as hard as I possibly could and let the chips fall.

"After nine holes, I'd cut the lead to one. I'm not going to say I was making Tiger sweat, but I was playing well. At the 10th hole, he hit his second shot over the green. I went into a front bunker. He got up and down; I didn't. That was pretty much it. He ended up winning by two. I was still pretty happy with myself on the day. I shot one shot lower than Tiger, and I hung in there, didn't get nervous, and finished second. In all, it was a great experience."

A few weeks later he made his first cut in a major, finishing 37th at the British Open, and went into the PGA Championship— also played outside Chicago that year, at Medinah—feeling great about the state of his golf game.

"The second place at the Western had taken Q-School completely out of the picture. I was closing in on a million dollars made for the year at that point," he said. "My swing felt great; my game felt great. I wasn't thinking about winning, just thinking I was ready to play really well."

He did just that for three days. He was 11 under par after

54 holes, which put him in a tie for first place with—you guessed it—Woods. Once again, they were paired in the final group. Only this wasn't the Western Open. It was a major, and Woods hadn't won one since his blow-away victory at the Masters in 1997, meaning he had gone zero for ten. Woods walked onto the first tee on that steamy August afternoon with a look in his eyes that let Weir know this was a very different setting than the one they had played in six weeks earlier only a few miles down the road at Cog Hill.

"You really can't understand what it feels like to be in the hunt on the last day of a major until you've been through it," Weir said. "I hadn't been there before, and I certainly hadn't been there playing with Tiger.

"I just wasn't ready for everything that's involved in being in the last group in a major. I mean, if you think about it, I'd gone from the last group at Q-School in December to the last group in a major the following August. That's a long way to travel in a few months.

"It was great that I'd done it, that I'd come so far, but I just wasn't ready for it—especially with Tiger. It was completely different than the Western. The pressure ratcheted way up; there were more people; there was more noise, more security. A lot of times during the day I had to back off shots because of people moving after Tiger had hit or because of noise. I'm not making excuses, but it is a little bit like a circus. Tiger didn't bother me at all. He was doing his thing; I was doing mine. He's not much of a talker out there—especially on Sunday at a major. But that was fine because I'm not a big talker out there either. It was just everything, the whole experience. I wasn't ready to handle it just then.

"I could have birdied the first hole, and I didn't. Then I three-putted the second and three-putted the fifth from eight feet. At that point I started pressing, and the day just got worse and worse."

By the time the day was over, Weir had shot 80 and had dropped to a tie for 10th place. Most players will walk away from that sort of debacle and insist it was a learning experience, without being able to explain what they learned—other than the fact that the pressure of the last day of a major is different from the pressure of the last day of any other tournament.

Weir, though, did learn, mostly by observing Woods. "As great as he is, I could see that *he* was nervous," Weir said. "I remember on 17 he had a key putt that he absolutely had to make or he was probably going to end up in a playoff with Sergio [Garcia]. I watched the way he stalked that putt, made absolutely sure he was ready to putt before he got over it, and I remember the look on his face when it went in. I remember thinking, 'I want to have a putt like that someday in one of these things.'

"You always know from the time you first pick up a club how important the majors are. I can remember watching the Masters as a kid and thinking how cool it would be just to play in one, much less contend or win one. By the time you become a pro, you know all four of them aren't like the other tournaments. You see what it does to a guy's career to win one. You hear players talking about them, telling stories.

"But after you experience playing late in one, you feel differently. It gives you a hunger to do it again that you didn't have before. That day made me rethink my goals in a lot of ways. I didn't want to just be a good player. I wanted to be a guy who had a real chance to win a major. Watching Tiger, especially those last few holes, seeing how much it meant to him and how exhausted and relieved he was at the end taught me a lot."

The irony of that Sunday afternoon was that it was really the first time Woods had felt the pressure of trying to hang on to win a major. At the '97 Masters he started Sunday with a nine-shot lead and, for all intents and purposes, needed to finish 18 holes standing to win the green jacket.

Over the course of the next ten majors, Woods never held a 54-hole lead, and seriously contended only twice—in the 1998 British Open and in the 1999 U.S. Open. In both cases, trying to come from behind on Sunday, he had finished third. This was different. He started the last day tied for the lead, and the man he was tied with—Weir—fell away fairly quickly. That left him trying to hold off Garcia, who was making his first significant appearance on the world stage at age nineteen. Watching Woods deal with that kind of pressure, seeing that it affected him too—he fought his way to an even par 72 that day to hang on and win by one shot—was most definitely a learning experience for Weir.

"Tiger was very gracious that day when we shook hands," he remembered. "He just said, 'Hey, you're playing great. Forget about today.'"

ONE OF WEIR'S STRENGTHS is his ability to forget—a trait Woods has all but perfected over the years. Like Woods, Weir never seems to get discouraged when things go wrong. He may get angry, and he certainly gets frustrated. But he never says, "This is too tough."

"I usually just say, 'Okay, that wasn't good enough. What do I do to get better?'"

Three weeks after he lost Sunday at the PGA, he found himself in contention again. The setting wasn't a major by any stretch, but for a twenty-nine-year-old Canadian the pressure was almost as great. The place was Vancouver, the tournament the Air Canada Classic, and Weir found himself in position to become the first Canadian to win on tour since Richard Zokol had won in Milwaukee in 1992. And, perhaps more important, he had a chance to be the first Canadian to win a PGA Tour event in Canada since Pat Fletcher had won the Canadian Open in 1954—sixteen years before Weir was born.

"People in Canada are very loyal and devoted to Canadian athletes," Weir said when the subject of that very emotional day came up. "I think a lot of it has to do with the fact that there aren't that many of us. Obviously our population is a *lot* smaller than the U.S. A lot of the biggest stars are hockey players, so when someone has some success—almost any success—in another sport, it's a very big deal."

One might not think of Canada as a rabid golfing nation, especially given the shortness of the Canadian golf season. But Weir points out that more people per capita play the game in Canada than in any other country in the world. "I've often wondered if because the season is so short, it makes us appreciate the game more than in some other places," he said. "When you talk about golf, it isn't as if the first country you think about is Canada, but up there, I can tell you, people really get intense about it."

The last day in Vancouver was intense from start to finish, Weir's countrymen cheering him with every step. When he holed out from 155 yards with an eight-iron on the 14th, the roars seemed to reverberate from coast to coast.

"I remember it was cold, really cold," he said, laughing. "Canadian summer—a gray August day where you could see your breath. People were wearing parkas all afternoon. I was tied for the lead on the 14th hole when I holed that shot with an eight-iron. The roar when that went in was like nothing I'd ever heard— at least for me. I might have heard a couple like that for Tiger. Then at 16, I made a long birdie putt, and that gave me enough cushion to get it done. I'm not sure if I was shaking from the cold or from nerves on 18. Probably a little of both. But I was definitely shaking."

Weir had always known that his first win on tour would be a big deal in Canada. But actually winning *in* Canada ratcheted the whole thing up exponentially.

"It was just overwhelming," he said. "There's just no way you can prepare for something like that. If the next week we'd been playing someplace in the States, I think I probably could have handled the extra attention because there wouldn't have been all that much of it. But the next week was the Canadian Open, and it seemed as if everyone in Canada wanted five minutes with me. I wasn't going to say no to people. I understood this was a big deal to a lot of people, and I also understood it was an opportunity for me.

"But there was no way I was going to be able to focus on playing."

Not surprisingly, Weir missed the cut. That was disappointing since the Canadian Open ranks behind only the four majors in importance to him. "It's *my* fifth major," he said, smiling. "Realistically, though, there wasn't much I could do. I think I might have hit ten range balls that week—if that."

The win not only established him as a star in Canada, it gave him security on tour. His two-year exemption guaranteed him a spot on tour—no more Q-School—through 2001. It also set him up financially, allowing him and Bricia to buy a house in Salt Lake City. There would be no more loading up the Camry for the summer.

For the year, Weir ended up making just under $1.5 million in prize money, which put him 23rd on the money list, a jump of 108 places from his rookie year. Armed with his two-year exemption and the confidence that comes from winning and making a lot of money, he played even better in 2000. He almost doubled his money, making more than $2.5 million for the year.

Perhaps more important than that, he won another tournament, and this time it was an international event that included all the top players in the world. It was played at Valderrama, in Spain, which had hosted the 1997 Ryder Cup matches, and Weir shot 67–67 the last two days to hold off Woods and Lee Westwood. As emotional as the victory in Canada had been a year earlier, this one, in a World Golf Championships event, with virtually every top player in the world, was a giant step forward.

"I had proven I could compete with the best guys, and I'd proven to myself that I could hold up under pressure trying to win a tournament," Weir said. "But to actually *beat* the best guys on a Sunday was almost as good as it could get. After that I felt like when my game was on, I could win against anyone, anytime.

"That meant there was really one goal left for me to accomplish—winning a major. At that point, I hadn't played in that many of them, but the win at Valderrama meant I was going to get into all four of them. No qualifying, no worrying about my world ranking—I was in. I just felt like my time was coming. I'd come a long way in a few years. But I still hadn't completely climbed the mountain just yet."

4

Climbing the Mountain

By the time the 2001 golf season ended, Mike Weir had established himself as one of the best players in the world. He had finished 2000 in sixth place on the PGA Tour money list and dropped only slightly—to 11th—in 2001. That had much to do with his decision to cut back on his schedule—from twenty-eight tournaments to twenty-three—after the birth of his daughter Lili in April 2000.

"It just got harder to travel with two kids instead of one," Weir said. "So, I tried to cut my schedule back a little bit to be home more."

For a third straight year he won a tournament, and, once again, it was an important one. This time it was the Tour Championship, the season-ending event open only to the top 30 money winners on tour. He shot 68 the last day to get into a four-way playoff with Ernie Els, Sergio Garcia, and David Toms. Els was a two-time U.S. Open champion; Toms had just won the PGA Championship; and Garcia, at twenty-one, was one of the game's rising stars. Pretty good company. (Tiger Woods finished tied for 13th.)

Weir won by birdieing the first playoff hole, becoming the first non-American to win the Tour Championship, and jumped to sixth in the world rankings. He was playing so well at that point that there was no reason to change anything in his game. But, like most golfers, he wanted to improve even more.

Going to Palm Springs to work with Mike Wilson had become an annual off-season ritual. As well as he had played, making just under $8 million in three years, Weir felt as though he needed to improve his ball striking a little bit more if he wanted to contend — seriously contend — in the majors.

Since the 10th-place finish at the '99 PGA, he had played in eight majors and hadn't matched that performance, his best finish being a tie for 16th at the '01 PGA. Having won on tour, having beaten the best players, having given himself financial security at age thirty-one, there was just one truly important goal left: win a major championship.

"I think every kid who ever picks up a golf club fantasizes about the majors," Weir said. "Maybe nowadays there are kids who stand on the putting green by themselves late in the day and say, 'This is to beat Tiger Woods,' but I think most of them proba-bly say, 'This is to beat Tiger Woods and win the Masters or the Open.' I think that's the way the game has always been. I'd gotten good enough by then that it wasn't just a fantasy anymore. But I felt like I needed something more to make it reality."

That winter, he and Wilson worked on changing his preshot routine, cutting back on the waggle with the hope that it would somehow tighten up his swing just a little bit and make him more consistent off the tee and with his long irons.

His first round of the year suggested that he might have been on to something. He shot 63 on the first day of the Mercedes Championships, tying the course record for the Plantation Course at Kapalua. But he couldn't back up the start and slid to a tie for 14th place on Sunday. That proved to be a harbinger for the whole year: he would come up with a good round, even a very good one, here and there, but he couldn't put four good rounds together.

"Early in the year I got into contention a couple times, but my swing didn't hold up under pressure the way it had when I was winning the previous three years," Weir said. "I realized after a while that, for whatever reason, the waggle was the trigger that got me into position and made me feel the most comfortable. I went back to it midway through the year, but by then I'd lost confidence in my putting. I just never could put anything together all year."

He wasn't awful; he simply wasn't as good as he had been. He made twenty-two cuts in twenty-five tournaments and was in the top 25 on eleven occasions. But, after making the top 10 in twenty-one tournaments from '99 through '01, he didn't have a single top-10 finish. Nine of those top 10s had been top threes, including his three victories. Needless to say, he didn't come close to finishing that high all year.

He ended the year with $843,000 in earnings, which dropped him to 78th on the money list and left him wondering what he had to do to get back to where he had been prior to the '02 season. He again went to Wilson during the off-season looking for answers.

"Nothing was working," he said. "Mike was trying, I was trying. We just couldn't make any progress. Finally, one afternoon I got so frustrated I just left Mike on the range, jumped on a cart, and drove out to an empty spot on the golf course. I needed a break from grinding, hitting balls, talking about the swing, hitting more balls.

"I finally stopped on a long par-three and just sat there for a while. Finally I took out my five-wood and decided to just try to relax and remember what my swing felt like when I was playing well. I hit one shot and liked it. So, I hit another. I ended up hitting six balls, shaping each shot a little bit differently, kind of telling myself, 'Okay, just hit this shot, no pressure, just hit it.'

"I'm not sure why, but something clicked at that point. The ball started going exactly where I wanted it to go. It was such a relief to see I could still do it. For some reason, after that I just felt more relaxed about my swing. I stopped grinding and started playing again."

Golfers often talk about the key to improving being the ability not to make golf work. Tom Kite once said, "You have never heard someone say, 'I'm going to go work golf.' You say, 'I'm going to go play golf.' You need to take that approach to your swing on the range. When it becomes work, you almost never get any better."

At some point during that session on the long par-three, Weir found his way back from working at golf to playing it. The Bob Hope Chrysler Classic was his second tournament in '03, since he had not qualified for the Mercedes Championship (for the first time in three years; tournament winners only), and he arrived feeling relaxed, confident, and fresh after starting the year with a solid ninth-place finish in Phoenix.

He played solidly all week but trailed leader Tim Herron by four shots entering the fifth and final day. The weather was windy that day, making the golf course unusually difficult. But Weir shot 67 and won the tournament by two shots over Jay Haas.

"Even if I hadn't won, I'd have come out of that week feeling really good about things," Weir said. "I felt like I was back to hitting the ball the way I had before '02. Plus, I made putts. You have to make lots of putts to win at the Hope [Weir's winning score over 90 holes was 30 under par], and I did. I made putts from all over. It had been a long time since I had done that."

If he had any lingering doubts, or if he wondered whether he could also win on a truly difficult golf course, they went away a few weeks later when he shot a five-under-par 66 on Sunday to catch Charles Howell III from seven shots behind (winning in a playoff) to win the Nissan Open at Riviera Country Club, one of the classic golf courses played on tour. That gave him two wins in four starts and put him on top of the money list early in the year.

It did not, however, make him a favorite going into the Masters. For one thing, he had never finished higher than a tie for 24th in three starts at Augusta. For another thing, there was only one favorite as tournament week began, and that was the two-time defending champion—the one player who had sur-passed Weir in victories on tour in 2003.

Tiger Woods had three wins—in San Diego, in the Match Play Championship, and at Bay Hill. He hadn't yet named a swing coach to replace Butch Harmon, but everyone knew he was spending time with Hank Haney, working on trying to take his swing more to the outside to avoid getting stuck coming down.

If Tiger was showing any signs of trouble because of the swing changes, no one had really noticed them yet. And even though Weir had won twice in 2003, he, like almost everyone else in the field, was able to fly under the radar during tournament week, which was fine with him.

"I've always had a pretty good relationship with the media," he said. "I get along with most of the guys I've dealt with quite well. But I'm fine if I'm not getting a lot of attention, especially the week of a major. I really want to get off by myself and work to get ready."

ANOTHER PLAYER WHO ARRIVED at Augusta unnoticed but full of confidence was Len Mattiace. While Weir had slipped in 2002, Mattiace had pieced together his best year, winning his first tour event in Los Angeles in February, then backing it up with a sec-ond win in Memphis in June.

Like a lot of players, Mattiace was a relatively late bloomer and had gone through the ups and downs that so many players go through before establishing himself as a solid moneymaker.

He had learned the game as a kid growing up in Mineola, on Long Island. His dad had started him playing right-handed at age six, even though he was a lefty, and he took to the game immedi-ately. "I think it's fair to say I've loved everything about golf since I was eight," he said.

By the time he was thirteen, he was good enough to make the

team at Jericho High School as an eighth grader. When he was a freshman, his family moved to Ponte Vedra Beach, Florida, which happens to be where the PGA Tour is headquartered. Given a chance to play year-round, Mattiace blossomed into an excellent junior player at Nease High School.

As a sixteen-year-old, he was one of the youngest players to qualify for the Northeast Amateur, which was played in Newport, Rhode Island. During the week, Mike Felici, one of the board members who helped run the tournament, introduced him to his eighteen-year-old daughter Kristen. Len was dazzled. Kristen was not.

"He was kind of a little kid to me," Kristen said, laughing. "I mean, I was getting ready to go to college. He was sixteen. He told me later that it was love at first sight."

Len was recruited by most of the top golf schools but chose Wake Forest, a program that had produced, among others, Arnold Palmer, Curtis Strange, Jay Haas, and Lanny Wadkins. As a freshman in 1986, he was part of a team that won the national championship coming from way behind on the last day to beat Oklahoma State.

A year later, Mattiace made the Walker Cup team, playing in the amateur equivalent of the Ryder Cup. The U.S. team easily defeated Great Britain and Ireland that summer, and the next April, at age twenty, Mattiace found himself playing in the Masters.

These days, only five amateurs—the U.S. Amateur champion and runner-up, the British Amateur champion, the U.S. Public Links Champion, and the U.S. Mid-Amateur champion—are automatically invited to play. In those days, as part of its commitment to amateur golf (Masters cofounder Bob Jones being the greatest player never to turn pro at any point in his career), the Masters invited the entire Walker Cup team to play. In 1988, all ten members of the '87 Walker Cup team were in Augusta.

Mattiace would talk later about how he just assumed back then that, once he turned pro, he would be at Augusta every year. "I was a young college stud at the time," he said. "I thought I'd be on the tour, be in the top 30 on the money list every year, and play the Masters every year."

Life is never quite that simple. Unlike a lot of top college golfers—including Palmer, Strange, Haas, and Wadkins—Mattiace graduated, getting his degree in sociology in the fall of 1990. While he was finishing his degree work, a friend of his named Barry Fabian, who knew Kristen, told him that the girl he'd had the crush on back in high school was now living in Jacksonville, where she had gotten a job as a teacher after earning her degree in elementary education. She didn't know anyone in town, Fabian said, and he suggested that Len give her a call. He did, and she agreed to have dinner with him. He was en route to Florida from Wake Forest, planning to pick her up to go out, when—unbeknownst to him—Kristen was taken to the hospital for an emergency appendectomy.

"I called his parents to tell them what was going on," she said. "I said, 'Look, you don't me, but I'm supposed to be having dinner with your son tonight, and I have to go the hospital.' Except they couldn't reach him. There were no cell phones, and he was in the car.

"Len got to town and called my apartment to let me know he was ready to pick me up, and he got my answering machine. He finally left a message saying, 'Well, I guess you're blowing me off.' My parents went to my apartment to get some things for me later and heard the message. They tracked him down and told him what had happened, and then his parents told him I'd called. He felt horrible and came to the hospital every day to see me. We started dating when I was better and just went from there."

Mattiace spent most of the next five years of his life wandering the backwaters of professional golf. He did make it through

Q-School in 1992 and spent 1993 on the tour. He didn't even play all that badly—he had two top-10 finishes, but one was at an event played opposite the Masters where the prize money was relatively low, and he finished the year 160th on the money list.

Injuries were frequently a problem. During '93, Mattiace was diagnosed with carpal tunnel syndrome and was often awake half the night because the pain was so bad he couldn't lie down.

He had gone back to Q-School at the end of '93 and again at the end of '94. Each time, he failed to make it back to the tour. He spent '94 playing minitours after he recovered from wrist surgery and '95 on the Nike (now Nationwide) Tour. He made it back through Q-School at the end of '95 and managed to stay on tour from 1996 on, even though he had to have carpal tunnel surgery on his other wrist at the end of '96.

Late in 1996, he was in a five-way playoff at the Buick Challenge after the last 36 holes of the tournament were washed away by rain. Michael Bradley won the tournament, but the money Mattiace made from his second-place tie, combined with a tie for fourth a few weeks later in Texas, jumped his earnings to $238,000 for the year and allowed him to finish 92nd on the money list and keep his card. The following fall, a tie for third at Disney solidified him again, and he moved up to 77th on the money list.

His first real brush with fame and with a serious chance to win came a year later at the Players Championship. His story was well chronicled that week. For one thing, he was a local boy making good. Beyond that, his mother, Joyce, dying from lung cancer, was there in a wheelchair. A Mattiace victory would have been a remarkable feel-good story.

He came close.

On Sunday, he arrived at the infamous island-green 17th hole trailing Justin Leonard by just one shot. The next fifteen minutes were brutal to watch. Mattiace put his tee shot in the water. He walked to the drop area, hoping to salvage a bogey and hit his third shot into a front bunker. Then, from the bunker, he flew the green back into the water. By the time it was all over, he made a quintuple-bogey eight. What many people forget is that he somehow shook off the disappointment to birdie the 18th, one of the tougher finishing holes in golf.

He finished tied for fifth — his biggest paycheck up until that moment on tour but, no doubt, his biggest disappointment. Three months later, his mother passed away. In stories written about that day, it is frequently pointed out that the last time she saw her son on a golf course, he was making a quintuple-bogey eight on national television. They forget to point out that, in truth, the last thing she saw him do was make a gritty birdie on the final hole.

"To this day I have people come up to me and say, 'I remember Len at the island green in '98,'" Kristen Mattiace said. "'What did he make, eight?' I say, 'Yes, he did, but did you know he made a birdie on the 18th hole?' I know people don't remember that because it hasn't been shown a million times on television the way the eight has been.

"What I remember vividly about that day is that Phil Mickelson was playing in the group behind us. Amy [Mickelson] had walked ahead to get to a good spot to watch and saw me as we were leaving the 17th. I was in uncharted waters. I had no idea what I should say or do when Len finished. Amy just looked at me and said, 'Just tell him you're proud of him.' She was right — and I was proud of him."

MATTIACE HAD GONE TO work on his swing with Jim McLean, one of the game's best-known teachers, after losing his card five years earlier in 1993. McLean had told Mattiace then that he had two options: try to get his technically imperfect swing to work for him — players like Jim Furyk and Bruce Lietzke had done that very successfully — or tear down his swing and rebuild it completely.

Mattiace opted to go back to square one.

"I knew there were guys who'd done well with unorthodox swings," he said later. "But the vast majority of guys who have been consistent players and winners have very technically sound swings."

His improvement was gradual. Each year he seemed to get a little better and a little more confident. He was consistently in the top 100 on the money list from 1996 to 2001 but was never really close to winning until 2002, when he came from behind on the last day at Los Angeles to catch Scott McCarron (who helped by bogeying three of the last six holes, including the 18th) and win for the first time in his 220th start on tour.

A gentle soul by nature, Mattiace couldn't help but feel sorry for McCarron when the tournament was over. "I wouldn't wish that finish on anybody," he said. "I especially wouldn't wish it on a guy like Scott."

Unfortunately for Mattiace, that win came during a period when the Masters had abandoned its long-standing tradition of granting an automatic invitation to anyone who had won a tournament on the PGA Tour. That change had come during a time when the Lords of Augusta were trying to "make over" their field. Selected past champions were sent letters informing them that although they were exempt into the field for life, the club was "suggesting" that they stop playing in the tournament. This came after Doug Ford, the 1957 Masters champion, continued to use his champion's exemption long after he could play the golf course competitively.

In his last five Masters before the letter was sent out, Ford's scores were 81–88, 85–94, 89–withdrew, 88–withdrew, and 94–withdrew. By the time he shot that last 94, he had played in a then-record forty-nine Masters, and people were screaming to find a way to get him off the golf course. Traditionally, past champions had sensed when it was time to stop playing in the tournament, usually sometime between ages sixty-five and seventy. Ford turned seventy-eight in 2000 but still teed it up that April.

The decision not to invite all tour winners beginning with the 2000 Masters also had a good deal to do with a push made by the powers that be in golf to reward long-term results rather than a hot week. Prior to the change, players who finished in the top 30 on the PGA Tour money list at year's end were exempt into the Masters the following April. Under the new setup, the top 40 were invited.

Mattiace had finished 84th on the 2001 money list, so he wasn't invited to the 2002 Masters even after his victory in Los Angeles. Until that point he had only played in six majors in his career, starting with that 1988 Masters when he had been, as he described it, "a young college stud."

It had taken him fourteen years to get from there to winning on the PGA Tour. Some players, even very good ones, never get that first tour win. All who do will tell you the same thing: the first win makes you feel as if you *truly* belong. Loren Roberts, who would go on to win eight times on the tour and has been a star on the Champions Tour since turning fifty, was almost thirty-nine when he won for the first time.

"Until you walk out on a Sunday evening holding a trophy, you feel almost like a day worker out here," Roberts said at the time. "Once you've won, you know you're a [PGA Tour] member for life, and you feel as if you've proven that you belong, really belong."

Mattiace was thirty-four when he broke through, and he felt much the same way Roberts had felt. Brimming with new-found confidence, Mattiace won again at Memphis in June, charging from behind on Sunday just as he had done in Los Angeles, shooting a 64 to again come from seven shots back to win. That victory wrapped up a spot for him in the '03 Masters because it ensured that he would finish in the top 40 on the money list.

"Everything really does change when you win a tournament,"

Kristen said. "It's not just financial. It's the way people look at you, the way they treat you. There is definitely a hierarchy among the wives, just like there's one among the players. I remember when Len was a rookie on tour, I was invited to a wives' luncheon. They asked all of us to stand up and say who we were and who we were married to. I stood up and said, 'I'm Kristen, and I'm married to Greg Norman.'

"Of course they all knew that wasn't true—Greg wasn't even playing that week for one thing. Afterward a lot of the older wives came up and said, 'Why did you say that?' I told them it was because I knew they'd like me better if I was Greg Norman's wife."

By the end of the year, Mattiace had won just under $2.2 million, almost triple the money he had made in his previous best year ($762,000 in 2000), and had finished 18th on the money list. That performance guaranteed that he would get the chance to play in all four majors for the first time in his career.

Unlike Mike Weir, who had not played especially well in 2002 but had started 2003 as well as any player in the world not named Woods, Mattiace had not gotten off to that good of a start. In fact, his only top-10 finish had come in Los Angeles, where he had tied for eighth while defending the title he had won the year before. Nonetheless, just being back in the Masters made him feel good about himself and his golf. Having learned from experience that taking a spot in the Masters for granted was a mistake, Mattiace planned to make the most of the opportunity.

Weir was in his fourth straight Masters and wasn't thinking so much in terms of getting to come back as improving on past performance. "I'd been consistently mediocre," he said, laughing. He was right: his previous finishes had been a tie for 28th, a tie for 27th, and the high-water mark tie for 24th.

Prior to arriving in Augusta, Weir decided to make one change to his Masters week routine. Like most players, he had always rented a house for the week. Weir's family and a couple of close friends shared the house with him, and everyone enjoyed the camaraderie of spending time together each night.

"We had a pretty good routine going," he said. "We'd cook out if the weather was nice, sit around, maybe drink a few beers, and tell stories after dinner. It was always fun."

For his fourth Masters, Weir rented the same house once again. The usual suspects would be there, but Bricia and the kids would stay home because it was just too much work to travel cross-country with such young children. This time, though, when dinner was over, Weir's plan was to sit around for a while and then leave—for a hotel.

"I just thought I'd sleep a little bit longer and maybe a little bit better," he said. "It wasn't necessarily going to be as much fun, but I wanted this Masters to be more than just fun."

In a sense, he was in a better position now than he had ever been in before going into the tournament. The two victories had been worth more than $1.6 million, and if he didn't win another nickel all year he had made enough money to clinch a spot in the 2004 Masters. All he had to do was worry about playing the best golf he was capable of playing. He went to bed in his hotel room on Wednesday night convinced he had a chance to seriously contend.

Of course, his name was hardly on the lips of any of the prognosticators. Tiger Woods—absolutely. Phil Mickelson, who had finished third two years in a row? Sure. Vijay Singh, another past champion; Ernie Els, who had won three majors and been achingly close at Augusta in the past; Davis Love III; Fred Couples; even Rich Beem who had won the last major played—the 2002 PGA—were all names being mentioned.

But Mike Weir? Nice player having a nice year but on the new supersized Augusta National (it now played 7,290 yards as opposed to the 6,925 it had played to when Woods won in 1997), a short, straight hitter had little chance. The same was true for Len Mattiace, who would, no doubt, be thrilled to finish in the top 16 and earn a return visit in 2004.

Woods was trying to become the first player in history to win the Masters three straight years. That was the story when everyone woke up on Thursday morning. It would be part of the story all weekend. But the tournament would not unfold the way anyone had imagined.

5

Battle Royal

THE SCENE WAS SET for a battle in Augusta, but the battlefield was in questionable shape. It had rained overnight, and it was still raining Thursday morning when the players woke up to prepare for their scheduled tee times. The tournament's planned eight o'clock start was pushed back to 10:50 in the hope that the weather would clear long enough to get some play in.

The rain did stop briefly, long enough for players with early tee times to hit a few balls on the range, but then the skies opened up again. By 11 a.m. the decision had been made to send everyone home for the day and try to get the golf course into playable shape so that players could be sent off two tees at 7:30 Friday morning. It was the first time since 1939 that the opening round had been completely washed out by rain.

The Masters doesn't like to break with tradition, and starting before eight in the morning and having players tee off on both the front and back nines simply isn't done, unless there's no choice. In this case, the weather forced a break in tradition.

Several years earlier, the club had abandoned the notion that it could play the entire tournament in twosomes and re-pair after the first round. Almost all golf tournaments send players out in threesomes for the first 36 holes and do not re-pair until the start of the third round, when the players are sent out in twosomes, the worst scores playing first, the best scores last.

Because pace of play on the PGA Tour had slowed so much throughout the 1990s, in 1999 the Masters finally gave up on twosomes for the first 36 holes, instead shifting to the more traditional threesomes and not re-pairing until after the second round when the cut had been made. But everyone still went off the first tee on Thursday and Friday rather than off the first and 10th as was done at most PGA Tour events. The Masters could afford the one-tee start because it rarely had more than ninety players in the field, compared to the 144 or 156 (depending on the time of year) in most other tournaments.

But the Thursday rainout left the Lords of Augusta with no choice: If players wanted to have any chance to complete the tournament by Sunday evening, they would have to start early Friday, go off two tees, and play as many holes as possible before it got dark Friday evening. The plan was to complete the second round on Saturday morning and—weather permitting—be back on schedule by the end of the third round Saturday evening.

The conditions weren't pleasant Friday morning. The weather was still misty, and the temperature was in the forties when the players began warming up shortly after sunrise. The golf course would play long and hard because of the wet conditions, and walking up and down the Augusta hills would certainly not be a treat, especially since everyone expected to play at least 27 holes by day's end.

"Not exactly the ideal way to start a major," Mike Weir said. "But it was the same for everybody."

Weir was paired for the first two rounds with two-time Masters champion Tom Watson and Irish Ryder Cupper Padraig Harrington.

For Weir and his caddy, Brennan Little, the pairing was both difficult and poignant. Bruce Edwards, who had been Watson's caddy for most of thirty years, had been diagnosed in January with ALS—Lou Gehrig's disease. Everyone in golf knew that Edwards had been handed a death sentence, and, in spite of his brave promises to caddy for Watson for another thirty years, they knew this would almost surely be Edwards's last Masters on Watson's bag.

"You could see how he was struggling, especially during that long day on Friday," Weir said. "He was having trouble talking, and even though he would never admit it, you could see how tired he was getting, especially towards the end of the day. I was actually kind of relieved when it finally got dark and we had to stop."

Weir played very solidly throughout the day. He shot a two-under-par 70 in the first round, which put him four shots behind leader Darren Clarke but only one shot behind Sergio Garcia and U.S. Amateur champion Ricky Barnes, who were tied for second place with 69s.

Weir's group was able to play 12 holes in the afternoon—going off the 10th tee—and by the time the horn blew at dusk, stopping play for the day, Weir was three under par on his second round and leading the tournament at five under par.

"I felt good all day," he said later. "I was finding fairways, which was important, because you didn't want to play out of the rough, even the Augusta rough, with the golf course so wet. And my putter was there right from the beginning. That gave me a real jolt of confidence."

ONE PERSON NOT FEELING at all confident when the horn blew on Friday was Tiger Woods. Right from the start, he had struggled. He wasn't finding fairways with any consistency—and Augusta's fairways are about as wide as any in golf—and he wasn't making putts to save par the way he always seemed to do when he was in control of his game.

He shot a horrific, four-over-par 76 the first 18 holes, his worst round at Augusta as a professional, and was still four over par after 27 holes when play was stopped. As the players trudged wearily to their cars, knowing they all had to return to take their places on the golf course at 8:20 the next morning, Woods trailed Weir by nine shots and was in danger of missing the cut if he didn't get his game in gear.

Woods's play—not the play of Weir or of any of the other players near the lead—was the talk of the tournament that night. No one could remember seeing Woods fight his swing for so long at Augusta National since his win in 1997. That year, he had shot 40 on his first nine holes, only to come back and shoot 30 on the back nine. He had taken the lead on Friday afternoon that year and never looked back. After he had finished off his stunning 12-shot victory, he had been asked if there was any way he could have played better.

"Well," he said with a shrug, "I did shoot 40 on my first nine holes."

Because of who he is, no one was ready to count Woods out at the end of the first day. Nine shots down with two and a half rounds to go was not impossible for him. He had once come from eight shots down in the final round in a tournament overseas, catching Ernie Els—not exactly a club pro—to win.

That said, no one had been prepared for the possibility that Woods would be fighting to make the cut on Saturday morning. He had missed the cut as an amateur in 1996 but since turning pro had been out of the top 10 just once in six Masters. He had three wins, a fifth, a tie for eighth, and a tie for 18th in 1999 when he had been going through his first major swing change. Now he was struggling to make the top 44 and ties (or to stay within 10 shots of Weir since the Masters has a 10-shot rule that allows anyone within 10 of the leader to play the last two rounds) in order to make the cut.

Len Mattiace hadn't played much better than Woods on Friday, but, at the very least, he appeared to be in good shape to make the cut. He had shot a one-over-par 73 in the first round and was at three-over-par for the tournament, with four holes to play at dusk. It appeared that the cut would come at four or five over par and that it would be the top 44 and ties, because there were not that many players within 10 shots of Weir's lead.

Saturday dawned clear and sunny, an almost perfect day for golf. The temperature was still a bit cool — in the low sixties — when the players returned to the spots where they had been when play was called, but the day was warming quickly with no clouds in sight.

Weir finished his second round solidly, shooting a four-under-par 68, which put him at six under par for 36 holes. No one else had been able to handle the new supersized golf course the way he had. Clarke had spun back after his 66, shooting 76, but was still in second place, trailing Weir by four shots. Phil Mickelson had shot 70 in the second round — only three players had broken 70, the same number as in the first round on the long, wet golf course — and had jumped into a tie for third at one under par with Ricky Barnes, the U.S. Amateur champion who had outplayed Woods while paired with him for two days.

Woods's Saturday morning was a lot like his Friday had been. While everyone waited for him to make a move, he appeared to be running in place. He had teed off on the 10th hole for the second round, meaning he would finish his round on the ninth green. He arrived at the eighth tee appearing to be safely inside the cut line at four over par. The cut was almost certain to be five over at that point. Since the par-five eighth is a birdie hole for most players — more so for a long hitter like Woods — it seemed out of the question that Woods would play the final two holes at any-thing worse than even par.

That almost wasn't the case. Woods's drive missed the fairway at the eighth, and he had to lay up rather than go for the green in two. He hit a mediocre third shot to 50 feet and then, shockingly, three-putted for a bogey six. Instead of making birdie to have a two-shot cushion on the cut going into the ninth, he now had to par the ninth to make the cut. By now it was late morning, the course was bathed in brilliant sunshine, and thousands of specta-tors—most of them stunned by what they were seeing—were ringing the ninth green waiting for Woods.

The ninth is a deceptively difficult hole. It isn't very long— 460 yards with a drive straight down a hill—but the second shot is straight uphill, a blind shot to a tricky green that tilts back to front. Land a shot too close to the front, and the ball will spin right off the green and roll down the hill. Land it too far back, especially with a front-hole location, and you can be left with a very long putt that can twist in four different directions before it reaches the hole.

The flag that morning was front right, almost a sucker pin in the sense that a player trying to hit a shot directly at it could easily watch his shot land a few feet from the pin and roll back down the hill in front of the green.

Woods had no chance to fire at the flag because he pushed his drive into the pine straw underneath the grove of trees to the right of the fairway. From there, he had to try to punch a shot toward the left corner of the green, hoping to somehow get the ball up on the green and then stop it before it rolled all the way over. It was the kind of Houdini-like shot Woods has made famous.

Only this time, Woods wasn't Houdini—he was human. The ball rocketed out of the trees, left of the green all the way, finish-ing in the left bunker. That made the math quite simple: Woods had to get up and down for par, or, for the first time in the twenty-five majors he had played as a pro, he would fail to make the cut.

The good news for Woods was that he had a lot of green to work with. He set his feet carefully and hit a wonderful shot from the bunker to within four feet of the hole. Not exactly a tap-in, but the kind of putt Woods rarely misses under pressure. This time was no exception: he rammed the putt into the center of the hole, took a deep breath, and headed to the champions locker room for a quick lunch.

WOODS WAS ONE OF the last players to finish the second round. There was a break of an hour and forty-five minutes before the third round began. Only four players were under par after 36 holes, led by Weir at six under. Then came Clarke, Mickelson, and Barnes, who not only held up quite well playing with Woods but had outplayed him by six shots. There was a host of big-name chasers not much further behind. Vijay Singh, two-time Masters champion Jose Maria Olazabal, and David Toms were among those at even par, and K. J. Choi, Jeff Maggert, and Ernie Els—who had shot 79–66—were at one-over-par 145. Len Mattiace had made the cut with two shots to spare at three-over-par 147.

When the players returned to start the third round at 12:50 in the afternoon, they found completely different conditions. The sun had dried the course, but it was still soft, meaning players could fire shots at flags knowing the ball was likely to stop quickly. The temperature was warm, now approaching eighty degrees, and the breeze was gentle. Ideal conditions for scoring.

Not surprisingly, the player who took advantage of the conditions first and foremost was Woods. Right from the start, playing in one of the first groups on the course, he looked like a different player. Starting on the 10th tee—the players again went off two tees in order to try to finish the round before dark—he drained a long birdie putt on the 11th and was off to the races. By the time he returned to the ninth green for the second time that day, he was six under par for the afternoon and was one under par for the tournament.

That put Woods on the leaderboard and had people talking about the greatest comebacks in major championship history. He had made up nine of the 11 shots by which he had trailed Weir, who struggled to a 75 in the afternoon round. That left Weir in second place at three under par behind the new leader, Jeff Maggert. Often a contender in major championships but never a winner, Maggert, who had birdied five of the last seven holes after a double bogey on the 11th, had equaled Woods in the third round with a 66 of his own and had jumped to the top of the leaderboard at five under par.

Maggert would be with Weir in the final pairing on Sunday. Singh and Toms, who were at two under par, would be in the second-to-last group. Woods and Olazabal, both at one under par, would go just after Mickelson, who was also at one under par, and Jim Furyk, who was at even par. Among those final eight players, four — Woods, Singh, Toms, and Olazabal — had won majors. Mickelson and Furyk were generally considered the best players in the world who had not won majors, and Maggert, even though he had only won twice on tour, had eleven finishes in the top seven at majors. Only Weir, with his 10th-place finish at the 1999 PGA, had not contended late on Sunday at a major.

The pairing directly in front of Mickelson and Furyk had even less experience in majors than Weir. Jonathan Byrd was twenty-five and playing in the first major championship of his life. He was even par through three rounds and would play the last 18 holes with Len Mattiace, who had played superbly on Saturday afternoon, shooting a 69 that put him at even par too, tied for eighth place with Byrd and Furyk — five shots behind Maggert.

Mattiace wasn't really thinking in terms of winning at that

point. A top-16 finish would guarantee him a spot in the '04 Masters, and that was well within reach. Still, all week Kristen had been pushing the "mojo" of the house they were staying in.

"We actually rented two houses," she said. "Len and I and the kids [Gracee was five and Noelle was two] were in one house, and our families were down the street. When we got to the house, there was a nice note from the lady who owned it saying that a lot of players who had stayed there had done really well in the tournament, including David Duval a couple of times. I kept saying to Len, 'Breathe in that mojo. Let it work for you.'"

Most of the players were exhausted on Saturday evening. They had played 54 grueling holes in two days, and now they would have to wait until Sunday afternoon to play again. Maggert and Weir, the last pairing, would tee it up at 2:30. CBS would come on the air at two o'clock, which would give the network just enough time to set the scene before going to the first tee to show the two players who had the 2:10 tee time. That pairing would consist of two-time Masters champion Olazabal and — surprise — Tiger Woods.

MIKE WEIR WOKE UP earlier than he wanted to on Sunday morning, but that didn't really bother him. He knew, even with a late tee time, that he would be too keyed up to sleep very late. He had talked to Bricia the night before, and they had decided that she should fly in to watch the last round, just in case.

"It wasn't as if I was thinking, 'I'm going to win,' or anything like that," Weir said. "But I did feel confident, even though I hadn't made anything at all on Saturday afternoon. I thought if I could make a putt or two starting out and get some confidence going, I'd have a chance. I think we both thought that if I didn't win, it would be nice for her to be there anyway, and if I did win, she certainly wouldn't want to have missed it."

Bricia was still en route when Weir left for the golf course, so he didn't get a chance to see her before going out to warm up and then play. He was able to spot her in the crowd early in the round, though, helped by the fact that the biggest galleries were following the Woods-Olazabal and Mickelson-Furyk pairings.

Maggert and Weir did have one thing going for them as they stepped onto the first tee: the Masters winner had come from the final twosome on the golf course for twelve straight years. That said, there probably weren't more than a handful of people wandering around Augusta National on a sun-splashed afternoon who thought that streak would continue.

The first true roar of the afternoon came for Mickelson. If there was anyone other than Woods that most fans wanted to see win, it was Mickelson. At age thirty-two, Mickelson was a true star. He had won on tour twenty-one times — the first time when he was still in college — and had finished second in the U.S. Open twice, third in the Masters three times, and second in the PGA once. But he still hadn't won a major championship, and the questions about his inability to do so had started to bug him.

Unlike some players who have won a lot but never in a major, Mickelson didn't rationalize the hole in his résumé. He didn't claim, as Colin Montgomerie had once, that "I'll have had a great career whether I win a major or not." He clearly understood the difference between a lucrative career and a great one.

Mickelson parred the first hole but then pulled his drive way left into the trees at the par-five second hole, the ball finding a small stream. Forced to take a drop, Mickelson, always the risk taker, hit a driver from the woods for his third shot and threaded it through the trees and onto the front of the green about 80 feet from the hole. Even at that, he stood to lose a stroke to most of the field because number two is a birdie hole for most players. Mickelson promptly rolled the 80-footer into the center of the hole, which prompted a rare fist pump and a wide smile.

Maybe, finally, this would be his day on a major championship Sunday.

The leaderboard on most major Sundays is an ever-changing puzzle. Nowhere is that more true than at Augusta where most of the holes—especially on the back nine—offer risk-reward opportunities that can send players climbing upward or tumbling backward in a matter of minutes. Even though changes to the golf course have taken some of that away, almost nothing is certain on a Sunday at the Masters.

There really are few events in sports that TV treats with the reverence of the Masters. It is only in recent years that the club has loosened the reins on the telecast a little bit, allowing CBS, which has televised the tournament every year since 1956, to show the entire front nine and to expand its weekend telecasts so that fans can see the leaders play their entire rounds.

What hasn't changed is the syrupy music, the hushed tones, and the sense that something slightly more important than the election of a president or a pope is about to happen.

And, of course, there are the "Augusta Rules." There are no front nine and back nine at Augusta but, rather, a first nine and a second nine. There's no rough but, rather, a first cut and a second cut. The Masters, unlike the other three majors, is *not* a championship—it is a tournament or, as ex-club chairman Hootie Johnson always called it, a "toonamint." And you had better believe there are no fans or galleries watching the toonamint. There are, and always will be, "patrons."

Several years ago when Sean McDonough was still working for CBS, he slipped one afternoon and referred to the crowd around the 16th green. Horrified and concerned he might go the way of Jack Whitaker (who once famously referred to the patrons around the 18th green as "a mob" and was banished forever) or Gary McCord (who referred to "bikini-waxed greens," and "body bags" behind the 17th green, for those who were foolish enough to go over the green, and was also banned), McDonough announced to anyone who would listen in the clubhouse the next morning that "there are going to be patrons *everywhere* at 16 today. There will be patrons behind the green, around the green, and perhaps *on* the green. There may be patrons swimming in the water next to the green."

The patrons had a big day at 16, and McDonough survived. Along with crowds, there is also no mention of money at the Masters. The total purse in 2003 was $6 million, with the winner getting $1,080,000 (those numbers had jumped to $7.5 million and $1,350,000, respectively, by 2009), but if you watch CBS you might think the players are playing strictly for the green jacket.

"Will it be a day that defines a man's career?" Jim Nantz said in his melodramatic opening. "Or will it be another day for a man who has defined his sport?"

Cue syrupy music.

Of course, there is some truth in all the syrup and breathlessness. As huge as the prize money is, what drives players on the last day of a major is knowing that a victory makes them a part of golf history. And that was the way Weir was thinking as he walked to the first tee on Sunday.

"I thought I was ready to handle the pressure of the last day of a major," he said. "In 1999, I hadn't been ready. Now, I thought I was. That didn't mean I was going to win, but I did think I was going to play well."

Weir and Maggert provided striking contrasts as they walked to the first tee: Weir in a black shirt, Maggert in a white one. Weir isn't exactly Lee Trevino, but he is friendly and warm to most people. Maggert was described by Nantz as "the taciturn Texan."

Both men overcame their nerves to hit good drives on number one, but Maggert was short and right with his second shot, and Weir was long and left, the ball skidding just over the green about 40 feet from the hole. Maggert pitched to 10 feet and made his putt. Weir's birdie putt rolled five feet past, but after a long look he also made his par putt.

"That was a key putt," he said. "Because the greens had really gotten fast by Sunday afternoon, and I knew I was going to be looking at putts like that all day, and I was going to have to make them if I wanted to win."

Up ahead, Woods had reached the second green in two and had made birdie to get to two under to tie Mickelson. Vijay Singh had also birdied the second and was tied with Weir at three under. As he had done throughout the tournament, Weir laid up at the second, then hit a wedge to two feet for a birdie that put him at four under. As they walked to the third tee, Weir trailed Maggert, who had failed to birdie the second, by one shot.

By the time they got there, the hole had already changed the tone of the day, and the tournament. Lanny Wadkins, who was CBS's lead analyst at the time, described number three as "the toughest short hole I have ever played in golf."

It is, indeed, a short but treacherous par-four, just 350 yards long. It is called "Flowering Peach" (each hole at Augusta National is named for a flower), and with the tees up, longer hitters can drive the green. The championship committee, which sets the tees and the hole locations each morning, had moved a number of tees up on Sunday to tempt players to go for spectacular shots.

The first person to give in to that temptation, surprisingly, was Woods. Very rarely does Woods make a mental mistake on the golf course. But he walked to the third tee brimming with confidence after his two-putt birdie at the second hole. He hadn't made a bogey since the eighth hole in the second round on Saturday morning, and he was feeling good about his swing. So was Steve Williams, his caddy. Except when talking to his boss or someone he deems important, Williams is one of the more unpleasant men you are likely to meet in any walk of life. His colleagues have dubbed him "the vigilante caddy," since he often takes it upon himself to yell at professional photographers for doing their job or to destroy cameras owned by fans who are not authorized to have them on the golf course.

He is, however, an excellent caddy. Sensing his player's confidence, Williams suggested to Woods that he go for the green, no doubt thinking he might pull off an eagle and, at worst, would get up and down from somewhere near the green for a birdie. Woods would later tell CBS that it had been Williams's idea—"Stevie talked me into it" were his exact words—but would take the hit for the decision himself since, in the end, it was his decision.

As soon as he saw Woods pull the driver, Lanny Wadkins questioned his choice. "I think this is a bad gamble," he said. He was right.

The shot never had a chance. It went straight right, smacked off a tree, and came to a stop in the middle of the trees that line the right side of the fairway. From there, even though he was only 103 yards from the flag, Woods had no chance to get the ball on the green, but managed to pitch it out from the trees to a spot a few yards short.

On most holes he would have had a reasonable chance for par. But Flowering Peach isn't most holes. The green is very shallow from front to back and has swales running through it. Finding a pin placement on a flat area can be a challenge. With the flag tucked on the left side, getting the ball close was tough. Woods tried to hit a pitch and run, but the ball never stopped. It ran all the way through the green, coming to rest on the fringe, leaving him with a straight downhill shot coming back.

Things didn't get any better after that. His next pitch ran through the green again, stopping 17 feet from the hole. He putted from there, missing by six inches, and tapped in for a double-bogey six. Just like that, he had gone from three shots behind Maggert to five shots back.

Neither Weir nor Maggert hit the ball long enough to even

think about hitting driver at the third. Weir hit an iron that ended up rolling just into the rough (first cut) on the right. Maggert's tee shot found the front of the fairway bunker on the left.

At the moment Maggert stepped into the bunker, Woods was three-putting the par-three fourth hole from 30 feet to fall another shot back. Mattiace, who had birdied number two and number three, was walking off the fifth green, having just saved par by holing a 12-foot putt. He was at two under par, tied with Mickelson and Toms, trailing Singh by one, Weir by two, and Maggert by three.

Maggert had a difficult shot. He had to clear the lip of the bunker and still hit the ball far enough to reach the green, which was 137 yards away, *and* get the ball to stop once it got there. Perhaps overthinking, Maggert hit the ball thin, and it didn't carry the lip. But that wasn't the worst thing about the shot. Before Maggert knew what had happened, the ball ricocheted off the lip and hit him in the chest.

Stunned, Maggert stared down at the ball, which now rested at his feet. It took a moment for him — and for everyone else — to realize what had happened. When he did, Maggert immediately called Weir over.

"The ball hit me," he said. "I'm going to call for an official."

Maggert was fairly certain he knew the rule, but he wanted to be sure. Too often on tour, players assume they know the rules, don't call for an official, and end up making a mistake. This rule was simple: if you get hit with your own golf ball, the penalty is two shots.

"Needless to say, I was stunned," Weir said. "I really didn't see what happened, but when Jeff called me over, I had a feeling maybe the ball had hit him. Otherwise, why would he need me?"

Players frequently check with other players if they are unsure about a rule or to inform them when they are going to penalize themselves. Weir knew the rule but didn't argue when Maggert said he wanted to ask an official. "The last thing you want to do is give a guy bad information," he said. "Jeff never asked me, but if he had I think I'd have said, 'I think it's two shots and play it as it lies, but let's check.'"

After confirming the two-shot penalty, Maggert played what was now his fifth shot from the bunker. He hit a superb shot, the ball rolling just over the green about 50 feet from the flag. Still a little bit shaken by what he had seen, Weir managed to put a pitching wedge on the green and two-putted from there for a par he was very happy to make. Maggert's first putt rolled 15 feet past the hole. Just when it looked as if he might take an X, he rammed in his second putt for what was the closest thing one could make to a "good" seven.

Suddenly, the entire tenor and mood of the tournament had swung because of one innocent-looking little par-four. Weir was now the leader at four under par, with Singh one shot back. Maggert had dropped to two under, and Woods was now behind a large group of players and was at one over par. What's more, the confidence he had felt standing on the third tee was in reverse.

The last six holes of the front nine at Augusta National are, generally speaking, not the place to try to make a move. The fourth and the sixth are two of the more difficult par-threes in the world; the fifth is a long, difficult par-four; and the seventh and ninth are shorter par-fours with treacherous greens. Only the par-five eighth is a birdie hole, and it is the longest and least reachable of the golf course's par-fives.

Every player in contention at the Masters on Sunday knows this. Barring a lucky or brilliant shot, the general approach is to hope to pick up shots at the two par-fives and be happy with par at the other seven holes. It can be tempting to attack the third because of its length, but as Woods and Maggert learned, any bold play can be disastrous.

Almost everyone in the field had some sort of hiccup working their way through the four through nine minefield. Mickelson hit his tee shot long and right at the sixth and made a bogey to drop back to one under. Singh made his first bogey of the day at the fifth to drop to two under. Toms missed the fairway at the seventh and bogeyed to fall to one under. Woods found the front bunker at the seventh and made bogey from there, and then, remarkably, bogeyed the eighth for a second straight day after driving his ball into the right fairway bunker. That left him at three over par and, shockingly, out of contention, barring a miraculous back nine. The disgusted look on his face as he walked to the ninth tee made that seem unlikely, even for him.

The three players who did the best job of not losing ground during the rest of the front nine were Weir, Mattiace, and, surprisingly, Maggert, who somehow managed not to lose his composure after the debacle at number three. He made a great par save at number four and then rolled in a 30-footer for a rare birdie at the fifth to get back to three under. That kept him within one shot of Weir who was doing what he knew he needed to do: make putts to save par.

At the fourth, Weir's 30-foot birdie putt went 10 feet past the hole, causing David Feherty to say, "That's the first real mistake he's made so far today." Weir quickly erased the error, though, by making the putt coming back. At five, he looked destined to make bogey when his tee shot found the left bunker and his second shot came up well short of the green. From there, he had a pitch-and-run shot that, seemingly, was almost impossible to get close. He cozied it to three feet and made the putt to maintain a one-shot lead over Maggert and Mattiace, who had just made a remarkable birdie at the eighth.

Mattiace had missed the fairway to the right with his drive, and, after pitching out, his third shot had come up well short and left of the green, leaving him with a tough pitch, especially since the flag was tucked behind a bunker on the green's left side. He pitched the ball onto the front of the green, hoping it would stop somewhere within 10 feet of the flag to give him a reasonable shot at par. Instead, the ball bounced onto the green and took a hop to the left. From there, it just kept rolling until it hit the flagstick and dropped in for a stunning birdie.

"I saw it with my own eyes, and I still couldn't believe it," Jonathan Byrd said. "He hit a really good shot with a lot of touch, but the way it bounced left was amazing."

Mattiace couldn't even see the ball go in from where he was, but he heard the shocked roar from the crowd and thrust a fist into the air. He walked onto the green with the kind of grin that is usually seen when someone talks a cop into letting him off with a warning. But in this case, the cop had handed Mattiace a $100 bill and said, "If you get stopped again, use this to pay the fine."

Until that moment, Mattiace had been gliding along unnoticed, even by the other players on the leaderboard. Weir and Maggert were waiting for one of the big names to start making a move, but Mattiace was now three under par for the day and tied for second with Maggert.

Weir expanded his lead to two shots when he hit a brilliant six-iron to four feet at the sixth, easily the best shot of the day at a hole where most players were thrilled to be within 30 feet. He made another miraculous par at the seventh, wedging to five feet from the same front bunker where Woods had found himself twenty minutes earlier.

Weir also missed the eighth green. After a mediocre layup, his chip from 70 yards came up short of the green, about 80 feet from the hole. His chip rolled six feet past, but he made the putt for par. At that moment, Weir had hit only three of eight greens, but he was two under par for the round.

"Which is what you have to do on the last day of a major, no matter which one it is," he said later. "You're going to make mistakes. You're going to miss fairways and greens. How you handle yourself on those holes is what ultimately decides your fate on the day."

The one person who was continuing to make it look relatively easy was Mattiace. After he parred the ninth, his second shot from the 10th fairway came up 80 feet short and right of the flag. The hole location on the 10th is almost always the same on Sunday: back left. If you go for the flag and carry the ball too far, you may find yourself with an almost impossible shot from behind the green. Most players take the conservative approach, trying to land on the front of the green, hoping the ball will roll to a reasonable distance. No one complains about making par on the tenth.

Mattiace's second shot had finished in a spot almost identical to where Ben Crenshaw's second shot had ended up on Sunday in 1984. From there, Crenshaw had rolled in what was arguably the most famous putt of his career, the putt bending right to left and diving into the hole. That birdie had given Crenshaw the momentum that carried him to his first major victory and the first of two Masters wins.

Mattiace wasn't thinking about Crenshaw as he lined up the putt; rather, he was thinking that he would be very happy to two-putt and run to the 11th tee. Only he didn't two-putt. The putt tracked almost the identical path that Crenshaw's had taken nineteen years earlier with the exact same result: the ball rolled into the center of the cup, for Mattiace's second breathtaking birdie in three holes.

Ever alert, CBS producer Lance Barrow almost instantly came up with tape of Crenshaw's putt to show the viewers how close to identical the two putts had been.

Playing the eighth hole at that moment, Weir and Maggert heard the roar for Mattiace's birdie but had no idea what or who it was for. "To be honest, I had no clue," Weir said. "You hear a roar that loud, there's a tendency to think it's Tiger or Phil, but I knew Tiger had dropped back some and Phil was probably still on the ninth, and the roar didn't come from there. So, I just didn't know."

The birdie at 10 put Mattiace alone in second place, one shot behind Weir. With everyone having made the turn except for Weir and Maggert, who were on the ninth, the standings looked like this: Weir at five under; Mattiace at four under; Maggert at three under; and Mickelson, Furyk, Singh, and Toms all still lurking at two under. Olazabal and Rich Beem were one shot further back.

One of the oldest clichés in golf is that "the Masters doesn't start until the back nine on Sunday." The reason that statement had always applied to the Masters more than to the other majors is the way Bob Jones and Alistair McKenzie designed the last (second) nine holes. There is water in play at five of the nine holes (11, 12, 13, 15, and 16), and players have risk-reward options on a number of holes, most notably the two par-fives — 13 and 15. Those holes are often referred to as "par-four-and-a-halfs," because they often can be reached in two but not without dealing with potential water troubles.

Even with the lengthening of the golf course, 13 and 15 were still holes where players could make a major move in one direction or another. The two par-threes often play an important role in deciding winners and losers. The tiny par-three 12th almost never requires more than an eight-iron off the tee and is often played with a wedge, depending on the wind. But the green is narrow, and there are water and bunkers in front, and bunkers and a flower bed behind. Any error, any gust of wind one way or the other, and a player can be in deep trouble. The 16th isn't nearly as daunting, and the Sunday pin is often back left, near the water, but in a spot where a shot that lands right of the flag may funnel toward the hole if it lands in the correct spot.

There had already been talk that the lengthening of the golf course had taken some of the romance out of the back nine. More players were laying up at 13 and 15 than in the past, and 18, once a hole with some birdie potential, had been stretched out to the point where birdies were few and far between.

Even so, with a tightly bunched leaderboard—there were nine players within four shots of the lead, five of them past major champions—it was clear that this was one Masters that would be won on the back nine on Sunday.

"What's hard about it is that there's no chance to take a deep breath," Weir said. "Part of it is the situation, but a lot of it is the golf course. There are birdie holes out there, but there isn't a single hole where you can lose any concentration at all and not get burned by it. It can wear you out mentally."

That's why it isn't at all uncommon to see players sneak up the leaderboard on Sunday and then suddenly plunge—undone by "Amen Corner," or, almost as often, by other less famous holes.

Weir finished his front nine with a solid par at the ninth, hitting an eight-iron to 18 feet and two-putting to go out in 34, two under par. As he and Maggert (who had also parred the ninth) walked through the ropes that run behind the 18th green to get to the 10th tee, CBS showed a graphic on the highest finishes by Canadian players in major championships: George Knudson had tied for second in the '69 Masters behind George Archer, and Dave Barr had tied for second, one shot behind Andy North, in the '85 U.S. Open.

Weir was still a long way from matching or topping them as he walked to number 10. The 34 on the front nine meant that he had played the front nine in six under par for the tournament. Through three rounds, he was one over par on the back, including the three-over 39 on Saturday that had knocked him out of the lead.

He began the back nine with another par, while Maggert, who had been quietly hanging in, rolled in an 18-foot birdie putt to get to four under, one shot back. Singh was also at four under at that moment.

Up ahead, Mattiace had stayed away from trouble to make par at the 11th, and then caught the kind of break at the 12th that a Masters champion often needs. His eight-iron looked for a moment as if it might come up short of the green, but it landed just over the bank that would have almost guaranteed a wet finish and stopped 18 feet from the hole.

"That was four feet from disaster," CBS's Bobby Clampett said.

"He got away with one there," Lanny Wadkins said in response.

"Looks like it's turning into a magical day for Len Mattiace," Clampett added.

Mattiace two-putted for par and walked to the 13th tee still trailing Weir by a shot. He hit a perfect drive, drawing the ball toward the corner where the hole doglegs left. From there he had 224 yards to the hole and decided to go for the green with a five-wood. He hit a gorgeous shot, the ball landing on the front of the green and rolling to within 10 feet of the cup. At that moment Mattiace was the twentieth player in the field to go for the 13th green in two on Sunday and only the second to find it.

The "patrons" were by now beginning to sense what Clampett had brought up on the 12th hole: that this was indeed becoming a magical day for Mattiace. With Woods out of contention and Mickelson still a couple of shots back but not making a big move, they were as happy to root for Mattiace as anyone else. When his eagle putt went into the hole putting him at six under par for the day and for the tournament, the cheers echoed off the giant trees all the way back to the 10th green, where Weir and Maggert were at that moment.

"I guessed that it was Len and that he'd made eagle because it wasn't a birdie roar," Weir said. "I could tell it was coming from 13 green, and I had a suspicion he'd just taken the lead."

He had. Weir knew he had to stay patient and make sure he got through 11 and 12 without making a mistake. His chance at

13 would come soon enough, and there were still plenty of holes to play — for everyone.

Weir and Maggert both parred the 11th. Singh had birdied 11, but then bogeyed 12 from the back bunker and bogeyed 13 after a poor drive that forced him to hit his second shot left-handed. Olazabal and Beem had both gone into the water at 13. Mickelson and Furyk were still at two under par, along with Singh. It was beginning to look like it was a three-man tournament: Mattiace, Weir, and Maggert.

Weir found the green at the 12th and breathed a sigh of relief. The hole was playing longer than usual because of the wind, and Maggert decided to go with a seven-iron to make certain he didn't come up short. He didn't, but the ball flew into the back bunker. There may not be a more frightening bunker shot in golf than one played from the back bunker at the 12th hole, which has the innocent-sounding name "Golden Bell," because the shot is straight downhill to the pin, and if you try to baby it you can leave the ball in the bunker. Play the ball boldly at all, and it can easily end up in the water.

That's what happened to Maggert. His second shot rolled through the green and straight into the water. As a result, he had to walk all the way around the green and Rae's Creek to the drop area between the tee and the green. Clearly unnerved, he plopped what was now his fourth shot into the water. Memories of Tom Weiskopf's 13 on the tiny hole began to surface in people's minds. Maggert finally found the green with his sixth shot. He missed his 20-foot putt for seven and tapped in for an eight.

Two holes — the shortest par-four on the course and the shortest par-three — had destroyed Maggert's chance to win the Masters. As he walked off the 12th green, Maggert had played 10 holes in the last round in two under par. He had played the third and the 12th in eight over par, meaning he was six over par for the day and one over par for the tournament.

Weir watched Maggert unravel with some measure of shock and an equal measure of sympathy. He knew he had to keep his focus, which wasn't easy since it took Maggert quite a while to play from bunker to water to water to green. Weir took a deep breath when Maggert finally found the green and began lining up his 60-foot birdie putt.

His putt went about five feet past the hole, but, just as he had done all day, he was rock solid on the putt coming back and walked to the 13th tee still trailing Mattiace by one.

At that moment, however, Mattiace was on 15. He had parred 14—often a difficult task for players pumped up after making an eagle at 13—and then hit a perfect drive at the 15th, leaving him only 219 yards from the hole.

"This may well be the most important shot of his life," David Feherty told the TV audience as Mattiace lined up his four-iron on a slight downhill lie. The shot rocketed over the pond fronting the green and rolled just over the putting surface. Many players are so concerned with coming up short of the 15th green that they go over the green and find water on the other side. Mattiace was close enough to the green that he could putt, and he cozied the ball to within 18 inches of the cup for a tap-in birdie. He was seven under par and two shots clear of Weir. No one else was within three shots of him.

But Mattiace knew the tournament was far from over since Weir had yet to play 13 and 15. Weir knew exactly what the situation was at that moment. "I knew I had to at least make a birdie at 13 and make one at 15 and make sure I made no mistakes coming in," he said. "Lenny had played a perfect round up until that point, but I still thought I could catch him."

Unless Mattiace completely collapsed, it was unlikely anyone other than Weir was going to have a chance to catch him. Mickelson had reached both 13 and 15 in two but hadn't converted either eagle putt. He was in third place at four under par, but the more likely birdie holes were behind him. Furyk was at three under. Everyone else had gone backward on the back nine.

Weir hit a good drive on 13, although it was a little bit left of an ideal spot, and he had to steer around some overhanging tree branches with his second shot. He hit a four-iron from 193 yards, and the ball bounced through the green into the deep swale to the left. Peter Kostis quickly noted how tough the shot was by pointing out that it was possible to put the ball into the water fronting the green if the shot was played too boldly.

Clearly aware of that, Weir decided to putt rather than chip from the swale. The ball tracked all the way across the green and barely stopped before reaching the fringe on the other side, leaving a tricky 12-footer for birdie. Fully aware of what was at stake, Weir stalked the putt for a while before calmly stroking it into the hole. As it went in, he shook his fist, as if to say, "This isn't over yet."

Which was exactly what he was thinking.

Mattiace had other ideas. Wanting to be sure not to come up the least bit short on the par-three 16th — "Redbud" on the scorecard — he took a five-iron, with the hole playing 183 yards to its normal Sunday back-left pin position. His ball landed in exactly the right spot, dead center on the green, and trickled left, stopping 8 feet under the hole. The birdie putt was never going anywhere but in the hole. At that moment on Sunday at the Masters, Mattiace had played 16 holes in eight under par. He led Weir by two and everyone else by at least four.

Mickelson and Furyk were in trouble. They both parred 16 and 17, leaving them too far back with too few holes to play. "Realistically, when I didn't birdie 16 or 17, I knew it was over with Len [two groups ahead] on 18 at eight under," said Mickelson, who would finish third for a third straight year. "I needed to birdie those two and the 18th and hope he made five at 18 to have any shot at all."

Weir had parred 14 while Mattiace was playing 17. Seemingly

nerveless, Mattiace had hit another perfect drive at 17—which CBS somehow missed showing live—and then watched his second shot from 156 yards roll just off the green. From 40 feet he calmly putted to within a foot and tapped in. A par at 18 would mean Weir would have to play the last four holes in two under par to catch him.

Mattiace stood on the 18th tee fully aware of where he was and what he was on the verge of doing. The course record at Augusta National is 63—before the extra length was added— held by Greg Norman (1986) and Nick Price (1993). Neither man had won the tournament that year. The low Sunday round by a winner was the 64 Gary Player had shot in 1978, years before the course was lengthened. Mattiace needed a par to shoot 64 and, in all likelihood, win the Masters. He had not made a bogey all day: he had one eagle, six birdies, and ten pars.

On the 18th tee, the moment finally got to him a little bit. His drive went right, bouncing into the trees and the pine straw on the right side of the fairway. If the ball had bounced differently, he might have had a shot to the green, but when he got to it he could see that he had no chance and no choice but to punch out and try to get up and down for par. He did so, leaving himself 120 yards to the flag, which was in a new location—back right. The usual Sunday placement was front left.

The new location had given the players fits all day. There had been one birdie—by 1998 champion Mark O'Meara—and a slew of bogeys. Trying to make sure he didn't leave his wedge short of the upslope in front of the flag, Mattiace watched the shot fly over the flag and stop in the back fringe, 18 feet from the flag.

Badly wanting to make the putt, Mattiace looked at it from all angles and then, nerves clearly taking over now, left the putt a good seven feet short. All of a sudden he had a tough putt for *bogey*. He managed to slide that one into the hole. He breathed a deep sigh of relief, waved his cap in appreciation as the fans stood to cheer his remarkable round, and was in the scoring hut intently watching as Weir played the 15th hole.

Weir's drive on 15 had faded a little bit left into the rough, forcing him to lay up—not the play he wanted under the circumstances but the only play he had. From 92 yards he was able to skid his wedge to a halt five feet away, and, as he had done all afternoon, he coolly nailed the putt to get to seven under. That meant he and Mattiace were tied. Weir was walking off the green when he heard the crowd murmuring. He looked behind him at the giant scoreboard that is right off the green and saw the red "7" next to Mattiace's name, indicating he had bogeyed 18. He took a deep breath.

"New ball game," Weir said to Little as they walked through the tunnel underneath the stands that leads to the 16th tee.

6

A Life-Changing Moment

LEN MATTIACE WAS SITTING in the scoring cabin adding up the numbers on his card to be sure they were correct—golfers are especially careful about this at the Masters, where Roberto De Vicenzo's 1968 gaffe, signing for a score one shot higher than he actually shot, has never been forgotten—when Mike Weir made his birdie putt at the 15th to tie him for the lead.

Mattiace knew it would take Weir at least forty to forty-five minutes to play the last three holes and that a playoff was a distinct possibility. Traditionally, when a player is tied for the lead late on Sunday after finishing 18 holes, the tournament committee has him taken by cart to the Bobby Jones Cabin, which sits in the woods to the left of the 10th tee. The player doesn't stop to talk to the media because he is considered to be playing as long as a playoff remains a possibility.

So Mattiace got into a cart with Jack Webber, his caddy, riding on the back, and headed for the Jones cabin. While Mattiace was in transit, Weir hit a shot that made it look as if a playoff might not be needed, absolutely nailing a six-iron shot at 16, the ball landing 10 feet below the hole. Given the way Weir had putted all day, a birdie and a one-shot lead seemed not only possible but likely.

Except that this time he missed—the first putt he had missed from inside 15 feet all day. "It was a putt I thought I could make. I just wasn't quite as aggressive with it as I'd been with other putts," Weir said. "Still, I didn't feel badly. You can't make every putt, and I had made a lot of them. I just knew I had to grind out the last two holes, hope for a birdie, but make sure I at least went par-par."

Weir is not one of those players who doesn't check scoreboards on Sunday. Most players keep a close eye on where they stand on the leaderboard throughout a Sunday round because it can affect decision making, especially coming down the stretch. Every once in a while, a player will make a conscious decision not to check scoreboards, thinking it will somehow make him feel less pressure.

That can be dangerous. At the 1994 British Open, Jesper Parnevik came to the 18th hole needing only a par to — at worst — playoff. Having not looked at a scoreboard all day, he decided he needed to make birdie and played an overly aggressive second shot that led to a bogey. He ended up losing by one shot to Nick Price.

Weir wasn't about to make that mistake. Throughout the day he had been aware of what Mattiace and everyone else were doing. As he walked to the 17th tee, he knew exactly what the situation was. He knew he was the only man who could take the Masters away from Mattiace.

In the Jones cabin, Mattiace decided that watching Weir and perhaps stiffening up while he watched was probably not the best strategy. He asked to be taken to the range, where he was joined by his longtime teacher Jim McLean. With McLean sitting in a chair and Webber standing nearby, one might have thought the three were having a casual late-afternoon teaching session rather than killing time and trying to stay loose in case Mattiace had to play off to try to win the Masters.

Woods and Olazabal were finishing on 18 as Weir and Maggert walked to the 17th tee. Maggert had somehow not lost his cool after the debacle at 12 and had birdied 14, 15, and 16 to get to two under par, which put him in fifth place. He wasn't going to win, but no one could dispute his mental toughness.

Woods had never recovered from the gaffe at three and tapped in for a final par and a round of 75. "I thought if I could shoot 65, I'd win the tournament," he said. "Just like Jack did back in '86."

Woods was right: if he had shot 65 he would have won the tournament by one shot.

Back on 17, Weir had split the fairway with his drive and, like Mattiace a little earlier, left himself with a long birdie putt. He charged it five feet past the hole but, not bothered by the miss at 16, made the par putt coming back.

As he walked off the green, Weir felt a surge of pride. He knew the math was simple: If he birdied 18 he would be the Masters champion. If he parred it, he and Mattiace would play off.

"I turned to Butchie and said, 'Hey, I've got a real chance to win the Masters in the next few minutes. How great is that?'"

Making par or birdie at 18 — as Mattiace could attest — was no lock. The character of 18 had been changed radically by the new tee, which was a good 50 yards back from where it once had been. Before Tiger and new equipment, the yawning bunker on the left side of the fairway had been something players had to seriously think about standing on the tee. For most, if a solidly struck tee shot drifted left at all, the bunker came into play. If one aimed too far right, the trees on that side were an issue. Some players took the safe route and layed up with a three-wood before playing a middle iron to the green. Only one player in recent Masters history — Sandy Lyle in 1988 — had birdied the 18th to win the tournament, and he had done that from the fairway bunker.

But the new distances players were hitting the ball changed the hole in the late 1990s. Players routinely took driver and blew the ball over the bunker, knowing that even if they lost the ball left, they would still clear the bunker and have a short, relatively easy shot into the green. It was as if the bunker had become invisible.

That wasn't the case from the new tee. Many players couldn't reach the bunker, and those who could often went back to the old play of hitting three-wood off the tee. Weir had no idea that there had been only one birdie at 18 all day, and if he had he wouldn't have cared. All he knew was that he needed to make sure his drive found the fairway.

It did, coming up short of the bunker to a safe spot. He still had 199 yards to the flag and chose a four-iron, knowing that if he came up short of the ridge, the ball would roll back to the front of the green.

"I thought I had enough," he said, "but sometimes, no matter how many times you play the hole, you forget that it's basically straight uphill from the bunker to the green, and, on that day, the hole was way back. I think the fact that I wasn't used to playing to that pin position might have been a little bit of a factor. Plus, I didn't want to go over the green and have to chip back."

Playing just a little conservatively, Weir watched his shot land on the ridge in the middle of the green and roll backward until it stopped about 50 feet short of the pin. Realistically, that took birdie out of play.

As Weir and Maggert walked up the hill to the 18th green, bathed in cheers, Mattiace was standing on the putting green. He had given up trying to hit balls and decided to hit a few putts so his second warm-up of the day would feel as normal as possible. Most players hit balls on the range before they play, and then go to the putting green—which is almost always near the first tee—to hit some putts before their tee time. Mattiace knew his tee time was probably a few minutes away, so he was on the putting green.

Finding a place to putt wasn't that easy. The awards ceremony is always held on the putting green, and dozens of chairs and a podium had already been set up in anticipation of what was to come. Mattiace finally found a hole that wasn't covered by chairs in a corner of the green and hit a few putts. Mostly, though, he watched Weir as he lined up his birdie putt.

Weir knew he had a long uphill putt, and he didn't want to leave it short. He also knew that most of the day his longer putts had gone past the hole, and he didn't want to leave himself a downhill putt of any length coming back, simply because downhill putts are tougher to control than uphill putts.

He thought he had rammed the putt when he hit it, but he could see it quickly losing speed as it tracked up the ridge toward the hole. It stopped about six feet short, leaving him a putt similar to the one Mattiace had made for bogey forty-five minutes earlier. Only now Weir had to make it, or, after not three-putting all day, his final memory of the '03 Masters would be a three-putt on the final hole that cost him a chance to win the tournament.

While Maggert was finishing, Weir stood to the side and waited, his face showing no emotion. Inside, he was churning. When it was his turn, he circled the green, trying to read the putt, but also having a talk with himself.

"Whatever you do now doesn't change anything you've done all day," he said to himself. "Stay with your routine, make sure you hit a solid putt, and if you do that, whatever happens, you can walk away feeling good about yourself. Just stay in the moment and make the putt — don't think about what's going to happen next, one way or the other."

As he got over the putt he could feel the tension, and he took a deep breath to settle himself down. Finally, amid deafening silence around the green, he drew the putter back, put a perfect stroke on the putt, and watched it go straight into the center of the hole. Just as every putt under 15 feet — other than the one on 16 — had been all day, this was a never-in-doubt putt. Weir pulled the ball out of the hole and shook his fist, knowing there was still work to do but extremely satisfied with what he had accomplished in the past four hours.

Mattiace saw the putt go in and forced himself to look down and hit some more putts. He knew he had a few more minutes to wait while Weir signed his scorecard. They would be on the 10th tee—which is only a few yards from the putting green—in a matter of minutes. Soon after that, one would have a green jacket and a place in golf history forever. The other would be, well, the other guy: Dan Pohl to Craig Stadler, Ed Sneed to Fuzzy Zoeller, Scott Hoch to Nick Faldo.

IT WAS A FEW minutes after seven when Weir joined Mattiace on the 10th tee. The two men shook hands and congratulated each other on their play. Mattiace won the draw—reaching into a hat and pulling out the number one—so he had the honor. By now, every inch of possible space outside the ropes was packed with people, fans having raced over from the adjacent 18th hole the instant Weir's final putt went in.

Bricia Weir was standing outside the ropes at that moment, escorted by a club member. She hadn't gotten to the golf course until Mike was making the turn. She waved to him as he walked off the 10th tee to let him know she was there. Mike waved back. Later, when they discussed the day, Mike had no memory of seeing her at that moment.

"I was very happy to be out there, but I was trying not to get too caught up in the whole thing," Bricia said. "I knew what was going on, but it was almost as if I was in denial about what was at stake. I'm not one of those golf wives who analyzes everything her husband is doing. I've never gotten into that. When I'm out there, I do try to channel positive energy in Mike's direction. My hope is it starts with me and ends up coming out of his putter.

"By the time he got to the 18th, I was past being able to pretend this wasn't a big deal. All you had to do was look around to know. Standing there on the 10th tee when he and Len walked out there, I could definitely feel the tension of the moment."

Kristen Mattiace wasn't there. She had walked the entire 18 holes with her family and Len's family, often standing back from the ropes and listening for sounds, because trying to get close became more difficult as Len moved up the leaderboard. "At the 13th hole, I knew he had to decide whether to go for the green over the water," she said. "I'm afraid of water. Maybe it's left over from the 17th hole at TPC in '98.

"My mother isn't shy about shouldering her way into a crowd. She worked her way in there, and I said, 'Is he going for it?' She said, 'He's going for it.' I thought, 'Oh God.' I couldn't see the ball in the air, but then I heard the roar, and I knew he'd hit a great shot. I remember thinking, 'Why you little so-and-so, you just might pull this off yet.'"

Kristen managed to stay calm as Len negotiated his way—with the lead—from 14 through 17. At 18, her nerves kicked in again. "He'd struggled on the 18th tee all week," she said. "I knew what a good drive at that moment would mean. It was just a tough driving hole for him. Once he made the putt for bogey, I took off to go to day care to get the kids.

"I knew it would be at least forty-five minutes before there was a playoff or before anything else happened. I wanted to get the kids back there. When I got back and realized there was probably going to be a playoff, I had two thoughts: how in the world is he going to be able to play after waiting that long, and there is no way I can walk down that tenth hole with the girls."

The men in the green jackets understood and took her to the Bobby Jones Cabin. By then, Len was on the putting green waiting for Weir to finish.

———

THE TEE WAS COVERED in shadows by now, and Mattiace took his time looking for a spot to tee his ball up. He finally settled on a spot on the far right and, almost an hour after hitting his final tee shot on 18, cracked a perfect drive, drawing it down the middle so it would catch the hill and take a big bounce in the direction of the green. The drive was measured at 307 yards.

Weir decided that Mattiace's spot was just right for him too, although he had to put the ball down a bit farther from the tee marker since he was left-handed. Weir was trying to become the second left-handed golfer in history to win a major — Bob Charles had been the first when he won the 1963 British Open. Like Weir, Charles was a righty who played the game left-handed. One of golf's better trick trivia questions is to ask, "Who is the greatest lefty to ever play golf?" The answer is Ben Hogan — a lefty who played right-handed. Mattiace was also a lefty who played right-handed, and, while he had no dreams of matching Hogan, he now had a chance to be something that Hogan had been: a Masters champion.

Weir's drive was almost identical to Mattiace's, the ball bouncing down the hill and going exactly one yard farther than Mattiace's drive had gone. The two men marched down the fairway into the fading sunlight, the temperature dropping as dusk approached. It was a spectacular setting for a moment that meant so much to the two players involved.

Mattiace was away by exactly one yard. The 10th, even though not as famous as some of Augusta National's other holes, is historically and statistically the toughest hole on the golf course. It has been played through the years to an average of 4.29 — one of six holes on the course that has played over par since the Masters began in 1934.

Mattiace had enjoyed more luck on the hole than Weir, having birdied it on both Saturday and Sunday, most recently with the Crenshaw-like 80-footer a couple of hours earlier. Weir had played the hole sixteen times in four Masters and had birdied it just once.

It was a lot cooler now than it had been when the players had come through the hole in the late-afternoon sun. Mattiace pulled a five-iron. He was 188 yards from the hole and, ideally, wanted to draw the ball into the middle of the green, hoping that it would bounce back someplace close to the pin.

Only instead of starting right and moving left, the ball started left and kept going left. In player terminology, he had "overcooked" the draw, the ball flying way left of the target and the green. It took a big hop into the swale left of the green and came to a stop almost directly behind one of the huge loblolly pine trees that casts the green in shadow, especially late in the day.

Mattiace stared at the ball as it headed left and muttered "Damn" when he realized how far off target the shot was. He knew he probably had to figure out a way to get up and down from a very difficult spot because now Weir could play for the center of the green.

Weir did just that, aiming a six-iron at the front of the green, not wanting to do anything fancy with the shot. His shot was right on line, but, much like at 18, he played it a little too conservatively. The ball bounced on the front of the green and skidded to a quick halt about 50 feet below the hole.

Not a great shot but, at that moment, plenty good enough given where Mattiace's ball was located.

The two men continued their walk down the hill in the direction of the green, cheered every step of the way by the appreciative fans (patrons). As upset as Mattiace was with his second shot, he still paused to tip his white cap in response to the cheers. He walked over to check on his ball, then walked up on the green to survey his shot. It was not an encouraging sight. The flagstick was on the back left, meaning he had very little chance to stop the ball if he landed on the green, and he couldn't put very much loft on the ball because it might go straight up into the trees and leave him completely dead. If he landed short, there was a distinct possibility that the ball wouldn't even make it up the hill onto the green.

"It's almost impossible for him to get this close," Lanny Wadkins said. "He has to be sure he gets it on the green and hope he can make a 10- or 15-footer to save par."

That was what Mattiace was thinking. He knew if he left the shot short, he would need a miracle chip-in to avoid bogey, and he was fairly certain that Weir wasn't going to three-putt. He got over the ball and took three quick practice swings and a deep breath before drawing the club back.

His pitch landed on the green, but, even though he had put the ball as close to the fringe as he dared, it skittered all the way across the putting surface, leaving him a 20-foot putt for par.

Weir now had a huge advantage, knowing that if he two-putted he was likely to win the Masters. That advantage created pressure he hadn't felt until that moment.

"They always teach you in match play to expect your opponent to do something when it's least expected," he said. "So, I told myself, 'Lenny's going to make the putt.' I didn't want to catch myself thinking a two-putt was good enough to win, because when you do that, all of a sudden two-putting can become really hard."

His putt was on almost the same line as the one Mattiace had made earlier, though not as long. It was going to break hard to the left en route to the hole and pick up speed as it got close. As he lined the putt up, Wadkins noted that the 10th was traditionally one of the faster greens on the golf course because the trees kept it in almost constant shade.

What the players didn't know—because no one had told

them — was that the green had been rolled before the playoff began, making it lightning fast, especially with the close-to-dusk shadows now engulfing it.

Sure enough, trying to make certain he didn't baby the putt, Weir put too much speed on it. The line was good, but the ball skipped past the hole, leaving him seven feet coming back. Regardless of how good Weir had been on those putts all day, Mattiace clearly had life again.

The problem for Mattiace was that his putt was straight downhill, and, like Weir, he had to assume his opponent wasn't going to miss if he had a putt to win. He had watched from a few yards away while Weir banged in his putt on 18, a putt that involved a lot more pressure since a miss would have meant defeat. So, he tried to make the putt and, like Weir, put too much speed on it, especially given that it was downhill and playing fast.

The putt sped past the hole, moving faster and faster as it went, and didn't stop until it bumped against the fringe 18 feet away. The crowd gasped, stunned that Mattiace, who had been so brilliant all day, was suddenly looking like a weekend hacker.

Mattiace was still away. He now had to make the bogey putt or Weir would only have to two-putt from seven feet to win. By that point, Mattiace was mentally and emotionally gassed. He had been so good for so long all day and had waited so long for the playoff, only to see his second shot put him in an almost impossible position. His bogey putt looked for a split second as if it might have a chance, but it slid by the hole, stopping three feet away.

If it had been true match play, Mattiace would have told Weir to pick up his ball at that point and congratulated him. But in stroke play, the winner has to hole out to make the result official. Weir had been stroking putts that hit the back of the hole all day. He wasn't about to do that now. He cozied the putt up to the hole, stopping it about 10 inches away. He walked up to the ball, looked at it for a moment, and tapped it in. Both his arms shot into the air, and he walked over to offer his hand to Mattiace.

A couple of green jackets came onto the green to shake Weir's hand. He was now looking for Bricia, who suddenly appeared, sprinting from the crowd to run into his arms for a hug and a kiss. It was the first time they had seen each other up close all day.

At most PGA Tour events, the winning player's wife and kids are encouraged to charge the 18th green as soon as the final putt goes in the hole, for a family TV photo op. That's not the case at Augusta. In fact, one of the members is assigned to make sure that the wife and kids of any player in position to win are escorted to the back of the 18th green and also is given the job of explaining to the wife that she is to wait for her husband to come to her as he exits the green, not the other way around.

Bricia Weir had walked down the 10th hole escorted by one of the members. When Mike's last putt went into the hole, she completely forgot about Masters decorum and charged onto the green, thus becoming the first wife of a Masters winner to kiss her husband on the green.

"A couple of years later, I was at one of the pre-Masters parties, and the member who had been escorting Bricia came up to me and said, 'You know, your wife got away from me when your last putt went in,'" Weir said. "He was laughing about it, but I'm pretty sure it won't happen again anytime soon."

"I'm glad I got to go out there," Bricia said. "Not because I wasn't supposed to, but because of the look in Mike's eyes when I got there. I remember he just looked at me and said, 'I did it,' as if he couldn't believe it. It was an amazing moment for both of us."

Once the handshakes and the hugs were over, both players were taken by cart back up the 10th fairway. When they got to the top of the hill and reached the putting green where Mattiace had watched Weir make his putt on 18 a few minutes earlier, they went in opposite directions — literally and figuratively.

Mattiace's cart turned left to go past the clubhouse and down the hill that leads to the press building. There he would conduct one of the most wrenching and heartfelt post-Masters interviews anyone had ever witnessed.

Weir's cart veered to the right and went down the path that leads to Butler Cabin. Waiting for him there were Woods, the 2002 champion; Jim Nantz; Ricky Barnes, who had finished in 21st place and had been the low amateur; and Hootie Johnson, the club chairman. Not to mention TV cameras that would show this version of the green-jacket ceremony to people watching around the globe.

There may not be a more awkward awards ceremony in the world than the Butler Cabin ceremony. For years, the club insisted that the chairman be present but also that he ask the first question of the new champion. That tradition was finally done away with when then-chairman Hord Hardin opened the champion's interview in 1983 with Seve Ballesteros by saying, "Seve, there's a question I've always wanted to ask you.... Just how tall are you?"

To be fair to Hardin, he was also the chairman who said in the wake of the corporate takeover of golf and sports in America, "This will *never* be the Pizza Hut Masters. If it ever came to that, we'd just shut her [the tournament] down."

Nowadays, the chairman still starts the ceremony. But he quickly welcomes "my good friend Jim Nantz," who takes over from there. Even with a TV pro in charge, the brief interviews are about as stilted as you can possibly imagine.

Weir could have cared less. All he knew was that he was sitting next to Woods, who had one green jacket on and another draped over his arm. When the questioning had ended, everyone stood up, and Woods stepped behind Weir to put the jacket on him.

"Great playing, Weirsy," he said, as a chill ran through the kid from Sarnia.

———

MATTIACE WOULD BE ADDING $648,000 to his bank account but nothing to his wardrobe. He had locked up a spot in the 2004 Masters — the top 16 and ties are all invited back the next year — but knew he had been inches away from a place in the Champions Locker Room, for life.

He was predictably emotional talking to the media, breaking down as he spoke about what the day had meant to him and how he felt about playing so superbly, only to come up that much short of victory. He had kept his emotions in check for the entire day, but as it hit him what had happened — or perhaps, more specifically, what had *not* happened — the tears came in a flood.

Kristen had left the Jones Cabin and been taken to the press building as soon as Weir's final putt went in. But she'd needed some time to get the girls organized, and when she got there Len was a puddle. She wasn't surprised.

"He's Italian," she said. "He's a cryer. He cried when the girls were born, and I was pretty sure he was going to cry, win or lose, after this. But when I saw him, my first thought was, 'Oh God, they asked about the TPC and his mom again.' That was the first thing they had asked him about after he won in Los Angeles. But it wasn't that. It was just the whole day.

"When I think of that day, I really don't think that much about the playoff hole. I think about the fact that he shot 65 on Sunday at the Masters and came so close to winning. I was as proud of him that day as I've ever been."

This time, Kristen Mattiace didn't need Amy Mickelson to remind her to tell her husband how proud of him she was. That was never in doubt.

Weir had little time to think about his emotions. As soon as the ceremony in Butler Cabin was over, he took off the green jacket and then was escorted to the putting green where the official awards ceremony took place. The other three majors require that the runner-up take part in the ceremony. The Masters is merciful enough not to require the presence of the runner-up.

The bad news about the Masters award ceremony is that it takes forever. Virtually every golf official in the world is recognized, along with the club membership—all decked out in green jackets of course—and those who work at the club, in addition to all the volunteers who work the tournament. Then the green jacket ceremony is reenacted, and the winner speaks briefly.

Once the ceremony was over, Weir was taken by cart to the press building. Mattiace was long gone by then, and Weir first did TV interviews outside the building, then went inside to speak to the print media. From there he was escorted to the clubhouse, where he and Bricia joined the members for the "champions dinner."

It was closing in on eleven o'clock by the time all the toasts and speeches were finished, but Weir still wasn't finished with his workday. Several TV outlets are always granted a one-on-one sit-down with the champion at the end of the champions dinner, so Weir had to go through that before he was finally allowed to leave.

"I was fried by then," he said. "Honestly, I barely remember the dinner. I know I had a smile on my face the entire time because it was starting to sink in a little bit, but if you asked me anything that was said or anything I said in the interviews afterward, I couldn't possibly tell you."

From the club, he and Bricia drove back to the house where the group that had been there all week had already been celebrating. They joined in and watched the sunrise a few hours later. It was at that point that Weir remembered that he had to get to the airport, where a chartered plane was waiting to fly him to Toronto.

"I had made plans months earlier to unveil a clothing line in Canada through Sears on the day after the Masters," he said, laughing. "They were sending their plane for me, and they had a whole day lined up in Toronto. I just about had time to take a shower, pack, and get to the airport. I wasn't in the best shape of my life when I got there."

He managed to sleep a little en route to Toronto and was whisked into a car to head to the Sears store in a downtown mall, where he was going to make the announcement and sign a few autographs.

"We walked into the mall on the upper level and had to go down an escalator to get to the entrance of the store," he said. "I was still a little bit groggy, but as we headed down the escalator I saw this line of people coming out of the store and snaking down the hallway there for as far as the eye could see.

"I turned to the guys I was with and said, 'Hey, what do you think that's about?' I remember one of them gave me a funny look and said, 'Mike, that's about *you*. They're all here to see you.'

"*That* was when it really hit me. You're so focused on the task that you don't even think about how people on the outside are reacting to what you're doing. I've always known that Canadians love their star athletes. A lot of it is because we're a small country in terms of population. If you win an Olympic medal as a Canadian, you're a hero. The star hockey players, obviously, are huge. And I'd gotten a good deal of attention, especially after I won at Vancouver and started having success on the tour.

"But this was like nothing I had ever seen. I just hadn't thought about the notion that my winning was the lead story in every paper in Canada and what it meant to people. When I came down that escalator, it was as if a light went on in my head. I remember thinking, 'Oh my God.' I walked into the store, and people were cheering from every direction—the employees, everyone.

"It was an unbelievable feeling. It also made me understand

something I hadn't thought about until that moment: my life was now completely different. I was no longer 'Mike Weir, successful golfer,' I was 'Mike Weir, Masters champion.' I was in a new world."

With a brand-new set of challenges. But that would all come later. That night, as planned, Weir and some of his friends went to a Stanley Cup playoff game between the Toronto Maple Leafs and the Philadelphia Flyers in Toronto's Bell Centre. Leafs officials asked Weir if he'd like to drop a ceremonial opening puck before the game began. Needless to say, Weir was thrilled. Since he'd been wearing the green jacket all day, he wore it onto the ice.

"When I walked out there, the place just went nuts," he said. "The players were all lined up at their blue lines, and they were all tapping their sticks [hockey player applause] on the ice. I got out there, and I was standing between Mats Sundin [Leafs] and Jeremy Roenick [Flyers] who are each about 6 foot 5 in street shoes, which makes them about 6 foot 8 on skates.

"I looked up at the two of them and thought, 'Boy, did I make the right call choosing golf.'"

At that moment, there was absolutely no doubt about that.

7

Best Player to Have Never Won

MIKE WEIR'S VICTORY AT the Masters was heartbreaking for Len Mattiace. For Phil Mickelson and Jim Furyk, it was only disappointing, but it did force both of them to go through yet another round of "How does it feel *still* not to have a major title?" questioning.

It was more acute for Mickelson for obvious reasons: not only had he won twenty-one times in eleven years on the tour, he had been achingly close in majors on several occasions, most notably at the 1999 U.S. Open when Payne Stewart made a 15-foot par putt on the 18th hole to beat him by a shot, and two years later at the PGA Championship when David Toms made a 12-foot par putt on the final hole for a one-shot win.

Furyk was five weeks older than Mickelson and had been a model of consistency since arriving on tour in 1994. He had won nine times and had finished fourth in majors five times, missing playoffs by two shots on three different occasions. He didn't get asked about not winning a major as often as Mickelson did, but it certainly came up in conversation.

"The first couple times I seriously contended in majors was 1998," he said. "I had chances at the Masters and at the British Open that year and couldn't get it done. To be honest, I'm not sure I was ready for what comes with winning a major back then, although I'm sure I thought I was ready, and both times I was extremely disappointed. By the time 2003 rolled around, I thought I was ready."

There was another difference between Mickelson and Furyk: Mickelson had been a prodigy, a top junior player growing up in San Diego who had won on the PGA Tour as a twenty-year-old junior at Arizona State. In 1990, he had been the first lefty to win the U.S. Amateur, and he was the first player to win both the Amateur and the NCAA individual title in the same year. He was one of four players in history to be a college All American for four straight years. His bio in the PGA Tour media guide began with the phrase, "started hitting golf balls when he was eighteen months old."

Furyk's father, Mike, was in the golf business. He worked as a club pro and then as an equipment representative and began teaching Jim the game when he was seven. But he didn't want his son to play too much at a young age, and Jim was at least as interested in football and basketball anyway, so he didn't really get into the game until he was twelve.

"To be honest, when I was young, the major attraction of golf for me was driving the cart," he said with a smile. "If I'd been good at football, I probably would have stuck with it."

Jim's favorite golf-course trick as a little boy was to put the cart into reverse while Mike was hitting a shot. Mike would jump back into the cart, hit the gas, and find himself going straight backward. "He never got mad at me for it," Jim said. "He figured if he wasn't smart enough to check, it was on him when it happened."

When his father first began giving him lessons, Jim had what would politely be described as an odd-looking swing. It looked sort of like a roller coaster, the way it looped and rolled en route to the top and then back down to the ball. His dad never tried to change it.

"Almost from the beginning, he hit the ball solidly," Mike said.

"I knew it looked funny, but I also knew he was comfortable with it, and he could repeat it. Until that changed, I wasn't going to try to make him change."

When Jim did start to play golf more regularly, he improved rapidly. Even so, he still liked football a lot too. Fortunately for golf and Furyk, he went to a football camp run by then–Philadelphia Eagles quarterback Ron Jaworski when he was thirteen. Jaworski took one look at Furyk's throwing arm and suggested he find another sport. Which may explain why Furyk grew up to be a fanatic Pittsburgh Steelers fan.

Regardless, Jaworski's advice was sound. Within two years, Furyk was one of the best junior golfers in Pennsylvania, and he was widely recruited by the major golf schools as a high-school senior. He chose Arizona, where he often encountered Mickelson over the next four years, and had a solid college career, making All American as a senior.

By then he knew he wanted to take a shot at the tour. He made it through the first two stages of Q-School in fall of 1992 (Mickelson went straight to the tour with a two-year exemption, when he graduated that same year thanks to his win in Tucson two years earlier) but failed to make the 72-hole cut at the finals. He struggled for most of 1993 with partially exempt status on the Nike Tour before breaking through late in the year with a win at Gulfport, Mississippi. That helped him finish 26th on the Nike money list, but he still had to go back to Q-School in the fall.

At the finals he made the 72-hole cut on the number and then made it to the tour—also right on the number. From there, Furyk never looked back. He tied for seventh in his second tournament of 1994 at Tucson—a homecoming for the Arizona grad—and went from there to finish 78th on the money list as a rookie. He had only gotten better after that, finishing fourth on the money list in 1997 (while making his first of six straight Ryder Cup teams) and third the next year. Going into 2003, his worst finish on the money list in the previous six years had been 2000 when he made just under $2 million and finished 17th. In short, he was a human ATM machine.

But he hadn't won a major. He had been extremely consistent and often very good. Just not quite good enough. Through the '03 Masters, he had played in thirty-one majors and made twenty-six cuts. He had finished in the top 20 on eighteen occasions and in the top 10 twelve times, six of those in the top five. That was an admirable record, except for the one glaring omission.

He knew how frustrating it was for Mickelson, who had become a friend during their years on tour, and seeing players like Weir and Rich Beem win majors added to his sense that something in his career was missing.

"I don't think it was something he ever lost sleep over; he's not that way," said his wife, Tabitha. "But when you've made a good living on tour, and you've won on tour, there's one thing left to do that's really important, and that's win a major."

Jim and Tabitha had met at the Memorial Tournament during Jim's rookie year on tour. Jim had been signing autographs after his first round when he noticed a pretty blonde watching him, or at least he hoped she was watching him. He took a leap of faith, stepped out of character ("I never did stuff like this"), and walked over to introduce himself. It turned out that Tabitha, a schoolteacher, had been watching him, impressed by the way he handled himself with the kids as he signed for them.

They have been together ever since, and Caleigh, their first child, was born shortly after the end of the 2002 U.S. Open. That had been a frustrating week for Jim, a rare missed cut at a major. He had shot 73–80, the 80 coming on a miserable, rainy Friday afternoon. It was the first time in eight Opens that he had failed to make the cut. Perhaps he had been distracted by the impending birth of his daughter.

But he had started 2003 in typical Furyk fashion. The fourth-place finish at the Masters was his seventh top-10 finish in nine tournaments. That included losing a playoff to Scott Hoch at Doral. By the time he flew into Chicago to begin preparing for the Open, he had already made $2.3 million for the year, even though he hadn't won yet.

The USGA had decided to return the Open to Olympia Fields Country Club for the first time in seventy-five years. The championship had been played in the Chicago area frequently—at Chicago Golf Club and Medinah Country Club—but only in 1928 had it been played at Olympia Fields. That had been a memorable Open, with Johnny Farrell beating Bobby Jones in a playoff.

The USGA hadn't gone back to Olympia Fields because it wasn't considered a classic golf course. Most people liked Medinah better, but one exception was executive director David B. Fay, who had made a habit of breaking longtime traditions when it came to course selection. Fay wasn't crazy about Baltusrol, which had hosted five Opens in the New York area (Springfield, New Jersey), so he dropped it from the Open rotation and replaced it with Bethpage Black, a municipal course on Long Island. He wasn't a fan of Medinah, so when executive board member Buzz Taylor (a Chicagoan) brought up Olympia Fields as a potential site for the '03 Open, Fay and the rest of the committee were receptive to the idea of going back.

One person who liked Olympia Fields was Furyk. "I liked the way it set up the first time I saw it," he said. "It wasn't that long, and the holes all set up pretty well for me. After I played my first practice round, I felt as if I had a good chance to play well." The only problem he had going into the week was *his putter.* The model he had been using had been declared illegal (for technical reasons), so he had pulled out an old one from his closet. Fortunately, it felt comfortable right away.

The putter issue resolved, Furyk went about preparing, his confidence growing each day. Olympia Fields is not a bomber's golf course, and it rewards consistent driving and good iron play. That suited Furyk just fine. By the time he played his last practice round on Wednesday, he was about as confident as he had ever been going into a major.

"You never know what's going to happen once the tournament starts," he said. "And I don't think anyone, except maybe Tiger, ever goes in thinking, 'I'm going to win.' But I did feel pretty confident."

So confident that he stunned his wife that night as they were getting ready for bed. "He just walked in and said, 'I'm going to win this thing,'" Tabitha Furyk remembered. "We had been together for nine years at that point, and I had never heard him say anything like that.

"When we were first dating, he was playing in this one-day exhibition, and he had a putt to win on the last hole. He walked over to where I was and gave me a kiss, as if to say, 'I'm going to win this for you right now.' Then he missed the putt. He never did anything remotely like that again.

"He's a pessimist by nature. He'll come in after struggling through a round where he puts up a decent score, and I'll say, 'Hey, you hung in there.' I'm the cheerleader. Usually his response is something like, 'No, I left it out there.' That's Jim. He's a glass-half-empty kind of guy most of the time."

Now, Furyk was telling his wife the glass was about to over-flow. Her response was simple: "Let's do it," she said.

Furyk had a late tee time on Thursday. He was in the 12:30 pairing on the 10th tee, along with Darren Clarke and Phil Mickelson. This was no accident. The USGA likes to have fun with its Thursday–Friday pairings. Once upon a time, when Fay was still putting together the threesomes, there was something known as "the prick pairing." Fay would put three players together generally considered to be, well, pricks. Only when word got out about the pairing did Fay and his successor, Tom Meeks, stop doing it.

But Meeks still put players together for a reason. In this case, Mickelson, Furyk, and Clarke were generally ranked one, two, three in the unofficial world rankings as the Best Players to Have Never Won a Major. All of them knew that was why they were together, and none of them really wanted to talk about it very much.

"On the one hand, it's an honor, because it means people think you're a good player," Furyk said. "On the other hand, it's a reminder whenever it comes up that you haven't won a major yet."

The Thursday weather conditions were perfect for scoring—the temperature never got above the sixties, the humidity was low, and there was almost no wind. Bret Quigley, playing in the morning, shot 65 to take the lead, followed by Justin Leonard and Jay Don Blake at 66. Australian Stephen Leaney was at 67. The biggest surprise of the morning was Tiger Woods struggling to shoot an even-par 70.

Furyk was having a very solid round, already a couple under par on the back nine, when he heard a huge roar coming from several holes back. It was the kind of roar usually reserved for Woods or Mickelson doing something spectacular. Furyk knew Woods had played in the morning, and he knew Mickelson was playing with him, so he was somewhat baffled by what he heard. Only when he checked a leaderboard soon after did he begin to piece together what had happened.

Everyone in golf was aware that Bruce Edwards, who had been Tom Watson's caddy for most of thirty years, had been diagnosed with ALS—Lou Gehrig's disease—early in the year. There were very few people in golf as well liked as Edwards. He had been one of the first of the truly "professional" caddies in the 1970s. He had an easy smile and a quick wit and a friendly word for almost everyone.

The news of his diagnosis was devastating for golf people. Even at that point, he had admitted to close friends that walking

18 holes carrying a forty-pound golf bag was getting more and more difficult. Watson had cut back on his practice rounds and lightened his bag—taking out things like umbrellas, extra balls, and anything not absolutely necessary—to make it as easy as possible for Edwards.

Watson was fifty-three and was playing in the Open on a USGA exemption. He had won the tournament in 1982, beating Jack Nicklaus at Pebble Beach when he chipped in for birdie at the 17th hole, one of golf's most memorable shots. He knew this would quite possibly be his last Open, and it was almost certain that it would be the last one for Edwards. Time was running out fast.

Watson had also started on the 10th hole, exactly an hour after the Best Players to Have Never Won a Major threesome of Furyk, Mickelson, and Clarke. He bogeyed the 10th hole, then saved par with an eight-foot putt on the 11th. On the 12th, he had 170 yards to the hole following his drive and decided to hit a six-iron, even though Edwards thought he might need to hit a soft five.

Watson's call was right. He holed the six-iron for an eagle two. That was the roar Furyk heard.

As the afternoon wore on and Watson's name popped up on the leaderboard, everyone noticed. In fact—especially with Woods already finished for the day—fans began flocking in the direction of the threesome that included Scott Verplank and Argentina's Eduardo Romero. In the locker room, players who would usually sit and talk with the TV as background noise stopped what they were doing to watch.

Furyk noticed Watson's name on the board and could see that something special was going on. But it wasn't until he finished his round—shooting a very solid 67 to join Leaney in a tie at that moment for fourth place—that he had a chance to watch Watson play his final few holes.

"Normally, especially with an afternoon tee time, I'd grab

something to eat and go right to the range to meet my dad and Fluff [caddy Mike Cowen]," Furyk said. "But when I walked in, everyone was sitting around the televisions, watching, which you never see on a Thursday. It was one of those things you just had to see."

By the time Furyk got into the clubhouse, Watson was on the fifth hole (his 14th of the day), and he was four under par, one shot behind Quigley. Like everyone else, Furyk knew something special was happening. "We all knew by then just how sick Bruce was," he said. "It didn't seem likely that he was going to be able to keep caddying for much longer. Knowing that, seeing how emotional both Tom and Bruce were getting those last few holes, it became emotional for me to watch."

On the seventh hole—Watson's 16th of the day—his 20-foot birdie putt appeared to stop an inch from the cup. While the crowd groaned, Watson began walking in the direction of the ball. Verplank, standing a few feet from the hole, could see that it was still moving ever so slightly. "It's going in!" he screamed at Watson, afraid Watson might tap it in prematurely. Watson had no intention of doing that. He was going to wait the full ten seconds that was allowable once he reached the ball before tapping in.

Just as he reached it, the ball—as if on cue—dropped into the hole. Watson kicked his leg in the air euphorically, and Edwards began to laugh and cry at the same time. (One of the things ALS does is make it very difficult to control or conceal one's emotions.) Seeing a close-up of Edwards with tears in his eyes, Furyk felt himself choking up, as did millions of others watching on TV around the country.

Those watching the telecast weren't the only ones struggling with their emotions. The people producing the telecast were struggling too. Tommy Roy had been the executive producer for NBC's golf telecasts since 1990. When he had been promoted to executive producer for NBC Sports, he accepted the job on the condition that he would continue to produce golf.

"I still love the adrenaline of the truck," he said. "That part's never changed for me through all the years."

Roy knew Watson well, and he knew Edwards too. When he saw the shot of Edwards with tears in his eyes, he felt himself beginning to choke up. "I had to wait a second before I hit the button to talk to the guys in the booth at that moment," he said. "I knew I had tears in my eyes, and I knew a lot of the guys around me did too."

By the time Watson got up and down from a bunker at the ninth to shoot 65 and tie Quigley for the lead, he and Edwards had become the story of the Open. It almost didn't matter how Watson played the next three days; the sight of he and Edwards hugging on the ninth green after the 65 would be an indelible memory for everyone watching.

Furyk was happy for Watson and Edwards. The thought that Watson might somehow impede his path to winning the championship didn't really cross Furyk's mind. With the exception of Woods, no one looks at another player on Thursday and thinks, "He's the guy I have to beat."

Woods had shot a 70 on Thursday, and Furyk was aware of his presence, five shots behind the two leaders and three shots behind him. But it was much too early to worry about anyone or any-thing—other than trying to post another good number on Friday.

Which is exactly what he did. He had a very early tee time on Friday—7:30—and once again the conditions were about as benign as could be. Mickelson and Clarke were both playing rea-sonably well: Mickelson would shoot 70–70 and Clarke 70–69. Furyk was the hot player in the threesome. He bettered his open-ing round by a shot, shooting 66. That put him at seven-under-par 133, the lowest 36-hole total in U.S. Open history.

It did not, however, put him in the outright lead. Vijay Singh, who had been back in the pack on Thursday after shooting 70, went hyperlow, shooting a 63. That matched the lowest round ever shot in a U.S. Open. Only Johnny Miller, in the final round at Oakmont in 1973 (on a rain-softened golf course), and Jack Nicklaus and Tom Weiskopf, on the same day at Baltustrol in 1980, had ever gone that low in an Open.

Singh's 63 and the fact that he and Furyk had both broken the 36-hole scoring record caused a lot of buzz around the locker room. What was going on here? This was the U.S. Open, where par was supposed to be sacred. Players who frequently complained that Open conditions were too difficult were now grumbling that the golf course was too easy.

"I thought it was the conditions as much as anything," Furyk said. "Those first two days there was very little wind, but they'd had rain the week before, and the golf course was still pretty soft. You combine no wind with soft greens on any course, and you're going to get some low scores."

Watson had also played in the morning wave. Clearly exhausted from the emotionally draining day he'd had, he shot 72 and dropped back, although at 137 he wasn't out of contention.

Furyk almost made it look easy that morning, finding fairways consistently off the tee, hitting greens, and putting well. He was never in any serious trouble all day.

"If you hit it way off line, you'd get in trouble like at any Open course," Furyk said. "But I felt in pretty good control of my swing all day. I was very comfortable."

"The Open, maybe more than any other tournament, is like a marathon," he said. "The old cliché that you can't win the golf tournament on Thursday or Friday but you can lose it applies even more than normal. You really want to stay out of your own way. To see that Vijay had put up a 63 was surprising, even in mild conditions. My thought that day was that I was in a good place. Whether it was the lead or not, I felt good about the way I was playing."

Furyk was happy to be at the top of the leaderboard, but he knew there were far more 36-hole Open leaders who had been nowhere to be found late on Sunday than there were Open winners, so he wasn't jumping for joy.

"That's not his way anyway," Mike Furyk said. "He's almost always calm regardless of the circumstances. It's one of his strengths."

Furyk had played in enough Opens—nine—to know that staying calm going into the final 36 holes was critical.

8

The Kid from Nowhere

Two shots back of Jim Furyk and Vijay Singh heading into the weekend were two players with very little experience in majors and even less experience at the Open. In fact, although Jonathan Byrd and Stephen Leaney were paired in Saturday's second-to-last group, they might as well have been playing in their backyards for all the attention they received. Behind them were the two leaders, and just in front of them, after a Friday 66 had put him three shots off the lead, was the man still considered the favorite—Tiger Woods.

Byrd and Leaney were afterthoughts to all but friends and family.

Byrd, the twenty-five-year-old tour rookie who had played so well at the Masters—finishing tied for eighth—was in his second major and his first Open. He had gotten in by surviving the 36-hole sectional qualifier at Woodmont Country Club outside Washington, D.C. He had shot 69 on Thursday and backed it up with a 66 on Friday to pull into a tie for third. It was evident that he was a rising star, but few people expected an Open rookie to end up with the trophy on Sunday afternoon.

Even fewer people gave any thought to the notion that Stephen Leaney, who had followed his opening 67 with a 68, might be the winner. Much of that had to do with the fact that very few people in the United States had ever heard of Leaney or knew anything about him or his golf game.

He was a thirty-four-year-old Australian who had been playing on the European Tour for seven years, in large part because he hadn't been able to find his way to the PGA Tour. This was the 10th major he had played in (six of them British Opens), and he had made a total of two cuts—finishing 68th in the 1998 PGA Championship and tied for 37th in 2002 at the British.

He had been to Q-School for the U.S. Tour three times, missing "comfortably," as he put it, in 1998 and 2000, before missing by one shot in 2002. He had gotten into the Open by finishing 11th on the European Tour's Order of Merit the previous year. The top 15 on the Order of Merit are exempt into the next year's U.S. Open. Leaney had been quite successful in Europe, winning six times there in seven years, but his dream was to play on the PGA Tour.

"I think if you're a golfer, that's where you want to be and where you need to be," he said. "It's the best tour with the best players. Ever since I was a kid, my dream was to play on the PGA Tour. There's absolutely nothing wrong with the European Tour. I made a very good living there. We [Leaney and his wife, Tracey] loved living in London, but I knew in my heart if I didn't make it to the U.S. at some point, I would feel a void. I felt as if I was starting to run out of time a little."

What's more, he and Tracey were expecting their first child in September, so if a move to the United States was going to be made, sooner would be a lot better than later.

Leaney's was certainly not your typical golf story. He had been born in Busselton, a country town of about ten thousand in western Australia. His parents, Peter and Freda, had migrated to Australia from Great Britain soon after they were married. Andrew, their first child, was born in 1966, and Stephen came along two and a half years later. Peter Leaney was an electrician, and his wife was a high-school English teacher. Soon after Stephen was born, they moved to Sydney, where they lived for seven years, while Peter did his work in the coal mines, before moving back to Busselton; the mining work there was less dangerous and paid better, and the cost of living was less.

"I had a wonderful country upbringing," Leaney said. "It was the kind of town where you never locked your doors, the kids played all sports, and we went to the beach all the time. We lived in a house that wasn't more than three hundred yards from the water."

Like a lot of Australian kids, Leaney's first love was cricket, which he first learned in the backyard from his dad and older brother. Later he played some Aussie Rules Football, basketball, tennis, and—finally—golf. He remembers going to the golf course with his dad as early as age seven but says he didn't really get hooked on the game until much later.

"I would hit a few shots, go around in the buggy with dad when I was small, but that was about it," he said. "My dad was self-taught. He had learned the game by reading two Ben Hogan books, *Five Lessons: The Modern Fundamentals of Golf* and *Power Golf,* and he taught me how to play. He was a good player, had a handicap as low as three.

"But I didn't get into the game much until I was about twelve. I played everything else. My brother was a very good cricketer, good enough to play at the state level, though not good enough to be a test cricketer. I liked golf, but I knew it wasn't considered cool. I remember when I started high school, people would give me a hard time about playing golf. They'd say, 'Why do you want to play golf?'

"It wasn't until [Greg] Norman became a big star in America that people changed. After that, golf started to get cool."

By the time Leaney reached high school, he was hooked. He would get on his bike after school and travel the seven miles to

Busselton Golf Club so he could play and practice until dusk. Once he started to play regularly, he saw rapid improvement. By the time he was seventeen, he was a solid five handicap, but he was hardly looked at by people as a future pro.

"I was a pretty good country player, that was it," he said. "But I had this crazy dream that I could go to America someday and play on the PGA Tour. If you think about it now, it made no sense. I wasn't even one of the better players in my state."

In spite of that, Leaney convinced his parents to let him move to Perth when he graduated from high school to get a job and work on his golf game. The plan was to give it five years to see what happened.

"They were always very supportive of my brother and me when it came to sports. When I was in high school, there were clinics in Perth, sometimes on the weekend, sometimes for a couple of hours on a weekday. Without ever complaining, one of them would get in the car with me and drive to Perth—about three hours each way. On the weekends, we'd stay in a hotel Friday night so I could be there first thing Saturday morning."

The first thing Leaney needed in Perth was a job. As luck would have it, the president of Busselton Golf Club was friends with the president of Royal Perth Golf Club. He made a call that got Leaney a job as a printer and a place to practice—Royal Perth.

"I wasn't making very much money, and, at first, I had daytime hours at the printer's," he said. "I would get through at three o'clock and go straight to the golf course and play until dark. After about two years, when I started to show some potential, they gave me night hours, which meant I got off at midnight, went home and slept, and then played and practiced until I had to get back to work at four.

"I never went out—I mean never. For one thing, I didn't have much money, but for another I would always think, 'Do I want to stay out late and not be able to get up to play, or do I want to get up to play?' The answer always was that I wanted to get up to play.

"I was homesick a lot. I didn't go home much because that took time and cost money. After the second year, I started to see some progress. I started winning amateur tournaments within the state. Even then, I wasn't the best player in the state by any means."

Leaney's progress was steady but hardly meteoric. By year three, he began playing well in amateur events around Australia and was picked to play on several national teams. He became friends with Stuart Appleby and Robert Allenby, contemporaries who also dreamed of playing, as the Aussies say, "in America" someday.

In 1991, during year four of his five-year plan, Leaney broke through, winning a pro tournament—the Western Australian Open—as one of a handful of amateurs in the field. That same year, Allenby and Appleby also won tournaments as amateurs. Allenby turned pro at the end of that year after finishing second in the Australian Open against an elite field. Leaney decided he wasn't quite ready.

"By then I'd gotten good enough that I was working only four hours a day at the printing plant, and my boss was paying me as if I was working eight hours," he said. "I thought I was ready to turn pro, but I decided to wait until the end of '92 because I still wasn't sure if I was ready. Being from the country, I'd always had that mentality that the city kids were better than the country kids at things. I guess I felt the same way about turning pro."

When he did turn pro at the end of '92 he easily made it through Q-School for the Australian Tour—in part because one hundred players made it. "If you showed up and signed for the right score, you probably made it," he said. "I think I finished seventh or eighth."

The catch was that making it onto the tour didn't mean you were in tournaments. The Australians were still using the prequalifying system that the U.S. Tour had used until the early 1980s. A few players were exempt into the tournaments. Everyone else played in a Monday qualifier for the remaining spots. Leaney didn't make it to Thursday for a couple of months, but when he finally broke through he not only made the cut, guaranteeing himself a spot in the following week's event, he finished high enough to make $20,000.

"I felt like I'd won the lottery," he said. "The most I'd made in a year working as a printer was probably about $8,000. I felt rich. I went out and bought myself new blue jeans to celebrate."

He played steadily better after that and qualified for tournaments on the Australasian tour, one big step up from the Australian Tour. He was playing in a tournament in Malaysia when he developed a bad cough. Thinking he had a cold or perhaps the flu, he came home to play in the Victorian Open in Adelaide.

"I was sharing a room for the week with Greg Chalmers and Steve Collins," he said. "We were paying thirty bucks apiece. I woke up one morning, and my right arm was completely swollen. I had no idea what it was. I went to see a doctor who sent me right to a specialist. He said, 'You've got a blood clot; we have to get you to the hospital right away.'

"Next thing I know, I'm in intensive care with tubes and needles all over the place, and they're telling me I could die if the clot went to my heart. That's why I was in intensive care. It took a week for them to get the clot down. Obviously, I missed the tournament. They charged me $700 a night while I was in the hospital, and it wasn't covered by insurance."

He smiled. "When I got out, I heard straight away from Chalmers and Collins. They wanted to be sure I knew that I still owed them for the room."

Doctors told Leaney there were two ways to ensure that he

wouldn't clot on the other side of his body: take blood thinners for the rest of his life or have surgery to remove parts of two ribs that would open up blood passages to keep a clot from happening again. He opted for the surgery.

"The doctor came in and told me, 'You'll probably not play golf again,'" he said. "He seemed to think it would be too painful. I was shattered when he said that. I'd just been starting to get close to becoming a player and now this."

Leaney was pleasantly surprised by how quickly he recovered from the surgery. He was playing golf again—pain free—within a few months. But he still hadn't recovered mentally. "In a sense, I was lucky it happened when I was very young because I had time to recover and didn't really believe my career was over," he said. "But, even though the doctors told me it was very unlikely, I kept worrying it was going to happen again. Even after I started to play well, I still worried."

He won the Western Australian Open for a second time at the end of '94 and then won the Victorian Open—the tournament he never got to play for his $30 a night—at the end of '95.

"That was when I felt like I was back," he said. "It had been two years since the attack, and more than eighteen months since the surgery. I felt like I was ready to go forward from that point."

A year later, after winning the Victorian Open again, he decided he was ready for the next step: Europe. "Back then, there were still only a handful of Australians on the U.S. Tour," he said. "Norman was obviously a star, and Finchey [Ian Baker-Finch] had done well, and Stuey [Appleby] went over there and played the Nike [now Nationwide] Tour before he made it. But most Aussies went to Europe first. It was as if we all thought you had to take a step before going to America to prove yourself worthy. I know I felt that way."

He didn't make it through European Tour School in 1996 but was invited to play in Challenge Tour events there (the equivalent of the Nationwide Tour) in 1997. He decided to take a shot, even though he was making good money playing Australasia during the early part of the year and the Canadian Tour during the summer months—Australian winter. He played well enough on the Challenge Tour to earn his card for the big tour in Europe in 1998 without going back to Q-School.

"I remember I played thirteen tournaments in a row at the end of the year to make sure I made enough money to get my card," he said, smiling at the memory. "It was exhausting. The travel was tough, the golf courses weren't great, and we were playing for purses that totaled about 50,000 pounds a week. I think I made 25,000 pounds for the year and finished 10th on the money list."

That trial by fire—and exhaustion—made him into a much better player. He began his rookie year on the European Tour by winning in Morocco. That allowed him to relax a little since he was exempt for the next two years. He won again a few months later in Holland and moved up high enough in the world rankings to get into the PGA Championship, which was in Sahalee, Washington (outside Seattle) that year.

"It was my first trip to America," he said. "I'd played in Canada a couple of times but never the U.S. I was overwhelmed by it all. The golf course was very tough, and every time I turned around on the range or [in] the locker room there was Tiger [Woods] or Phil [Mickelson] or Vijay [Singh] or some other big star. I was intimidated."

He managed to make the cut and thought he might make that year's Presidents Cup team since his world ranking had climbed to number 60. But captain Peter Thomson chose Frank Nobilo and Greg Turner, two players who hadn't played as well as Leaney that year but had far more international experience.

"Looking back, Peter was probably right," he said. "I'd probably have taken one look at the Americans and been so awestruck I wouldn't have been able to hit a ball. By then, I'd played with Norman and with Seve [Ballesteros] in Europe, but, to me, the Americans were a completely different story."

Leaney's pairing with Norman had happened fairly early in his pro career in a tournament in Australia. "That was scary," he said. "I mean the guy had been my hero for years. First hole, there was water down the left, it was windy, and I hit my tee shot right into the water. I hadn't slept. I was a mess.

"But when we got to the 14th hole, Greg hit, I want to say, three balls in the water. It was almost like the ending of *Tin Cup*. I think he was hitting a one-iron off a downhill lie into the wind. Impossible shot, but he kept trying it. When he finally got the ball on the green, it was the loudest roar I think I'd ever heard. I think he made an 11."

Leaney won a third tournament at the end of 1998 at Royal Queensland. During the course of that year, he had noticed an attractive young woman named Tracey Camporelae, who worked for Bob Tuohey, the man in charge of a number of tournaments on the Australian Tour.

Leaney was too shy to ask Camporelae out. Sensing that, she decided to ask him out at the end of the tournament at Royal Queensland. "But then I won, and she was afraid I'd think she was some kind of gold digger," he said, laughing. "So she didn't ask."

The following spring, Leaney decided it was time to ask Camporelae out. So, he sent the head rules official from the Australian Tour to ask on his behalf. "I just couldn't do it myself," he said. "I told him to just say I was too shy. Fortunately, she thought that was sweet, I guess, because she said yes."

They dated briefly, and Camporelae traveled to Pinehurst for the U.S. Open that year. They broke up for a time while he was back in Europe playing that summer, but then got back together for good the following year. They were married in 2001.

At the end of 1998, not long after his first date with Camporelae, Leaney had taken his first swipe at U.S. Tour school and didn't come close. The difference in the golf courses affected him, and he was never in serious contention to get a card. He returned to Europe and didn't play as well in '99. His play in Europe the previous year got him into the U.S. Open (Pinehurst), the British Open (Carnoustie), and the PGA (Medinah). He missed the cut in all three and decided not to bother with U.S. Q-School at the end of the year because he wasn't playing well enough to make it worth the effort.

He also qualified for the Match Play Championships that year at La Costa and had to play David Duval in the first round. Duval was coming off a win at the Bob Hope Desert Classic in which he had shot 59 in the last round. On the day before the match, ESPN's Jimmy Roberts interviewed Leaney.

"Isn't it an awfully long flight [from Sydney] to here to play one round of golf?" Roberts asked, echoing what most people were thinking.

"I didn't come here to play just one match," Leaney answered, insulted by the question.

As it turned out, they were both right. Leaney did only play one match, but Duval had to make a long birdie putt on the 17th hole to beat him two and one. The loss was disappointing. Staying that close to Duval—who was ranked number one in the world at the time—told Leaney that he could play against Americans.

He bounced back in 2000, winning in Holland again. As before, though, he couldn't handle Q-School in Palm Springs.

"I was beginning to think I was going to spend my career in Europe," he said. "That wasn't a bad thing. I was making a good living there, and I wasn't at all unhappy. I was thirty-one, and it was beginning to look like the U.S. tour just wasn't going to happen for me. What made it hard was seeing Rob [Allenby] and Stuey [Appleby], who were my contemporaries and my friends, guys I'd come up with who I thought I was comparable to as a player, doing so well in the U.S. I was happy for them, of course, but a bit jealous."

He decided to give Q-School one last shot in 2002 after he had won the German Masters—which is a European Tour major, meaning he had a five-year exemption—figuring he had nothing to lose. All week he was right around the qualifying number, and he went into the sixth and final round at eight under par, which at that moment was right on the qualifying number.

"You're always guessing at Q-School because there are no scoreboards," he said. "The conditions were mild that day, and I figured the number would come down one more shot to nine under. I didn't think it would be 10 because last-day nerves would be involved, but I was fairly certain it would be nine."

Leaney arrived on the ninth tee at PGA West (his 18th hole of the day) still at eight under par, convinced he needed a birdie to ensure his card. "I had just missed a four-foot birdie putt on the 8th and really thought I had to make one more birdie," he said. "I drove the ball into the rough and had to wedge out. I hit my third shot to about 20 feet and missed the par putt. I thought I'd missed it by two at that point, and then, when I got in the scoring tent, they told me the number was going to be eight. All I'd needed to do was play conservative off the tee with an iron and make par, and I'd have been fine."

When he realized what had happened, Leaney was devastated. "I was thirty-two; I really thought it was my last chance," he said. "I couldn't believe the number had stayed at eight. Tracey and I went back to the hotel room and cried for a long time. Going back home to Australia for Christmas after missing like that was *so* hard. I didn't want to play, I didn't want to practice. I'd never been that down about golf in my life."

Leaney finally went to see Neil MacLean, who had been his sports psychologist for years. They had a long talk. Leaney was still in the 60s in the world rankings, meaning if he played well in the first tournament of the year on the European Tour, he could qualify to return to San Diego for the World Match Play to see if he could stick around for more than one round of golf.

"That was my incentive," Leaney said. "Neil said I had to tell myself every time I dropped a shot, I was one more shot away from making the match play. When I made a birdie, I was a shot closer. It worked. I finished second to Ernie [Els]. I shot 19 under par, which is a pretty good score until you realize that Ernie was 29 under."

Second was second, regardless of margin, and Leaney found himself back at La Costa as the 48th seed in the sixty-four-man field. He drew Bob Estes—the 17th seed—in the first round and beat him two and one. Then he played Justin Leonard—a past major champion who was seeded 16th—and crushed him, six and five. That put him in the round of 16 against the number one seed—Tiger Woods.

"Actually I wasn't as nervous as the first time I'd played with Norman," he said. "I only wish the first time I played with [Tiger] it had been in stroke play, because you can kind of slip along not being measured against him on every hole. In match play, they call out who won the hole on every green. I went out there hoping not to get my ass kicked—and got my ass kicked."

Woods, who would go on to win the tournament, was having one of his superhuman days. In 13 holes, he made two eagles and six birdies. If he hadn't won the match seven and six and had played all 18 holes, he might have broken 60.

Even after that defeat, Leaney was encouraged. He had beaten two good players to get to the match with Woods, and he wasn't the first person to get his ass kicked by Woods. A few years later, after making the mistake of saying that Woods might have slipped a little, Stephen Ames played him in the first round of the match play and lost nine and eight.

Leaney was invited back to the U.S. to play in Jack Nicklaus's Memorial Tournament two weeks before the Open. He played well there, even though he only finished tied for 34th. "I was hitting the ball very well," he said. "I just didn't make anything happen on the greens, but I felt really well about my game. I was finding every fairway, it seemed, and I knew how important that was at an Open."

Rather than flying back to London for a week, he and Tracey opted to spend the week in Chicago, relaxing and doing some sightseeing. On Saturday, Leaney decided to drive out to Olympia Fields to get an early look at the golf course. He figured it would be a lot less crowded than on Monday, when most of the players in the field would arrive.

His first look at the golf course was something of a shock. "I remember thinking, 'This is really playable,'" he said. "My first Open, at Pinehurst, had been a disappointment in a way. I mean, I'd been watching Opens on TV since the mid-80s, and to me the Open was always about really high rough and narrow fairways. At Pinehurst, the rough wasn't high at all. Of course, that was because the shape of the greens protected the course so the rough didn't have to be all that high.

"I expected Olympia Fields to be a more typical Open course. High rough, narrow fairways. But it really wasn't that way at all. It wasn't easy. There was rough, and you could see if the greens got fast, and they put the pins in certain spots where it could get hard. But I found it very playable right from the start. I was hitting irons off a lot of tees and still in good shape coming into the greens. It wasn't like every hole was a 500-yard par-four. I was comfortable playing there both days."

He played on Sunday with six-time major champion Nick Faldo. Both noted that the two hardest par-fours on the course — the ninth and the 18th — were playing dead into the wind. "I hit driver, three-iron to number 18 that day," Leaney said. "Everyone

at the club told us that the wind usually played just the opposite
of what it was playing that day. I figured if that was the case during the tournament, you'd be hitting more like eight-iron into the
green if you hit a good drive."

Having played 18 holes on both Saturday and Sunday, Leaney
took it relatively easy on the three official practice days, playing
only nine holes each day. Such a move isn't that unusual for players leading to a major, especially if they arrive early and play on
the weekend before the golf course gets crowded.

"I was still hitting the ball really well when I played on Saturday and Sunday," Leaney said. "I mean, I was flushing it. I felt like
I knew the golf course, and I didn't want to tire myself out fighting the crowds on the practice days."

When players bring up "fighting crowds on practice days" at a
major, they aren't talking about fans. They mean the other players
on the golf course. This is especially true at a U.S. Open, where a
majority of the players are unfamiliar with the golf course and are
practicing putts from different spots on almost every hole and trying to get a feel for the greens.

Furyk almost always arrived early at majors sites for just that
reason—he didn't want to get stuck playing a six-hour round on
Tuesday or Wednesday and be exhausted by the time he teed it
up on Thursday. Leaney's early arrival was mostly happenstance:
the schedule put him in Chicago early, and he took advantage.
Thus, he didn't have to fight the crowds.

"I felt good about the way I was hitting the ball, but I didn't go
out Thursday with any particular expectations," he said. "My hope
was to play well, make the cut, and go from there. In the back of
my mind was the notion that if I had a good week, I might make
enough money to have a chance to play a few more tournaments
in the U.S. and make enough money to get on the tour without
going back to Q-School."

One of the ways for an international player to get to the U.S.

Tour is by making enough money on sponsor exemptions or through majors or World Golf Championship events (like the Match Play) to get what is called "special temporary membership." To get that, a player must make as much money in U.S. tournaments as the 150th ranked player on the previous year's money list had made. In 2002, Tom Scherrer had made $356,657 to finish 150th on the money list. Leaney had played in three official tour events leading into the Open—the Match Play, Bay Hill, and the Memorial—and had earned just under $200,000. That meant he needed to make about $160,000 at the Open to be an exempt player for the rest of 2003. If he then earned enough to finish in the top 125 for the year, he would be a full-fledged tour player for 2004.

"I really didn't want to seriously think in those terms," he said. "It was all too complicated. I just went out the first morning and focused on playing well. Friday afternoon, I did the same thing. At the end of the day, I was in great position. I had achieved my first goal—making the cut. That was nice. But that's all it was— nice. I hadn't really done a thing yet, and I understood that."

Everyone understood that. One hole can feel like a lifetime in major championship golf—ask Jean Van de Velde (1999 British Open) or, for that matter, Jeff Maggert. Thirty-six holes was more like an eternity.

9

Always on Father's Day

STEPHEN LEANEY WAS BACK at his hotel getting ready to go out to dinner on Friday night when his phone rang. His caddy, Justin Boyle, was in the hospital. He'd had chest pains soon after the second round at Olympia Fields ended and had gone there for tests. The doctors didn't think he was having a heart attack, but he had "murmurs" in his heart. They wanted him to stay at least through the weekend so they could monitor him.

That would make caddying on Saturday and Sunday difficult.

Leaney was concerned, even though Boyle assured him he was okay. The more immediate problem was finding someone to caddy for him in the middle of the U.S. Open.

It had already been a tough year for Leaney in terms of caddies. Player-caddy relationships are a lot like marriages. They are volatile, emotional, and often end in divorce. Frequently there are reconciliations once a player or caddy moves on to someone new and realizes the old relationship wasn't as bad as he thought.

A month prior to the Open, Leaney had been in London, preparing to play in the European PGA Championships at Wentworth, when Steve Rawlinson walked into the locker room on Wednesday evening as Leaney was getting ready to leave. Rawlinson had caddied for him for two years but said he needed to tell

Leaney something before the tournament began: Colin Montgomerie had offered him a job, and he had accepted it.

Leaney was stunned, and angry, at both men. "I was pissed at Steve for not giving me some warning that he was thinking about it," he said. "I thought he would at least say, 'Monty has offered me this; do you want to match it?' or something along those lines. He didn't. But I was really pissed at Monty for not coming to me before he talked to Steve. That's usually standard procedure when you're going to talk to someone who is working for another player. I wouldn't have tried to stand in his way if he wanted to go, but it was a matter of courtesy, player to player. Obviously Monty was a bigger name than me and was making more money, so I understood Steve's thinking. I certainly wouldn't have said no to either one of them if asked. I just resented not being asked."

Rawlinson told Leaney that he would work for him that week—since the tournament began the next day—before moving on to Montgomerie. Leaney told him not to bother.

"I didn't want to spend the whole week walking around feeling pissed at my caddy," he said. "You're supposed to be a team. He'd quit the team. I needed to move on right away."

He found a local caddy to work for him that week and began asking around to see who might be available long term. The answer was Boyle, an experienced Australian caddy who had worked for Greg Norman and Seve Ballesteros. The new partnership had gone well. Now, sitting in a tie for third place midway through the U.S. Open, Leaney was again looking for a caddy.

Finding an emergency caddy early in a tournament week is not usually that difficult. There are always caddies hanging around outside the clubhouse who don't have a bag for the week. Some are kids, looking for a break, but many are veterans who have just split with a player or who work for a player who is hurt or is simply not playing that week. Players can afford to take weeks off during the year; most caddies cannot.

But this wasn't Tuesday or Wednesday; it was Friday. The caddies who didn't have bags for the week had taken off. Leaney was thinking he was going to have to call the USGA and ask for help finding a local caddy, when he remembered that Matt Goggin, one of his Australian friends who had been an alternate but had not gotten into the field on Thursday morning, had decided to stay to watch the tournament. He wondered if his caddy, Alistair Howell, had stayed too.

"I knew that Alistair had been staying with Matt, so I called him," he said. "Sure enough, they were both still there. Alistair hadn't walked [to measure for yardage] the whole golf course, but he had walked 10 holes. I figured at that point I was fortunate to get an experienced caddy, even if it was someone I only really knew away from the golf course, not on the golf course."

As with any close relationship—player and caddy generally spend about six to seven hours a day together for six days at every tournament—knowing one another is often a key to success. A good, experienced caddy knows when to soothe a player, when to yell at him, and how to tell him he's got the right club in his hands. It can often be as subtle as tone of voice.

"I think that's right" can come out sounding doubtful or certain.

Leaney and Howell would be flying blind on a golf course Howell hadn't really seen from inside the ropes. But the good news was that Leaney, having played a total of 99 holes there in a week—two 18-hole practice rounds, three nine-hole practice rounds, and 36 holes in the championship—probably didn't need as much help as he might have under other circumstances.

"I have to admit that it didn't help me sleep Friday night," Leaney said, laughing. "I was already dealing with how much was at stake and trying *not* to think about any of that. Now I also had to worry about working with a new caddy the next day. It's a good thing I had such a late tee time because I didn't sleep especially well."

Jim Furyk slept fine that night. He had been in contention at majors before, and he had no concerns about his caddy. In ten years on the tour, Furyk had worked with two caddies. The first was Steve Duplantis, known to everyone on tour as "the kid," because he looked and often acted like one. Duplantis was bright, engaging, and a very good caddy. But he also enjoyed going out at night, and that often led to late arrivals at the golf course.

Because Furyk liked him and because he was a good caddy, Duplantis had received numerous last chances. When he didn't show up at all one morning at Bay Hill in March 1999 (he later said he couldn't get there because of an accident on I-4; unfortunately, every other player and caddy in the field did make it to the golf course that morning), Furyk felt he had no choice and fired him.

As luck would have it, Mike Cowen was out of work at that moment. Cowen—known to all as "Fluff" because of his bushy hair and even bushier mustache—was one of the tour's most respected caddies. He had worked with Peter Jacobsen for seventeen years and had then gone to work for Tiger Woods when he first came on tour.

That was another case of a player not consulting with another player before offering a caddy a job. Jacobsen had offered to let Cowen work for Woods when Woods first came on tour in 1996 because Jacobsen was recovering from an injury. Woods was so happy with Cowen that he offered him a full-time job. It was Cowen who called Jacobsen to tell him he'd been offered the job.

"How could I tell him no?" Jacobsen said. "I mean, he was being offered the chance to make huge money working for the game's next great player, and I was forty-two with a questionable playing future. I just wish Tiger had picked up the phone and called me. I put it down to a rookie mistake."

Cowen was on the bag when Woods won the Masters by 12 shots in 1997 and became something of a celebrity himself, being as recognizable as he was and because he had an outgoing, friendly personality. Unfortunately, there is only one star on Team Woods, and it is not the caddy. Woods fired Fluff early in 1999 and hired Steve Williams, an excellent caddy who no one would ever mistake for being friendly to anyone except his boss.

After letting DuPlantis go, Furyk asked Cowen to come work for him, and by the 2003 Open, the two men had been together for more than four years.

WHILE FURYK AND VIJAY Singh were both highly respected players ranked in the top 10 in the world, theirs was not the pairing that was going to get the most TV time, at least at the start of the day, on NBC. There were four players three shots back, including Eduardo Romero and Fredrik Jacobson—both respected international players—Nick Price, and, of course, Tiger Woods.

At forty-six, Price was no longer the star he had been when he was the number one player in the world in 1993 and 1994, but he was still a threat, especially in a major. He had won two PGA Championships and a British Open and had 18 PGA Tour wins in all, the most recent at the 2002 Colonial.

And then there was Woods. His 66 on Friday had changed the way the tournament felt—the way it always did when he was on a leaderboard. Thursday had, without doubt, been about Watson and Edwards, and, even though Watson was still only four shots out of the lead at 137, there weren't many people who thought he was going to seriously contend on Sunday.

Tommy Roy, NBC's executive producer, knew that having Woods teeing off among the leaders was a boon to his telecast and his ratings. "It's no knock at all on the other guys," he said. "It's just a fact that people like to see Tiger. I've had people tell me they'd rather watch Tiger stand next to his golf bag waiting to hit than watch someone else actually hitting a shot."

The son of a golf pro, Roy dreamed of playing on tour himself, until a fluke injury turned him in the direction of a television career, so he appreciated the grinders and the guys for whom the game came a lot harder than it did for Woods. As a golfer and fan himself, he'd have been delighted to see how Jonathan Byrd and Stephen Leaney fared playing in the second-to-last group of the third round at the U.S. Open. As a TV producer and director, he knew he didn't have a dozen viewers who felt that way.

"We actually had a very good tournament shaping up going into Saturday," Roy said. "The leaders were very good, very established players. You had guys like Price and Mickelson still in contention. You still had Bruce and Watson, and, of course, Tiger was right there."

In TV fantasy world, Saturday would have been the day Woods made a big move on the leaders, rolling in birdies while the crowds roared and he pumped his fist repeatedly. But Woods was still struggling with his swing changes and establishing himself with Hank Haney, his new teacher, even though there had been no official announcement of the new arrangement.

Right from the start, Woods was in trouble that day. He was spraying tee shots all over the place and wasn't close to threatening to make a birdie on the front nine, even at the two par-fives. He managed to par the first four holes, but then bogeyed the fifth and the ninth. The look of frustration on his face made it clear what kind of day he was having, even if one didn't know that he was on his way to shooting a five-over-par 75.

Looking at the leaderboard, Furyk could see that Woods was going backward. He was surprised but knew he didn't have time to focus on it. The player who had made a big move on the front nine was Price, who had birdied five of the first six holes and had actually taken the lead at nine under par soon after Furyk and Singh began their round. That lead was a bit deceptive though. The first two days had made it clear that Olympia Fields played like two different golf courses: the first six holes were for going low; the last 12 were for hanging on.

Price had birdied both par-fives (one and six), two relatively short par-fours (two and three), and Olympia Fields's shortest par-three (the fourth at 164 yards). After six, there really are very few birdie holes left on the golf course. There are no par-fives, and the remaining par-threes are all over 200 yards long. Price came back to the pack quickly on that stretch of holes, playing the seventh hole through the 17th hole (the monstrous 247-yard par-three) in five *over* par. A brilliant second shot to within a foot at the 18th allowed him to finish with a birdie and a one-under-par 69.

Furyk wasn't shaken by Price's early birdie skein. He knew there were birdies to be made on those first six holes. He and Singh both played well on the front nine. Singh had taken a quick lead by birdieing the par-five opening hole, but Furyk answered with a 35-foot birdie putt at the fifth. They both birdied the par-five sixth hole before Furyk took the lead for the first time when he birdied the difficult 495-yard ninth, hitting a wedge on his second shot (the hole was playing straight downwind) to within two feet.

At that moment, it was beginning to look like a two-man tournament even with 27 holes still to play. Furyk was at 10 under par, Singh was at nine under. Price had gone backward, and Woods was reeling, having bogeyed the 10th and the 13th to trail Furyk by 10. If Furyk was being honest at that moment, he would concede that Woods trailing him by 10 didn't suck.

The only other contender hanging close was Leaney, who was quietly plugging away, new caddy and all, and was only two strokes behind Furyk as the leaders made the turn. Jonathan Byrd was hanging in, even par for the day, but that left him five shots behind Furyk and four behind Singh.

"It was way too soon to think that it was just Vijay and me and that it was going to be match play," Furyk said. "But I was certainly aware of what the leaderboard looked like. I also knew that if it did come down to Vijay and me on Sunday that I'd be dealing with a guy who had a lot of experience and who knew how to handle himself on Sunday at a major. But that was way down the road. At that moment, my only thought was that I had to keep hitting good shots and scoring because there was no reason to think that [Singh] was going to go backward."

Except that he did.

The toughest stretch at Olympia Fields is the beginning of the back nine: five straight par-fours, none of them easy. Neither Furyk nor Singh made a birdie during this stretch, and each made a bogey: Furyk at 10, Singh at 13. That still left them a stroke apart as they came to the closing holes.

Furyk hit a gorgeous five-iron to 10 feet at the par-three 15th and made a birdie to get back to 10 under and stretch the lead to two. He played the last three holes reasonably well: missing a short par putt at 17 (his only truly bad putt of the day) to make his second bogey of the round, then coming right back to birdie the 18th. In all, he had made five birdies and two bogeys for a very solid 67.

In the meantime, the usually steady Singh came apart on the final three holes. He finished bogey-bogey-bogey, a stunning change that turned a two-shot deficit with three holes to play into a five-shot deficit. That finish meant that Furyk and Singh would not be paired in the final group on Sunday, which everyone had expected until the last forty-five minutes of the afternoon.

Instead, Furyk would be paired with Leaney, who was called "the unknown Aussie" so frequently on NBC, it almost sounded as if his full name was "the unknown Aussie Stephen Leaney."

Leaney laughed at that thought. "They weren't wrong," he said.

Leaney had almost fallen apart at the start of the back nine. He had hit his worst drive of the week at the 10th and that had led to a double-bogey six. Shaken, he bogeyed the 11th, and suddenly he had fallen back into the pack at five under par. But he steadied himself with birdies at the 15th and the 18th, and, with Singh's poor finish, that left him alone in second place, three shots behind Furyk.

"After 10 and 11, I told myself to take it easy, that I was still in good shape," he said. "I reminded myself that no one went through an entire U.S. Open without a tough patch, and I'd just had mine. The birdie at 15 really settled me down. After that I was fine."

No one else was within five shots of the lead: Singh was tied with Price at five under. Byrd, Eduardo Romero, and Canadian Ian Leggatt were another shot back at four under, and Mark Calcavecchia, Mark O'Meara, and Billy Mayfair, all of whom had matched Furyk's 67, were at three under.

Tom Watson, clearly drained by all the emotions of the week, shot 75 on Saturday, which dropped him back to two over par for the tournament. He and Edwards went into Sunday holding out hope that a good round would get Watson into the top 15 and give him an automatic spot in the 2004 Open.

Tiger Woods had also disappeared from the leaderboard. He had made one more late bogey coming home and was now 11 shots behind Furyk at one over par and completely out of contention. Perhaps the only person holding out faint hope for a Tiger rally was NBC's Tommy Roy.

"When we got the tee times, I noticed that Tiger was going to be teeing off just as we came on the air," he said. "I thought, 'Maybe Sunday will be the day that someone finally shoots 62 at a U.S. Open, and if it's Tiger...'"

Even if it was Tiger, Furyk would still have to shoot three over par just to create a tie, and, based on his first three rounds, that wasn't likely. Of course in golf, as Roy could attest, nothing was impossible.

In a sense, Furyk's 10-under-par score, which was a 54-hole

record, just as the seven under he and Singh had shot for 36 holes had been, was a reflection of what the players had been saying about Olympia Fields not being a typical, punishing U.S Open course. But it was also a reflection of how well he had played, especially given that only one player was less than five shots behind, and only six were within seven shots of his lead.

Furyk was extremely happy with the way he had played, especially pleased with the birdie on 18 after the bogey on 17. And he was surprised by Singh's finish. More than anything, though, he knew he had put himself into a position he had never been in before: a major championship was now his to lose.

"It was definitely a different feeling," he said. "I'd been in contention in majors before, believed I had a chance to win, but now I was 18 holes away, and it really had become my golf tournament to lose. I was certainly happy to be in that position, but it also made me very uptight. I knew when I left the golf course Saturday that if I didn't win the next day, it was probably going to haunt me for a good long while."

Furyk's family could sense the added pressure at dinner that night. "Jim's always a little quieter than usual the last night of a major when he has a chance," Tabitha Furyk remembered. "But he was even quieter than that. I think without saying it, we all knew what he was thinking: 'If I don't win now, then when?'"

Leaney was just as tense as Furyk but for different reasons. Like Furyk, he was in a place he had never been before: not only in contention at a major but in the final twosome. He was well aware of what it would mean to win, but he was almost as aware of what second place or even a high finish would mean: a spot on the PGA Tour, since a top-four finish would mean he had made enough money to earn exempt status for the rest of 2003. A second-place finish (worth $650,000) would also give him enough money to clinch a spot in the top 125 and, thus, fully exempt status in 2004.

That was a lot to think about. Which was exactly why he didn't want to think about any of it.

"I tried very hard to rely on my experience of being in contention at other tournaments," he said. "It's silly to tell yourself it's just another tournament, because you know it's not, and you know when you get out there, it's not going to feel like just another tournament. What I tried to do was tell myself to go out and play to win and not think about anything else."

Leaney often sits down at night before an important round and writes out on paper things that can happen and how he will handle them when they do. On this Saturday night, knowing he wouldn't be teeing off until three o'clock Chicago time, he sat up late trying to think through his round.

"I wrote down things like 'first bogey'—how to deal with that. I wrote down what I'd try to tell myself if the other guys started to get close to me or caught me. There were some very good players not far behind me: Vijay, Pricey, Byrd, [Mike] Weir (who was two under). I didn't want to look up and see them making a move and panic. I also wrote down what to do if I caught Jim and found myself really close to having a chance to win.

"I've always found if I write down all the things that can possibly happen in an important round and think about how to deal with them the night before, then when they happen I'm better prepared mentally to deal with what comes next."

He smiled. "I had also found in the past that once I'd written things down and gone through it all mentally that I slept better. That didn't happen this time. I barely slept at all."

Exhaustion finally caught up with him in the middle of the night, and he slept—relatively late—which was a good thing given the late tee time. "Even so, I was jumpy and wanting to get to the golf course," Leaney said. "I usually like to go out on the putting green about an hour and fifteen minutes before my tee time, hit a few putts, then go to the range."

On this Sunday, he was greeted by a number of TV crews and some writers from Australia when he arrived. The good news about most of the first three days was that he had been completely under the radar. Watson and Edwards had been the story the first day; Furyk and Singh the second day and most of the third— with Woods an uncertain sidebar for everyone.

"It wasn't until Vijay faded there a bit at the end on Saturday and people realized I was in the last group that anyone really wanted to talk to me," he said. "Now, I had become at least part of the story, which didn't bother me, although it was another reminder that this was a very big day in my life."

He finished talking to the media, did a brief "unknown Aussie" interview with NBC's Jimmy Roberts, and went into the locker room to get something light to eat. Soon after, he walked out to the putting green to begin his preround routine.

"I went onto the putting green, hit a few putts, and looked at my watch," he said. "I still had an hour and forty-five before we teed it up. I said, 'Hold on here, you need to slow down.' So I went back inside and just sat in front of my locker for half an hour. There was no one in there. Everyone else was either playing or out warming up. I didn't look at television or anything. I just sat there and tried to keep myself calm."

Furyk was having at least as much trouble staying calm. He killed time in the morning playing with his eleven-month-old daughter Caleigh, watching a movie, and reading the paper, the way he normally did with a late tee time. But his father could see he was struggling.

"I don't think I'd ever seen him so tight," Mike Furyk said. "Usually, the first thing he says to me on Father's Day is 'Happy Father's Day, Dad.' He never said it to me that morning. I knew it was going to be an emotional day for him—leading the Open, his first Father's Day as a father. There was just a lot going on. I could almost see him churning inside."

Furyk was trying as hard as he could to keep himself together emotionally, not wanting anything to spill out before he went to play the last round of the U.S. Open. NBC likes to show the leaders as they walk from their cars to the locker room on the final day. As Furyk made his walk, Dan Hicks, the 18th-hole anchor for the network commented, "He looks relaxed."

All of which proves that looks can be deceiving.

Furyk went into the locker room for a few minutes and then met his dad to walk to the range—just as they always did—to warm up. They were crossing the putting green when Jim stopped and pulled his father aside

"I'd wanted to say 'Happy Father's Day' to him all morning," Jim said. "I just knew whenever I said it that I was going to break down. Part of it was certainly that it was my first one as a dad, but really it was more about all the years we had worked together, all the hours, all the effort we'd both put in trying to get to a moment like this—a moment that was still a long way off—but still right there within striking distance.

"I couldn't say it at the house because I didn't want a scene with everybody there. But in the back of my mind, I didn't want to leave it unsaid before I played, because then it would be on my mind. I knew he'd understand if I waited, but I didn't want to wait. So, when we got on the putting green and there really wasn't anyone around at that moment, I just took him aside and said, 'Happy Father's Day, Dad.' I'm not sure I got all four words out before I started to cry."

As soon as Jim started to cry, Mike joined him, and the two men hugged. NBC, which has cameras everywhere during the Open, caught the hug and the emotional look in Jim's eyes. As luck would have it, Leaney was just finishing his pre-warm-up putting session when he saw the two Furyks.

Leaney's father had been on his mind all week—not because of Father's Day, which is celebrated in September in Australia, but because his father was in the hospital having just had surgery to remove part of his stomach after cancer had been discovered there. The prognosis, Leaney had been told, was good, but nevertheless he had been concerned all week.

"I saw the two of them standing there, and I could tell they were having a moment," he said. "Needless to say, it made me think about my dad. I knew he would be watching that morning [it would be 6 a.m. in Busselton when Furyk and Leaney began their round], and I knew if I played well it would make him feel a lot better. But seeing Jim and his dad also reminded me that this was a big day for Jim too, really for all of us who were on the leaderboard."

Mike Furyk wanted to be certain that the emotions of the day didn't overcome Jim before he got to the first tee. "Hey," he finally said to his son, "let's go out there and win a golf tournament"— purposefully not mentioning which golf tournament his son was trying to win.

"I wanted, as much as it was possible, to keep him in the frame of mind that he was trying to do something he'd already done," he said. "He knew how to win golf tournaments; he'd done that seven times on tour before that day. I knew it was going to be hard for him to take the 'it's just another tournament' approach, but I wanted to try to keep it on that level for as long as I possibly could."

That wasn't going to be very long. It was Father's Day. It was U.S. Open Sunday. "If he's not under par for the day after six holes," Johnny Miller said soon after NBC came on the air, "he's going to be very nervous."

In fact, Furyk was already very nervous. His tee time was still more than an hour away. If Mickelson was the Best Player to Have Never Won a Major, Furyk was now the BPTHNWAM who would take a three-stroke lead into the final 18 holes of one.

10

Make Sure to Get the Trophy Engraved

WHEN NBC WON THE rights to the U.S. Open beginning in 1995, it committed to wall-to-wall weekend telecasts. ABC had changed golf coverage in 1982 when, for the first time, it televised all 18 holes of the final two rounds, beginning the telecast just as the final twosome reached the first tee. But NBC's deal with the USGA for the Open took that concept several steps further, the weekend telecasts beginning long before the final group teed off. In fact, NBC went on the air at 1:30 p.m. eastern time, a full two and a half hours before Jim Furyk and Stephen Leaney were scheduled to tee off.

Normally a lot of the pre-leaders' airtime was devoted to features and a fluffy interview with that year's USGA president. Every Open Sunday on NBC included some kind of reminder that Johnny Miller, who was the heart and soul of their telecasts, had shot arguably the greatest round in Open history—a 63 on the final day at Oakmont in 1973 that had allowed him to come from seven shots behind to catch Arnold Palmer, among others, and win.

Since the final day at Olympia Fields was the thirtieth anniversary of the "Miracle at Oakmont," NBC had prepared a lengthy feature as a tribute to Miller. It also used the memory of that day and that round to set up what they hoped would be another miraculous afternoon.

"This golf course can give up a 61, 62, 63, or 64," Miller said at the start of the telecast. "It's vulnerable, especially those first six holes."

Then he added, "I think for Jim Furyk today, given the circumstances, even par is 72—which would tie the Open scoring record for four rounds at eight under par. If someone can go low, and he shoots that number, things might get very interesting."

Of course, the person NBC wanted to see go low happened to be on the first tee at the very moment NBC came on the air—karma as far as Tommy Roy was concerned. Tiger Woods was tied for 26th place, 11 shots behind Furyk, as he and Dan Forsman arrived at the first tee for their 12:30 (central) tee time. The largest margin any player had overcome on the final day of a major had been 10 shots. It had taken perhaps the greatest final-hole meltdown in major championship history—Jean Van de Velde's infamous triple-bogey 7 at Carnoustie in 1999—to allow Paul Lawrie into a playoff with Van de Velde and Justin Leonard, which Lawrie won, making him the answer to two trivia questions: who overcame the greatest last-day deficit in major championship history, and who is the least well-known British Open champion of the past fifty years?

Woods had kept his driver in his bag most of the first three days, not having a lot of confidence in it and hoping to hit fairways off the tee. Now, he hit driver on the first tee, pulled it a bit left, and caught a lucky break when it bounced from the deep rough and just caught the first cut of rough.

"I really think Tiger still believes he can win," said Mark Rolfing, who was walking with Woods and Forsman for NBC.

Woods's second shot caught a front bunker, and he blasted out to about 10 feet. "He has got to make this putt," Miller said, no doubt speaking for the entire network and most of the audience.

Woods made the putt. He trailed by 10. Furyk hadn't even arrived at the golf course yet, but on NBC — regardless of the twenty-four players starting the day between Furyk and Woods — it had practically become match play at that moment. Miller even saw hope in Forsman's first-hole birdie. "If Tiger is playing with someone who is also playing well, that will help him," he said.

Forget about what it might do for Forsman. That didn't really matter.

Woods took out his driver again on the 400-yard par-four second hole. This should hardly have been a surprise. He was 10 shots down on the last day, and his conservative strategy the first three days had gotten him a tie for 26th place. To do anything but play aggressively made absolutely no sense.

And yet when Miller saw the driver come out, he almost leaped from the anchor booth next to the 18th fairway. "This is a different Tiger Woods today," he exclaimed. Woods hit a perfect drive. NBC went to commercial. When they came back, and Rolfing informed Miller that Woods had only 76 yards left to the hole, Miller said (you guessed it), "This is a different guy today."

Dan Hicks joined in, adding, "He's clearly got his foot on the accelerator."

Unfortunately for NBC and the millions turning on TVs hoping to find Woods five under for the day after six holes, Woods's accelerator was jammed. He did manage to birdie the sixth — the easiest hole statistically on the golf course — but little else was happening for him. In fact, as he approached the end of the front nine and the leaders began their rounds, it was quickly becoming apparent that this was *not* going to be a day when 61, 62, 63, or 64 was likely or even possible. The USGA, with some help from the warm, dry weather, had seen to that.

Trip Kuehne, who had finished as the low amateur in the field at 10 over par, was the first to voice in his postround interview with Bob Costas what was becoming apparent: "The golf course is playing hard and very fast," he said, having shot a very respectable final round 73. "The guys are going to get welcomed to the U.S. Open today."

Almost at the exact moment that Kuehne was making his prediction, Woods came to the par-four ninth. He was still two under for the day, and Rolfing was noting that he needed to pick up the pace since he was still nine shots back of Furyk. Instead, after his second shot spun off the front of the green, Woods four-putted for double bogey. He then missed the fairway at 10 and made another bogey, leaving him one over par for the round and 12 shots behind Furyk with eight holes to play.

There would be no Tiger Miracle on this Sunday.

"Maybe this is the day that Olympia Fields exacts a little revenge," Hicks commented.

There was early evidence that that was what was happening. Ernie Els had started his day with a double-bogey seven at the first hole. Eduardo Romero almost hit his tee shot out of bounds and made a bogey on the first, as did Mark O'Meara.

The twosome that seemed most likely to make a move on Furyk and Leaney was the one directly in front of them: Nick Price and Vijay Singh. Price had won three majors, although it had been nine years since his last one, and at forty-six, he would be the oldest Open champion if he won. Singh had won a pair of majors and, having just turned forty, was still in his peak years as a player.

But neither man could birdie the first hole, which seemed to get tougher as the day wore on. Price bogeyed it, while Singh missed a seven-foot birdie putt. Price also bogeyed the second to fall seven shots back before his round was 30 minutes old. Singh caught a break at number two when his 50-foot birdie putt, traveling at full speed, slammed into the hole.

"If that didn't go in, it's off the green," NBC's Bob Murphy said. "I've seen ten or twelve of them just like that today."

Regardless, Singh was at six under and within four of the lead. He was also tied with Leaney, who had missed his tee shot to the right off the first tee and caught a bunker. That led to a bogey and his first discussion with himself about staying calm and in the moment and not letting one hole — good or bad — affect him.

Furyk had an excellent birdie chance at the first, but his 10-footer slid just past the hole. Even so, his lead grew by one, with Singh and Leaney tied for second.

By now it was apparent that this was a very different golf course than the one the leaders had trampled the first three days.

The first two days had produced the most ideal playing conditions possible — just enough cloud cover to keep the greens from getting too dry and fast, cool temperatures, and comfortable humidity. Saturday had been warmer and a little breezier, and the golf course had started to get a bit faster by the late afternoon.

Sunday was windier, with completely blue skies, meaning the greens would get fast early in the day. What's more, the USGA had looked at Furyk's 10-under-par score and, realizing that he would break the Open scoring record by two shots if he shot an even-par final round, had decided to go with some difficult pin placements, or, as the USGA calls them, "hole locations."

Generally speaking, the hole locations are decided by Wednesday. In 2003, three men were responsible for setting up the golf course: Tom Meeks, Mike Davis, and Buzz Taylor, who was the chairman of the championship committee and, thus, the USGA's executive board representative when the golf course was set up. Technically, he had final say, but, like most executive board reps, he usually deferred to the professionals, Meeks and Davis. After several days of putting on the greens from different locations, they had picked five spots on each green to place the pins, the fifth being in case of a Monday playoff.

Although golfers frequently refer to a difficult hole location as being a "Sunday pin," there's really no such thing. Neither the USGA nor the PGA Tour saves the eighteen toughest locations for Sunday. Instead, they usually spread them out across the four days. But they will also make adjustments based on how the weather affects the scoring and try to make the golf course a little bit easier or a little bit harder on Sunday.

The scoring had been much too low the first three days as far as the USGA was concerned. Even though everyone at the USGA claims to pay little attention to how far under par the leaders go or how many players are under par, they are well aware of it. That's one reason why the USGA frequently turns a par-five into a par-four for the Open—to make the golf course a par-71 instead of a par-72, or a par-70 instead of a par-71, and thus harder in relation to par. Olympia Fields was normally a par-71, but the 12th hole had been converted to a par-four for the Open.

In 2002, after 54 holes at Bethpage Black, two players had been under par: Woods at five under and Sergio Garcia at one under. Only once in Open history had a player finished in double digits under par. That had come in 2000 at Pebble Beach, when in spite of the fact that the second hole had been converted from a par-five to a par-four, Woods had shot 272—12 under par. The USGA had consoled itself that year by noting that no one else in the field had come close to breaking par. Ernie Els and Miguel Angel Jiminez had tied for second at three-over-par 287, a jaw-dropping 15 shots behind Woods.

"We knew it was just a matter of Tiger putting on a once-in-a-lifetime performance," Mike Davis said. "The golf course held up fine against the rest of the field."

This was different. No fewer than nineteen players entered the final round at Olympia Fields under par, with Furyk in position to become the first player in Open history to break 270 just by shooting 69—two shots higher than he'd shot in any of his three previous rounds. That sort of scoring is fine at a regular PGA Tour event. It is *not* fine at a U.S. Open. In fact, Furyk was only the third player in Open history to reach double digits under par at any point. Woods had done it in 2000, and Gil Morgan had done it during the third round in 1992 when Pebble Beach played as a par-72. He had fallen back on a brutal, windy final day, and Tom Kite's winning score that year was three under par.

That was more like what the USGA wanted and expected. And so, when Meeks, Davis, and Taylor made their choices on hole locations for Sunday, they opted for whatever was the toughest spot remaining in their arsenal. They weren't going for unfair, but they were certainly hoping to make the golf course more difficult than it had been.

"As soon as I saw the pin sheets, I knew the course was going to play hard," Furyk said. "When we got out there and I felt the wind kicking up, I knew it was going to be a long day. But it didn't surprise me. It was pretty much what I had expected."

The golf course setup and the weather pretty much ensured that no one was going to match Singh's Friday 63 or the 64 that Woody Austin had shot that day or, for that matter, the 66 that Dicky Pride, the 444th-ranked player in the world, had produced on Saturday. That was good for Furyk and Leaney as long as they could stay somewhere close to even par.

All of that left Furyk and Leaney not so much wondering where a challenge might come from but trying to be careful not to start thinking the championship had become match play between the two of them too early in the day.

"You really don't want to get caught up in that, but sometimes it's hard," Furyk said. "You tell yourself to keep attacking the golf course the same way you did the first three days, but that can be easier said than done."

Furyk's first show of nerves came on the second hole, when he pulled his drive into deep rough just in front of a bunker. He punched out and found rough on the other side of the fairway, then pitched to 20 feet.

Leaney, having taken a deep breath walking off the first green, played the hole perfectly. His drive split the middle, and he hit an eight-iron to 10 feet. "It occurred to me that if Jim missed and I made, the lead would be just two with a lot of holes to play," Leaney said. "I had a chance to put some pressure on him if he missed and I made mine."

Furyk didn't miss. He has one of golf's most unorthodox putting routines, standing up to the ball as if he is ready to putt, then backing off to read it—sometimes he'll do it twice—before stepping up to take the cross-handed putting grip he's used since boyhood. This time, not wanting to make an early bogey, he rolled the par putt into the hole. Leaney managed to keep himself together and make his birdie putt, so the margin was three.

Up ahead, things were starting to come apart for Singh. A poor drive and an awful second shot led to a double bogey at the short par-four third hole, and, a few minutes later, he bogeyed the fifth too. Leaney didn't seem to want to make a par: he bogeyed the third but again bounced back with another birdie at the fourth.

Leaney hadn't made a par yet, but Furyk was just the opposite, grinding out pars on the first four holes. If someone had been making a move, those pars might have given Furyk pause since he had played the first six holes in nine under par the first three days, the rest of the golf course in one under. But as he and Leaney walked onto the fifth tee, Singh, Mike Weir, and Billy Mayfair were tied for third place—seven shots back.

"It's almost become a little golf tournament between Furyk and Leaney," Miller commented.

That, of course, was the last thing NBC wanted: Furyk way out front being chased by the Unknown Aussie.

NBC did spend a good deal of Tom Watson's last forty-five minutes on the golf course focusing on him and Bruce Edwards, which was certainly understandable. Watson was nearing the end of his round, and the roars for the two of them as they walked up 18 with Watson tied for 28th place at four over par were ear splitting. Kirk Triplett, who was playing with Watson, simply stopped 50 yards short of the green, took off his hat, and joined the applause.

Just as he had done on Thursday, Watson got up and down for par from a bunker on his final hole. The crowd was screaming *"Broooce,"* as he and Edwards walked off the green, most people understanding that in all likelihood it was the last Open for the two of them together.

With Watson finished and Woods a few minutes from completing his last round with a two-over-par 72 that would leave him one shot ahead of Watson in a tie for 20th place, the question was whether anyone was capable of keeping Furyk and Leaney from making it into a two-man tournament.

Leaney finally made a par at the fifth. Furyk was in trouble—again—and again saved par with a remarkable putt, twisting in a 12-footer that dropped at the last possible second. He laughed briefly when the putt dropped in, knowing he'd been a little bit lucky but relieved to have avoided giving up a shot.

"Looking back, the two most important holes of the day might have been two and five," Leaney said. "Both times Jim was in trouble, and if he made bogey I'd have been within two. But he made both those putts, and I think that helped his confidence a lot. I could see that even if he was tight, he was doing a very good job of handling his nerves."

After a shaky start, Leaney was doing a pretty good job himself, and the scoreboard was helping. Being four shots clear of everyone else made it a little easier for him to focus on the notion that his job was to catch Furyk, not to worry about the others catching him.

Walking around outside the ropes, Mike and Tabitha Furyk

were counting down holes, tryng not to get ahead of themselves with their thoughts.

"Usually I like to walk around by myself," Mike said. "I like to try to focus on what Jim's doing and try not to get uptight. If Jim's mom is with me, she's like any mom—she worries about every little thing—and that can get to me. Tabitha's usually with friends, so I just go off by myself.

"This time was a little different. The Exelon guys [the company whose name Jim wears on his shirt] were with me a lot of the day, and they actually did a good job of keeping me loose. Even so, I knew I couldn't allow myself to think 'He's got it,' no matter how good it might look."

It only got better the rest of the front nine. Both players hit the sixth green in two, missed long eagle putts, and tapped in for birdies. Furyk had now followed one of Miller's preround directives: he was one under par after six holes. So was Leaney, which was actually a surprise to most, who had thought the pressure would get to him.

In fact, while Furyk and Leaney were plugging along, the rest of the field was in full reverse. Singh and Price, the two players who had seemed the most likely candidates to make a move, were both two over par for the day after six holes and staggered through the rest of the front nine, both of them turning in 40.

Furyk, knowing he didn't have to take any chances, kept hitting fairways and aiming at the middle of the greens. He parred seven, eight, and nine and turned in 35, meaning he was 11 under par for the championship. Leaney bogeyed both the seventh and the eighth, actually making a great bogey on number seven after his tee shot buried in a bunker. He had to make an eight-foot putt to avoid a double bogey.

"That bogey probably feels like a birdie," said Roger Maltbie, who always walks with the final group for NBC.

The bogey at eight felt more like, well, a bogey. After a perfect drive, Leaney pushed his second shot into the right greenside bunker, yet another shot he had lost to the right. From there, buried again, he hit a superb shot to within 12 feet but missed the putt. Furyk's par gave him a five-shot lead over Leaney with 10 holes to play. Only Mike Weir, who was at three under at that point, was fewer than nine shots behind.

"You know if this was Tiger with this kind of lead we'd all be on our hands and knees talking about how great he is," Hicks said, as Furyk and Leaney walked to the ninth tee.

Miller was clearly bothered by the fact that no one was making a move. "The field is certainly folding as if Tiger's in the lead," he said in response to Hicks's comment.

Things didn't get any better for the chasers as they turned to the back nine. Singh, having bogeyed eight and nine, proceeded to bogey 10, 11, 12, and 13. Price had managed to settle down and was making pars, but that certainly wasn't going to make Furyk nervous. The only players making any kind of move were guys who had been back in the pack, like Kenny Perry, who shot 67 to get to one under par, and Justin Rose, who shot 69 to finish at even par. Leggatt and Pride, the two surprise late-starters who had been in the third-to-last group, both came down to earth, shooting 77 and 78, respectively. Eduardo Romero and Jonathan Byrd, who had both been six shots back at the start, each shot 76.

In fact, by day's end, not one of the nineteen players who began the final round in red figures for the tournament had shot even-par or better on Sunday. There was no doubt the golf course had played a lot tougher, but the fact that everyone went backward was stunning. "You hate to say it," Miller said later in the day, "but most of these guys have gone out and played, well, stinkers of a round."

The only person who had any chance at all to catch Furyk down the stretch—and it was the longest of long shots—was Leaney, who managed to stop the bleeding with a par at the ninth.

Furyk also made par, meaning he led Leaney by five, and everyone else by nine or more, with nine holes to play.

Knowing there would be no Tiger Miracle and almost certainly
no miracle at all, NBC was now clinging to Tom Watson and
Bruce Edwards as if they were a life raft tossed from the Titanic,
which, ratingwise, the telecast was about to become. If Woods
had been running away from the field, not only would everyone
be bowing and scraping, but the ratings would soar in the final
two hours. If Phil Mickelson had a similar lead, the ratings would
hang in because people would want to see him finally win that
first major.

Furyk was a player people knew and liked, but he wasn't going
to bring people running inside on a summer day to see him win
his first major. Perhaps if Woods or Mickelson had been chasing
him, but not with (to use his full name) the Unknown Aussie Stephen Leaney chasing him.

Furyk is a bright, thoughtful man who is well liked in the
locker room and by the media. To most fans, he's the guy with the
funny-looking swing, the move up and to the outside, followed by
taking the club down and inside in a reverse-C motion.

He is methodical. Everything with him is routine: check the
yardage, consult with Cowen, step up to the ball and take a practice swing, step back, tug on the pants, reset behind the ball without swinging, step up and swing. The bottom line is that it works.
The fact that it doesn't inspire screams has never bothered Furyk.

"It just wouldn't be me to do a lot of fist pumping or try to get
the crowd going," he said. "I think I've always understood that my
success means I have obligations to spend time with the media, to
sign autographs, to interact with fans. But it isn't something I'd
ever seek out."

Now his public persona was on the verge of becoming far more
scrutinized if he became a U.S. Open champion.

"You know the first U.S. Open I played in back in 1966, Arnold

Palmer was leading Billy Casper by seven with nine holes to play, and Casper was hoping to hang on and finish second," Miller said as Furyk and Leaney stood on the 10th tee. "Next day he beat Palmer in a playoff."

Palmer was always combustible, capable of shooting the 65 he had shot on the last day at Cherry Hills in 1960 to come from seven shots down to win his only Open; capable of blowing a seven-shot lead with nine holes to play. Furyk was much steadier than that.

And so, as the players headed for the back nine, NBC cut to an emotional, lengthy interview with Watson. Soon after, it followed with an interview with Edwards, who was struggling to talk because of the ALS but game to try his best to let people know how he felt about the outpouring of emotion he'd experienced for four days. Not long after that, NBC showed Edwards and his wife, Marsha, with a flag from the 17th hole at Pebble Beach, that Ron Read, a longtime USGA official, had found and presented to Edwards that day.

The flag was a duplicate of the one used at Pebble Beach during the 1982 Open during which Watson had famously chipped in at number 17 to beat Jack Nicklaus, arguably the most remembered and replayed shot in Open history. Edwards's house had been decorated with flags from Watson's most memorable wins, but he had lost all of them several years earlier in a fire that had been set by his ex-wife. Read, who lives at Pebble Beach, found another one and brought it with him to Olympia Fields.

WALKING TO THE 10TH tee, Leaney had another talk with himself. He had shot 37 on the front nine—one over par—and was still comfortably in second place, leading Weir by three shots at that moment and a handful of players by four.

"I looked at the board walking off nine and realized those guys were still in position where they could catch me for second," he said. "I had to have a talk with myself then, because I knew, absolutely knew, that if I started trying to protect second place I'd go backward. I didn't want to be one of those guys who skids on the back nine at a major and goes from second to 20th. There have been plenty of guys who have done that.

"So when I walked onto the 10th tee, I told myself that I could still win the golf tournament. Sure, five shots was a lot, and Jim was playing well, but it wasn't out of the question. There had been a couple holes on the front where there could have been a two-shot swing, and it didn't happen. If it happened just once, the lead would be three, and maybe he'd start to feel the pressure. As good a player as he is, he was still in a place he'd never been before."

Furyk's thoughts were far less complicated. In fact, he was doing everything he could to empty his mind of all thoughts other than yardages and club selection and reads on the greens. The only voice he wanted to hear was Mike Cowen's, discussing the next shot with him. He didn't want to think about his parents or about Tabitha, who was already fighting her emotions as the back nine began, or about his daughter, who was playing happily at the day-care center set up for the players and their families.

"I knew what was going on up ahead," Furyk said. "I didn't want to tell myself yet that it was just Stephen and me, because I figured the minute I did that someone would finish with four straight birdies and I'd get tight. I knew all the stories about guys getting ahead of themselves mentally. That was the one thing I wanted to make sure I didn't do."

Only at the start of the back nine did Furyk finally stumble a little. He had been the only player among the last thirty on the golf course to play the front nine without a bogey. Now, he bogeyed 10 after pushing his tee shot into a fairway bunker. Still, the lead went back to five after Leaney missed a five-foot par putt at the 11th and dropped to five under.

"Every time all day that I had any chance to put pressure on him, he either made a putt or I missed one," Leaney said. "A lot of it was him. It isn't as if I played badly, because I didn't. But I never was able to get myself into position where I was able to seriously think, 'I can do this.'"

At that moment he was trying hard not to look over his shoulder at Weir, who was having a fascinating, up-and-down tournament in his first appearance in a major as the Masters champion. On Thursday he had made back-to-back double bogeys at eight and nine but had managed to come back to shoot 73. He had followed that with 67 and 68, and, when he almost holed a wedge at 14 and made birdie, he was at three under, still seven shots behind Furyk but only two behind Leaney.

"I knew it wasn't likely, but I went to the back nine thinking, 'Get on one last little roll here, and get it to six and see what happens,'" Weir said. "As well as Jim was playing, I didn't expect it, but it's the U.S. Open and things do happen."

As Weir played the 15th hole, Furyk and Leaney were on the 12th, the toughest hole on the golf course, a long uphill par-four. Furyk's second shot landed just on the front of the green but spun back all the way down the hill in front of the green, leaving him with a long chip.

Knowing the potential damage of a short pitch, Furyk pitched safely past the pin, basically accepting his bogey—always a smart play at the Open when in trouble. The bogey cut his lead on Leaney, who parred the hole, back to four again.

Furyk wasn't about to panic. He wasn't happy about making two bogeys in three holes, but he hadn't expected not to make any mistakes all day. He hit a good drive at the 13th and an excellent second shot to within 10 feet. Leaney's second shot wasn't nearly as close, but he rolled in his 25-footer for birdie, allowing himself a modest fist shake for the first time all day. When Furyk missed his birdie putt, the lead was down to three, and the NBC people, hoping for some drama—*any* drama—at the finish were practically jumping up and down for joy.

"The game is on," Miller shouted. "All of a sudden this has a different feel, doesn't it?"

"Big mo switch right there," Maltbie added.

The two players involved didn't see the three-shot margin as being quite that dramatic. "That was when it occurred to me that it really was match play," Furyk said. "We had four holes left, and everyone else was seven or eight shots back or more, and either in the clubhouse or almost there. Unless something crazy happened, Stephen was the only one who could catch me. It was clear by then, he wasn't going to go away. The guy was a good player, and he was playing a very solid round."

Leaney was, but he knew time was running out. "I had started the day three back with 18 to go," he said. "Now I was three back with five to go. Far from impossible, but I knew I had to play close to perfect to have any chance."

The 14th was a 414-yard par-four that was playing downwind. Both players hit good drives that allowed them to hit pitching wedges from the fairway. Leaney hit a reasonably good shot, the ball checking up about 18 feet short of the flag. "That keeps the pressure on," Maltbie said.

Furyk had hit a perfect four-wood down the left side of the fairway, the ball stopping just short and left of an in-ground yardage marker. It was clear that his swing was likely to be impeded as he followed through by the marker, so he called over Reed McKenzie—who, as the USGA president, was the walking rules official with the final group—to be sure he was entitled to relief. McKenzie agreed. As a courtesy, Furyk called Leaney over too to show him where the ball was.

"You okay with that?" he asked.

Leaney nodded assent.

Technically, since a rules official was right there and had

granted him relief, Furyk didn't have to call Leaney over, but he did it anyway—something a player might do in a match-play situation.

"I just didn't see any reason for there to be any doubt in his mind," Furyk said later. "It's the U.S. Open; I'm an American, Reed's an American. I just thought it was the right thing to do."

"Just shows you the kind of guy Jim is," Leaney said.

Once he had dropped his ball away from the yardage marker, Furyk took a lot of time discussing the shot with Cowen. He even backed off an extra time just to be certain he knew exactly what he wanted to do.

"This is a green-light hole location for him," Bob Murphy said, as Furyk fidgeted over the shot.

A green-light hole location means that the hole is in a favorable spot for a player's natural shot. Furyk plays a right-to-left draw, and the flag was on the left side of the green, a rare location where players had a chance to get the ball to hit and stop.

As soon as Furyk got the ball in the air, he was talking to it. "Be right," he said, a reference to being the right distance, not to going to the right. Walking forward, through almost clenched teeth, he said it again: "Be right."

It was right—close to perfect, in fact. The ball landed just short and right of the flagstick and rolled to within three feet before stopping, as the loudest roar of the day went up.

"I knew that I'd hit it perfectly," Furyk said. "That's why I was begging for it to be the right distance because I thought I had a chance to get it really close."

As his son followed through, Mike Furyk was staring, not at the ball but at him. "I could see it in his eyes right at that moment," he said. "The thing I always notice with the great players is their eyes. At that moment, Jim reminded me of Hogan, the way he would stare a ball down. What I've always noticed with Tiger when he's hit a great shot, and he knows it at a big moment, is his eyes. You can see them narrow because he's honed in on what he wants to see happen, what he knows is going to happen. Jim had that look. He looked like a bird of prey.

"Right then, for the first time all day, I allowed myself to think 'He's got it.' I turned to Linda and said, 'It isn't over yet, but right now the tournament is his.'"

Most of America had been thinking that all day long. But it is a lot easier to concede victory to someone when you are spectating than when you're in the crucible. All the Furyks had been in the crucible throughout the afternoon. Now, as he half walked, half ran to the green, Jim knew he was a lot closer to the finish line than he had been a few moments before.

So did Leaney. "I knew even if I made my birdie putt I was going to be three down with four to go against a guy who really looked like he was in control of his game," he said. "I knew the last couple of holes were very tough and things can happen, but the window was closing pretty quickly."

Leaney missed his birdie putt. Furyk looked his over carefully, going through his whole routine before knocking it in. Now the lead was four with four holes to play. The good news for Leaney was that Weir was struggling with the last two holes. On 17, the monster par-three, he hit a four-iron that looked as if it was going to bounce between the bunkers and end up close to the hole. Instead, the ball kicked dead right into a bunker, and he made bogey. Then, after finding another bunker off the tee at 18, he finished with another bogey, leaving him tied for third with the long-finished Kenny Perry at one under par.

Leaney and Furyk both made routine pars at 15 and 16, finding the middle of the green. NBC had stopped showing any names on the leaderboard except for the top two, as if it didn't want to remind viewers how far back the rest of the field was at that stage.

Standing on the 17th tee leading Leaney by four with no one

else in the field closer than nine shots away, Furyk knew that only an act of God was going to stop him from winning the Open. Still, he remained steely eyed, firing a three-iron just over the back of the green, knowing that the highest number he could make from there was four. Leaney found a front bunker, and both men, playing conservatively to take a high number out of the equation, walked off with comfortable bogeys.

There was no doubt now that the deed was done. Tabitha Furyk had started crying almost from the minute Jim had birdied 14, knowing her husband well enough to be sure he wasn't going to blow a four-shot lead with four holes to play. "Fortunately, I was wearing sunglasses," she said. "But I was a complete mess."

She had called day care and learned that Caleigh was the only child still there. Could they, she wondered, bring Caleigh to the back of the 18th green. Not only could they do it, they did it with a police escort. As her husband and Leaney walked to the 18th tee, Tabitha ran ahead to collect her daughter and prepare for her husband's triumphant arrival.

The 18th hole was really a coronation for both players. Furyk was going to be the U.S. Open champion. Leaney was finally going to realize his dream of reaching the PGA Tour. Furyk led Leaney by four, and Leaney led everyone else by four.

"I'd stuck to my strategy, hitting three-woods off the tee all day," Leaney said. "I looked at the board coming off 17 and figured, what the heck, I might as well hit driver."

Furyk went the other way. He too had been hitting three-woods — and the occasional four-wood — off the tee, both men wanting to stay short of the fairway bunkers as best they could. Now, as he walked onto the 18th tee, Cowen didn't even wait to be asked his opinion.

"I like three-iron right here," he said, pulling the three-iron out before Furyk had a chance to start a debate.

For the first time since his putt at the fifth trickled into the side of the hole, Furyk smiled. He knew Cowen wanted to be sure he couldn't reach any of the bunkers, especially knowing how pumped up his man had to be at that moment.

His three-iron went down the right side of the fairway. Leaney's driver blew over the bunkers. Furyk hit a seven-iron second shot, and the ball bounced to the back left side of the green, about 30 feet from the hole. Leaney also found the green with a nine-iron.

As soon as he saw his ball on the green, Furyk knew there were no more ifs, ands, or buts left. There would be no Arnold Palmer collapse or a Jean Van de Velde triple bogey or any kind of suspense. There hadn't really been much suspense all day, but now any last vestiges were gone.

"I didn't think I was going to six-putt from there," he said.

When the realization hit him that the dream was now an absolute reality, Furyk began to lose it. As he walked up the fairway, the applause washing over him, the tears started to come. Once he had hit his second shot, Leaney's first thought was to walk over and congratulate him, but when he saw Furyk crying, he decided to wait.

"I wanted to go and say 'Well done,' right then and there," he said. "But when I saw him crying, I thought I should just give him his space and let him drink it all in."

The adrenaline that Cowen had worried about on the tee actually kicked in on the green. Furyk rifled his first putt a good eight feet past the hole. By then he was able to joke with Cowen about how close he'd come to putting the ball off the green.

He missed the putt coming back, which meant he would not break the Open scoring record but only tie it. "Never gave it a thought," Furyk said. "All I knew when that last putt went in [it was about six inches long] was that I was a U.S. Open champion. No matter what happened the rest of my career, my name was going to be on that trophy."

He had shot the 72 Miller had predicted and had beaten Leaney (who also shot 72) by three, and Weir and Perry by seven. Nick Price and Vijay Singh, the two men most had thought might have a chance to go low and catch Furyk, had shot 75 and 78, respectively. Only four players had finished the championship under par.

The Furyks had a Father's Day moment on the green, Tabitha handing Caleigh to Jim, who hugged and kissed everyone.

"We did it," he whispered in his father's ear, and it was about as warm a moment as you could hope to see.

NBC would announce the next day that Sunday's ratings had been the lowest for an Open since it began televising the event in 1995. Perhaps the ratings would have been higher if the network had been able to track Woods as he left for the airport. His plane was long gone by the time Furyk accepted the trophy.

As Jim Furyk kissed it and held it up for all to see, he really didn't care what the television ratings had been. His name was on the U.S. Open trophy. And he knew it would be there forever.

BUT, AS IT TURNED out, Furyk's name was not on the U.S. Open trophy.

After he had accepted the trophy and spoken to the crowd and been put through all the media paces, Furyk finally made his way to the parking lot shortly after nine o'clock Chicago time.

Exhaustion was kicking in. He had been up early, partly to play with Caleigh, partly because of nerves, and it had been a long, draining day—albeit one with a joyous ending. There was still some light left—Chicago is on the eastern tip of the central time zone, and June 18 is one of the longest days of the year—but Olympia Fields was largely empty when Jim and Tabitha, accompanied by a USGA official carrying the Open trophy, finally made their way to the car.

The trophy had been wrapped up and boxed for the trip home. It isn't very big, and, like the trophies from the British Open and the PGA, it is the champion's for a year. (The Masters has no permanent trophy. Each champion receives one, a replica of the Augusta clubhouse, to keep. The green jacket is what comes back to the club after a year thereafter to be worn only on the grounds of the club.)

In the case of the green jacket, players are technically not supposed to have duplicates made, but all of them do so anyway. The other three championships allow players to order duplicates of their trophies but have rules about how they should be made.

"I think you can have it made at 90 percent the size of the original," Furyk said. "That's just in case something happens so there's no confusing the original with the duplicate."

That was fine with Furyk. What stunned him was what the man from the USGA said as he helped load the box with the trophy into the back of Furyk's car.

"It's your job to get it engraved," he said.

Furyk laughed. He figured that was a joke, maybe an old USGA tradition to give the champion a laugh at day's end. Except the man wasn't smiling.

"Get it engraved?" Furyk said.

"You got it," the man said, shaking Furyk's hand. "Congratulations. Great playing."

Furyk didn't really think much about it that night or the next day. There was a celebration with family and friends back at the house, and then he had to be up shortly after dawn to take part in an Exelon outing that had been planned long before anyone thought he would be there as the U.S. Open champion. Instead of a preouting clinic, Furyk did a Q and A with the Exelon clients at the outing and couldn't help but observe that they were hanging on his every word.

That night, after his parents had flown to Hawaii to spend a few days together, he and Tabitha and Caleigh finally flew home to Ponte Vedra. Furyk was supposed to play at Westchester that week, and he wasn't going to back out on the commitment. Normally, he would have gone straight from Chicago to Westchester to play a practice round, but he decided he needed a few hours at home to catch his breath.

When the Furyks finally walked into their house Monday night, Jim carried the trophy inside, took it out of the box, and put it on a table. "Just looking at it inside my house made me smile," he said. "Then I remembered what the USGA guy had said."

He took a close look at the trophy, and, sure enough, the last name engraved on it was Tiger Woods—the 2002 champion. There was no sign of his name. Upon closer inspection, he could even see evidence that different engravers had been used by different champions.

"Up until Steve Jones [1996], the names looked pretty much the same and the spacing was identical," he said. "After that, some guys' names were closer to the guy above, and some were farther. It was weird."

Furyk was amused and amazed at the notion that he was responsible for his own engraving. Like anyone who has ever played golf or watched golf, he had memories of watching the official engraver for the Royal and Ancient putting the champion's name on the Claret Jug—the British Open trophy—before the awards ceremony took place.

"I guess I just figured it was the same thing for our Open," he said. "I was wrong."

The engraving soon became a running joke among the Furyks and their friends, especially when they showed friends the unengraved trophy.

"We actually sat around thinking up a TV commercial," Tabitha said. "We had Jim walking around in the mall carrying the trophy looking for a place that would engrave it for him."

"I'd finally find a place," Jim added, "usually a kiosk or something, and I'd be standing there going, 'It's spelled F-U-R-Y-K.'"

It wasn't until January that Furyk finally boxed up the trophy and sent it off to be engraved. "It didn't cost very much," he said, smiling. "Actually, the insurance cost more than the engraving.

"I did wonder, though, what they would have done if I brought it back the next June and said, 'Sorry, I didn't get a chance to get it engraved.'"

Retief Goosen won the Open in 2004. Maybe the USGA could have asked him to take care of adding Furyk's name while he had his own engraving done. After all, having won the championship once before (2001), Goosen clearly knew where to find an engraver.

"I would never have done it, of course," Furyk said with a laugh. "After all, I like to tell people how much it means to me knowing my name is going to be on the trophy forever. I had to be sure I was right when I said it."

Furyk's first hint that life had changed had come at the Exelon outing, but it really started to hit when he got to Westchester.

He had flown in late Tuesday night and had a morning tee time the next day for the pro-am. After he played his pro-am round he was brought into the press room, his first meeting with the media since his name had been not exactly engraved on the U.S. Open trophy.

"Usually, when I would do a pretournament press conference, they'd run around and round up ten guys to make sure when I walked in the room it wouldn't be empty and everyone would feel embarrassed," he said. "That day I remember walking in, and it was packed—there wasn't a seat to be had or any place to stand. I remember thinking, 'Okay, things are a little different now.'

"It even felt like people were listening to me more closely." He smiled. "Of course, that could have been my imagination. But over the next few months, I noticed that I got a lot more questions—on a lot more subjects. All of a sudden people wanted my opinions on things that went beyond the condition of the golf course.

"But all that was okay. I think I was ready for it. It wasn't as if I'd never been in an interview room or had media demands before. It just ramped things up. But not in a way that I didn't think I could handle."

Furyk was very happy to get home the week after Westchester, where he ended up finishing tied for 22nd place. After all, he needed to get to the mall to get that trophy engraved.

11

From Nowhere to St. George's

THERE IS A FOUR-WEEK gap each year between the U.S. Open and the British Open. After Westchester, the PGA Tour moved on to Memphis, Chicago, and Milwaukee before those who had qualified headed across the Atlantic to Royal St. George's in southern England for the 132nd playing of the British Open — or, as everyone in the world who doesn't live in the United States calls it, "the Open Championship."

The number of American players who make the trip each year has been the subject of a good deal of controversy for a long time. It has only been fifteen years since the British Open became an "official" tournament on the PGA Tour, meaning that money won in the event counts toward a player's standing on the money list.

Even with that, many players opt to stay home because they don't like the long flights, don't like the food in Great Britain, don't like adjusting their golf games to the vagaries of links play, don't like the size of the hotel rooms, don't like driving on the right-hand side of the road, and don't like the relative lack of showers or how small they are when they can be found.

Sometimes life is really tough for golfers. One prominent player who makes the trip every year often does so without his wife. "She only comes the years when there's a hotel with a spa at the course," he said — completely serious.

In 2003 Royal St. George's had no spa. It is in the town of Sandwich, a rural area a few miles from Dover and the famous white cliffs. There's no spa, no Ritz, not even so much as a Fairfield Inn by Marriott in Sandwich. It is bed-and-breakfast country.

In 2004, the Royal and Ancient Golf Club, which puts on the Open Championship, created a qualifying event in the United States to encourage American players to make the trip. Until then, very few Americans who were not exempt into the field flew over to play in the 36-hole qualifiers held at four different sites near the Open golf course. The American theory, generally speaking, was that no one wanted to make the flight to play 36 holes, perhaps not qualify, and then turn around and go home.

A handful of Americans did play qualifiers. Peter Jacobsen and Brad Faxon both played on several occasions. One year, Faxon failed in the qualifier, flew home on Tuesday, played in the B.C. Open, which then was held the same week as the British—and won. Faxon was adamant that Americans, especially those who were exempt, play in the British.

"To me, it's probably the greatest golf tournament in the world," Faxon said. "If you're a golfer and you don't love it, something is wrong. It's the oldest championship there is, it's played on great golf courses with great fans. Sure, it's a different kind of challenge, but for one week a year there's nothing wrong with that."

In 1996 when Scott Hoch (who famously missed a three-foot putt that would have won the Masters in 1989) didn't go to the British and called St. Andrews and other links courses little more than glorified cow pastures, Faxon lashed out, saying—among other things—that any American who was exempt into the British and didn't play should not be allowed to play in the Ryder Cup. For his comments, Faxon was fined $500 by the PGA Tour for being publicly critical of another player. "I'd say it again and pay the fine again" was his response.

Ben Curtis didn't have to worry at all about the British Open in 2003. His one and only concern as the tour moved into the summer months was to improve his game enough so that he could keep his playing privileges for 2004. When the tour reached the U.S. Open—generally considered the midway point of the season—Curtis, who had not qualified to play at Olympia Fields, had played in ten tournaments and had made five cuts in his rookie season. His highest finish had been a tie for thirty-first in Houston where he made $24,975. In all, he had made a little bit less than $73,000 in prize money for the year and stood 212th on the money list, a long, long way from the top 125.

"The last thing on my mind was the British Open," he said, laughing.

Just the fact that Curtis was on the tour was something of a surprise to him and to others, since he had never even qualified for the Nationwide Tour prior to his trip to Q-School at the end of 2002. Like Mike Weir and so many others, he had hit the second-stage wall.

Curtis grew up in the rural northeast Ohio town of Franklin. His grandfather, Dwight Black, had built a nine-hole golf course there in 1973, on the farm where he lived. He built another nine holes four years later.

"When I played it growing up, it was 6,300 yards with flat, round greens," Curtis said, laughing. "It was the perfect golf course for a kid starting out, because you could shoot pretty low scores and build your confidence."

Curtis's parents, Bob and Janet, grew up in towns that were ten miles apart—Radnor and Ostrander—and had both attended Buckeye Valley High School. Bob Curtis played baseball and basketball in high school; Janet Black was a cheerleader. They graduated in 1974 and were married not long after that. Bob worked on a farm for a while, but after his father-in-law opened the golf course he went to work there, and eventually he and Janet moved onto the property. Ben was born in 1977, and his brother Nick came along twenty months later.

"Our house was right behind the 18th hole," Ben said. "My dad basically taught me a grip and a stance when I was a kid, and then I'd go practice on the range, which was about 150 yards away. I never really took lessons. My dad and my grandpa would just watch me sometimes when I hit balls. When I was a kid, Nick and I and some of our friends would go out at about six o'clock and play 18 holes before dark. We'd each get our own cart, fly around, and play for pizzas."

He was good at golf from the start but also played baseball and basketball. He stuck with basketball through high school and was a starter as a junior and a senior. "I was a starter," he said, "but we were never very good. We won seven games in two years, and six were when I was a senior. We had a new coach, and we got better."

Even though he played other sports, Ben was hooked on golf at a young age. His father's maintenance shop was right next to the putting green, and his parents often found him chipping and putting after dark, using the light from the maintenance shop so he could see. By the time he was ten, his father and grandfather began taking Ben to the Memorial Tournament, which was played just outside Columbus.

"Growing up in Ohio, Jack [Nicklaus] was a huge deal for me," he said. "One of my first golf memories is watching him win the Masters in '86. Back then, they used to have this Skins Game on Tuesdays at the Memorial, and because my dad worked at a golf course we were able to get in, even though they limited the crowd to like five thousand people. I remember one year it was Jack and Fuzzy [Zoeller] and [Lee] Trevino. I was right up against the ropes. It was very laid back and very cool.

"By the time I was in high school, I was going to the tournament itself. In the back of my mind was the idea that I wanted to be a pro someday, because I was starting to have a lot of success in junior events and high-school tournaments. But my dad and my grandfather would always say to me, 'It may look easy, but it's really hard to be good enough to get out there.' My grandfather was always on me. I would shoot eight under or something, and he'd find a couple of flaws in what I was doing. It wasn't so much to be critical as to remind me not to think I was all that good just because I was doing well against other juniors."

Curtis won state titles as a junior and a senior and was recruited by a lot of good golf schools, notably Oklahoma State, as well as places like Georgia Tech, Ohio State, Minnesota, Florida Southern (a Division 2 power), and his local school, Kent State. He was interested in Oklahoma State for a while but became discouraged when legendary coach Mike Holder told him what he thought of his game.

"He said, 'You've got the talent to come and play for us, but we're going to have to overhaul your entire game to get you to the next level.' I wasn't up for that. I liked Georgia Tech, but I didn't have the grades to get in. I wasn't a great student because I didn't work that hard and my ACTs were pretty mediocre."

He ended up taking four official visits: to Ohio State, Minnesota, Kent State, and Florida Southern. He eventually crossed Florida Southern off his list because, unlike a lot of golfers, he didn't want to go someplace where he could play twelve months a year. "I was used to putting the clubs up in the winter," he said. "I kind of liked the break. It kept the game fresh for me."

He was tempted by Ohio State. The coach, Jim Brown—not *the* Jim Brown (of the Cleveland Browns)—had started recruiting him when he was very young because he knew his grandfather. But Ohio State was a national power in the mid-90s and was just coming off a fourth-place finish in the NCAA Championships. "They wanted me to come and walk on the team at first," he

Mike Weir's finest hour: receiving the green jacket on the Augusta National putting green from Tiger Woods. (*Golf Digest*)

Even seven years later, it is still difficult for Len Mattiace to talk about his most brilliant day ever on a golf course. (*Stan Badz/PGA Tour*)

Jim Furyk's unorthodox swing has produced remarkable results through the years. (*Copyright USGA Museum/ John Mummert*)

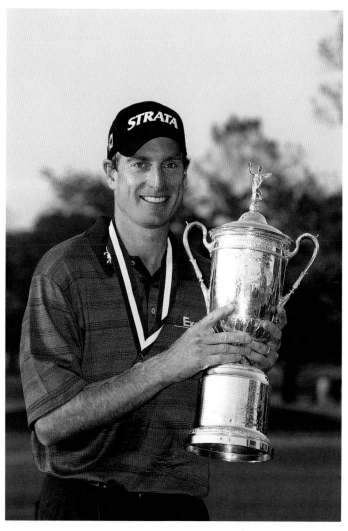

Furyk with the U.S. Open trophy he had to get engraved. (*Copyright USGA Museum/John Mummert*)

Jim and Tabitha Furyk, Tabitha's eyes *still* hidden behind sunglasses.
(*Copyright USGA Museum/Steven Gibbons*)

For one day, the 2003 U.S. Open belonged to Tom Watson and his
caddy, Bruce Edwards. (*Copyright USGA Museum/John Mummert*)

Stephen Leaney, "the unknown Aussie," kept it close at Olympia Fields on Sunday while everyone else faded. *(Copyright USGA Museum/John Mummert)*

Tiger Woods sought a new swing in 2003. It wasn't until 2005 that he again crossed the bridge to dominance. *(Copyright USGA Museum/ John Mummert)*

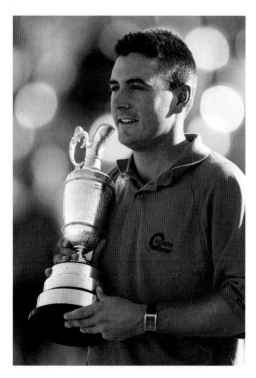

Ben Curtis with the Claret Jug, the trophy that put him in the same sentence with Francis Ouimet. (*Golf Digest*)

Years later, Thomas Bjorn can't bring himself to discuss what happened in the bunker at number 16 on the last day of the 2003 Open Championship. (*Golf Digest*)

Davis Love III had a chance to win after witnessing Bjorn's disaster but still couldn't believe what he had seen. *(Copyright USGA Museum/ Steven Gibbons)*

Shaun Micheel with the Wanamaker Trophy. Some still call his PGA Championship win at Oak Hill a fluke, even though he hit one of *the* great shots in golf history to clinch the victory.

said. "I didn't really want to do that. I wanted to go someplace and play as a freshman."

That someplace turned out to be Kent State. A number of players he had grown up with were there or were going there, and he liked the coach, Herb Page, a stocky Canadian who walked a little bit like a penguin according to his players. He had been a place-kicker at Kent State when Hall of Fame linebacker Jack Lambert had played there, and Curtis felt comfortable with Page from the beginning. So, he traveled across the state to enroll.

From the get-go, Curtis knew he'd made the right decision. Page held a two-week qualifiying tournament to determine places on the team, and Curtis won easily. "I finished second or third in my first tournament and kind of went from there," he said. "I was comfortable right from the start."

Most surprising was his academic performance. His first semester GPA was 3.8. "A lot of it was the weather," he said, laughing. "By the end of October, we weren't playing any golf, so I could concentrate on my classes. I figured it was important to do well in college. I had no idea if I was going to be good enough to make it as a pro, so I put some effort into it."

Curtis is one of those people who is sneaky smart. He's quiet, not the kind of guy who lights up a room with one-liners or stories when he walks into it. But when he has time to think about something, he usually figures it out and makes smart decisions. Unlike a lot of college golfers who put all their eggs into the "I'm going to be a millionaire pro golfer" basket, Curtis realized he had better work in the direction of a degree in case professional golf didn't work out, as it doesn't for so many college golfers.

He majored in recreation management, thinking he might someday run a hotel or a restaurant or a day-care center—or a golf course. He also minored in marketing, thinking that was an area that could be helpful to him no matter where he ended up after college.

Curtis had completed all his course requirements to graduate by spring of 2000 but had not yet completed the requisite thesis. By then he had won the Mid-American Conference tournament as a senior and been a two-time second team All American. After his junior year (1999), he made it to the semifinals of the U.S. Amateur, which was played at Pebble Beach, before losing on the 17th hole to eventual champion David Gossett—a can't-miss future star at that point.

"That tournament was when all the agents really started showing up," Curtis said, smiling at the memory. "I'd had some good results before that, but at the Amateur everyone is there and everyone is watching. I think what was important about it for me wasn't so much that agents wanted to sign me, but that I figured these guys had to know something about judging talent, and if they thought I was worth pursuing, I must have some ability."

If nothing else, his performance in the Amateur and the ardor of the agents convinced Curtis to at least take a shot playing on tour when he was finished at Kent State. He had planned to get his degree in the fall, so he wrote the thesis in the fall and sent it to his professor. "He either never got it or lost it," Curtis said. "Either way, I got a notice saying I wasn't getting my degree because I hadn't completed the thesis."

But by then he had turned pro and signed with IMG, the Yankees of management companies. It made sense for several reasons: IMG is a Cleveland-based company, so it felt right for an Ohio boy to sign with them. More important, IMG's tentacles are everywhere in the golf world. Frequently they are able to use their power to get their young players into tournaments on sponsor exemptions, and soon after signing with IMG, Curtis got a sponsor's exemption into the Buick Southern Open.

"Missed the cut," he said. "But it was good experience."

He made it through the first stage of Q-School in the fall of 2000 but missed at second stage. "The whole time I was a couple of shots outside the number," he said. "I just couldn't find a way to make a move."

He wasn't that disappointed, especially when he saw the number of quality players he had competed against in college who had also failed second stage. Since he hadn't made the Q-School finals, he had no status on either the PGA Tour or the Nationwide Tour (even IMG can't get that done). He was forced to go one level down to the Hooters Tour, getting through that tour's Q-School in January.

By then Curtis had started dating Candace Beatty. They had met on the golf course at Kent State when she had successfully walked on the women's team during his senior year. She was two years younger than he was and still in school when he came back in the fall to try to finish his degree work. So, Curtis headed out on the Hooters Tour—to places like Conover, North Carolina; Dothan, Alabama; Rogers, Arkansas; and Miami, Oklahoma— on his own.

"The Hooters tour was actually fun at the beginning," he said. "It was a lot of staying in Super 8s and Hampton Inns—that was upscale for us—in small towns, but I met a lot of good guys. We'd often stay three in a room to save some money and go out and find whatever chain restaurant was around to eat in at night."

The Hooters is actually a throwback to the early days of the PGA Tour—players driving from town to town, sharing rooms and cars and chasing a dream. One of Curtis's good friends starting in '01 was future Masters champion Zach Johnson, who had graduated from Drake in 1998 and was also trying to get his career started in golf's minor leagues.

The two were similar players and people, and they hit it off right away. "Ben and I both play what I call boring golf," Johnson said. "When we're on, we just hit fairways and greens, nothing very exciting. We're both grinders. But even though he was pretty quiet, I could see he had a lot of confidence. He was the kind of guy who could really go low when he was in contention because the pressure of the hunt didn't get to him. You could even see that in practice rounds."

It took Curtis a little while to adjust to life on the road. By midyear he began to find his comfort level on the tour, consistently finishing in the top 10 while making more than $40,000 — good enough to finish 18th on the money list. He went back to Q-School in the fall of '01, thinking he was ready to break through and at least make it to the finals.

Once again he cruised through first stage and headed for second stage in Stonebridge, Georgia. The weather was awful all week, the players dealing with rain and mud and standing water every day. There was so much water that the rules officials allowed players to lift, clean, and place their balls in waste areas around the course; usually lift, clean, and place is limited to fairways in wet conditions. Curtis and the other two players in his group — one of them being Gary Hallberg, who had been on tour for a number of years — thought the lift, clean, and place was allowed in the bunkers, which were also underwater.

"They called us in with a few holes to play on the third day because it was just too wet to play," he said. "That night a bunch of us were sitting around talking, and somehow the subject came up about how tough it was to play out of the bunkers. I can still remember my heart sinking. I went to a couple of friends who were playing who were also from Kent State and asked them, and they told me it was okay [to lift, clean, and place] in waste areas but not the bunkers. I went to Gary and said, 'I think we screwed up.'

"The next morning we went and told the rules guys. They said, 'We're really sorry, fellas; we have to DQ you.' I was right on the number at the time. I can still remember Gary screaming at the guys for not making it clear what the deal was, but the fact was everyone else playing got it right and we got it wrong. That one was tough to take. I really felt as if I was going to make it."

He went back to the Hooters for another year, won a tournament, and finished 10th on the money list. He decided to change his approach at the '02 Q-School, signing up for second stage in California, at a very difficult course called Bayonet, which is located at Fort Ord.

"I've always done well on tough courses," he said. "Plus, I'd tried the East Coast route twice and gotten nowhere. If nothing else, I thought it might change my luck."

It did. He played solidly for four days and was comfortably inside the cut line the entire time. That put him in the finals at PGA West, along with Zach Johnson, who had also broken through for the first time.

Like a lot of first timers at the finals, Curtis arrived early. The weather in Ohio — surprise — was terrible in early December, so he and Candace (they had gotten engaged at the end of '01) flew to Palm Springs on Friday night, dodging a snowstorm during a layover in Minneapolis to get there.

"I went out and practiced on Saturday and Sunday," he remembered. "On Monday I was practicing again, and I remember thinking to myself, 'This thing doesn't even start until Wednesday.' I needed to kind of back off and relax. If I hadn't, I would have been exhausted before I hit a shot that mattered."

Most of his family flew out for the week. His brother, Nick, who had caddied for him in both of his U.S. Amateurs, caddied again. During the fourth round on Saturday, Curtis holed out from 100 yards for an eagle on one of the par-fives. He was already playing well, but that really got him going. When he did it again on the 11th hole during the final round on Monday, he was almost certain he had clinched his card.

"That's when the wheels almost fell off," he said, shaking his head at the memory of Q-School terrors almost every player has felt. "The minute I thought 'I've got it,' I started to play scared. I bogeyed the next two holes. By the time I got to 17, I was pretty sure that two pars would do it, but two bogeys could get me into trouble. Nick was so nervous he was chewing on his nails, which didn't help me. I made par at 17, but I snap hooked my drive on 18 because I was trying to stay away from the water. I laid up and then hit my wedge over the green and ended up making double.

"I was quaking a little coming off, but someone told me everyone was struggling because it was windy, and I should be okay. As it turned out, I made it by a couple of shots. All I could think was, 'Thank God, you didn't blow it.'"

The Curtis family went to a nearby hamburger place to eat when it was all over. Ben was so drained, he couldn't think of anything else he wanted to do to celebrate. They flew home, where Ben proudly presented his PGA Tour card to his grandfather, who hadn't been healthy enough to make the trip to California.

"We took a picture of the two of us holding the card," Curtis said. "I'm very glad that we did that."

Because he had finished tied for 26th at Q-School, Curtis didn't get into the first few tournaments of his rookie year. He finally got in at Pebble Beach and missed the cut. He also missed the cut in San Diego and headed for Tucson, which was played opposite the World Golf Championships match play event, meaning there were lots of spots in the field for Q-School rookies.

He was playing a practice round in Tucson on Sunday afternoon (he had arrived early after missing the cut in San Diego) when he got a phone call. His grandfather, who had been dealing with heart problems for a while, had died. He flew home for the funeral and then, knowing his grandfather would have been very upset with him for not playing that week, flew back to Tucson to try to play.

Not surprisingly, he missed another cut. "It wasn't as if it was a shock when he died; he'd been sick," Curtis said. "And I was really glad that I'd been able to go home in December with the tour card, show it to him, and have our picture taken with it. But he spent all those years helping me with my game, right from the start, and he never got the chance to see me play on the tour in person. We would have been on the East Coast in a couple weeks, and he could have come."

When the tour got to the East Coast, things started to get better for Curtis. He was third alternate at the Honda Classic and spent all day Wednesday and most of the day Thursday hanging around hoping for withdrawals that never happened. A week later, though, the IMG connection kicked in again. Since Arnold Palmer was IMG's first client (he and the company's founder, Mark McCormack, were best friends), IMG runs his tournament at Bay Hill and controls the sponsor exemptions. Not surprisingly, those sponsor exemptions go, almost without exception, to IMG clients.

Curtis was able to take advantage of the free pass, making the cut and finishing in a tie for 42nd place, earning his first PGA Tour check. It was worth $14,130. That gave him a bit of a confidence boost, and he made his next four cuts in a row, his best finish coming at Houston where he made $24,975 for finishing in a tie for 31st.

"I wasn't exactly tearing things up," he said. "But at least I was playing on weekends and making a little bit of money." He missed his next two cuts—including at the Memorial where he got an exemption from Nicklaus as a local kid—and then failed to qualify for the U.S. Open. He was still way down the money list after making $10,300 at Westchester.

A week later at Memphis, he made another cut and appeared headed for another relatively small check when he shot an even-par 71 on Saturday. The TPC at Southwind, where the Memphis event is played each year, is one of those golf courses where an even-par round will usually cause you to lose ground. Curtis had managed a 67 on Friday to get him comfortably inside the cut line, but the 71 left him in a tie for 58th place. On Sunday, though, he got on a roll and shot the lowest round of his brief tour career, a six-under-par 65. That allowed him to pass thirty-one players and move up to a tie for 27th, earning him his biggest check of the year: $33,300.

"What was more important was that it reminded me I could go low at times," he said. "For a while I was wondering if I would ever shoot a low round. The golf courses we were playing were a long way from the Hooters Tour."

It also jumped him, for the first time, into the top 200 on the money list, moving him up to 141st place. That was still a lot of progress, especially given where he had been a year earlier on the Hooters.

In fact, many players who make the jump from either college (rare these days) or the Hooters to the PGA Tour without playing on the Nationwide Tour will tell you that the toughest adjustment is the quality of the golf courses. The greens are considerably faster, the rough a lot deeper in most places. Mistakes almost always cost you.

Curtis was getting the kind of on-the-job training that usually lands a player back in Q-School, but after his hot Sunday at Memphis, he jumped up on the money list, heading to Chicago for the Western Open. Cog Hill Golf and Country Club, where the Western Open was held until the tour did away with the event in a corporate big bucks shake-up in 2007, was one of the most respected venues on tour—a public golf course that many players thought was good enough and tough enough to someday host a major championship. The golf course was so respected by the pros that the Western was one of the few events Tiger Woods regularly played, strictly because he liked the golf course, with none of his corporate deals involved. That was the kind of course where Curtis had historically thrived, not unlike Bayonet, where he had broken through the second-stage wall six months earlier.

He made the cut with a shot to spare and then pieced together a three-under-par 69 on Saturday to move past a number of players into contention, and perhaps, he thought, to have his first top-25 finish.

"That's all I was thinking about," he said. "I wanted to play well, finish as high as I could, and get myself into the top 100 maybe on the money list. I had two weeks off coming up—I wasn't playing in Milwaukee or at B.C. [the event opposite the British Open], so I was looking forward to a break. I was tired because the weather had been hot and humid out there all week."

In fact, the tournament had been delayed a couple of times by thunderstorms, and with more in the forecast for Sunday, the players went out in threesomes, instead of the traditional weekend twosomes, to try to speed play. Curtis was paired with Fredrik Jacobson, an outgoing Swede he liked, and Vijay Singh, who was anything but outgoing but not a bad pairing for Curtis.

"[Vijay] was actually really good to play with," Curtis said. "He just kept saying, 'Keep it up, bro.' Freddy was great too. In fact, we became pretty good friends after playing together that day."

Play was stopped twice because of thunderstorms. The second time, Curtis was on the 16th green with a good round going. He was four under par and had moved into the top 20. As soon as the horn sounded, the players were carted back to the clubhouse where everyone sat and waited, hoping the tournament could finish before dark. There wasn't any doubt about who was going to win—Woods had a five-shot lead on Rich Beem—but there was more at stake than that.

At the start of 2002, in another attempt to get more American players—or at least players on the U.S. Tour—to play in the British Open, the Royal and Ancient had left eight extra exempt spots available specifically for the Western Open. The top eight finishers in the Western who were not already exempt into the British Open were instantly exempt.

With his play on Sunday, Curtis had played himself into the top eight among nonexempt players. As he walked into the clubhouse during the rain delay, he was blithely unaware of the fact that he had a chance to make the British Open.

"I had no clue at all," he said. "It was the furthest thing from my mind. A bunch of us were sitting around during the delay—Vijay was there, Freddy, and Stephen Ames was there too. Candace came walking in and said, 'You know, if you can par in, you'll make the British.'

"I had no idea what she was talking about. The other guys had to explain it to me. All of a sudden, I was nervous. When we went back out, the 17th [a par-four] was playing into a howling wind. I managed to get a five-iron on the green and make par there. On 18, I hit a three-iron that missed the green on my second shot and chipped it to four feet.

"When I got over the par putt, I was really nervous. I hadn't even thought about playing in the British, and now I'm thinking that if I make this I might actually get to go. I managed to shake it in, but I still didn't know if it was good enough because there were guys still on the course."

Curtis went into the locker room, packed up his things, and then went back to the players' dining area to wait for everyone else to finish. If he did make the British, there would be a lot to do, including figuring out a way to get Candace a passport since she didn't have one. The wait lasted about an hour. Finally, a tour official who worked in the scoring trailer came in and told him that he had actually finished seventh (13th overall) among the players not exempt for the British. He was in.

"Wow," Curtis said. "That's really cool."

Cool as it was, it meant changing plans—and making plans—very quickly.

Rather than fly home, Ben and Candace stayed in Chicago and spent most of the day at the passport office explaining why she needed a passport right away. They finally found someone sympathetic to their situation and got that done. They made a plane reservation for Thursday, figuring if they were going to make the trip, they might as well go over early and enjoy the experience.

"I figured it would be an adventure," Curtis said. "I thought we'd go early and do some sightseeing. I had no expectations. I had never played in a major, and I'd never played links golf. I thought, 'If we go over and have a good time, that'll be great. If I make the cut, that's a bonus.'"

He had no idea exactly what kind of adventure was about to unfold.

12

Miracle at St. George's

BEN AND CANDACE ARRIVED in London on Friday morning and made the two-hour drive to the town of Deal in the south of England—Ben keeping the car on the road in spite of having to drive on the right side—where they found the mom-and-pop bed-and-breakfast where they were staying. (Deal is one town over from Sandwich, the tiny village where Royal St. George's [the site for the 2003 Open] is located.) There was also the matter of finding a caddy. Danny Stahl, a teammate of Ben's from Kent State, had been caddying for him, but Stahl couldn't make the trip. Plus, it made sense for Curtis to try to find someone who had experience on links golf courses, since he had never seen one in his life.

Curtis called IMG. As luck would have it, one of their European clients, Andrew Coltart, hadn't qualified for the Open. His caddy, Andy Sutton, was available for the week. Curtis made plans to meet Sutton at Royal St. George's to play a practice round on Sunday.

"We slept most of the day Friday after we got there," Curtis said. "I had been in Europe once before for the World Amateur in Germany. Candace had never been there. The jet lag hit us both pretty hard."

On Saturday they decided to go to the golf course and at least find out what Ben would be getting into the following week.

The first time an American sees a links golf course can be a shock. It looks nothing like the lush, green, tree-lined courses Americans are used to seeing and playing. In fact, if you aren't looking carefully, it is easy to drive by a links course without even realizing it's a golf course. Most can pass for cow pastures, unless you happen to notice the flagsticks on the greens, which aren't terribly green under any circumstances.

Royal St. George's was virtually empty when Ben and Candace got there. Since Sutton wasn't due to arrive until Sunday, Ben took a pull cart, and they ventured onto the course together. More than any other course in the British Open rota, St. George's is famous for blind shots, one reason a lot of players don't like it. When Jack Nicklaus first saw the course in 1981, his comment was, "It's not that tough, as long as you pick the right church steeple or barn to aim at on most holes."

Curtis was aware of this, so, on most holes, Candace walked ahead of him as forecaddy to give him a line on where to hit the ball. "A lot of times she would stand on a spot, and I'd say, 'There ain't no way I should be hitting it there,'" he said. "But she was right. If she hadn't been with me, God only knows where I would have hit most of my shots."

The only other golfer Ben and Candace encountered all day was Australian Craig Parry, who was out playing by himself. The rest of the golf course was empty, which was fun and meant Curtis could linger, hitting extra shots when he wanted to in order to get more comfortable with links play—bouncing balls into greens, watching out for knolls and swales all the way around.

"I liked it," he said. "It wasn't that windy, and I figured it would be a lot tougher when the wind blew. It helped a little that the World Amateur I had played in had been on a linksey sort of course, but it was nothing like this was."

The next day Ben and Candace slept in, walked into town for a late English breakfast, and then met Sutton at St. George's. This time Candace took the afternoon off, and player and caddy set out to familiarize themselves with the golf course and one another. Curtis played 18 holes again, and he and Sutton walked onto the 18th green at about 5:15 p.m. The place was completely empty, and Sutton pointed at the clock behind the green as he handed Curtis his putter.

"If we can walk on this green at about this time a week from today, we'll both be very happy," Sutton said.

Curtis laughed. The thought of playing on Sunday still didn't seem all that likely to him. And the thought of being in one of the last groups—and arriving on the green late in the afternoon— had never even crossed his mind. Still, as he holed out and told Sutton that he and Candace were heading to London the next day to go sightseeing, he felt pretty good about where he was at that moment.

"I was playing well," Curtis said. "My swing felt good, and I thought I had adapted pretty well to links golf, even though it had only been two days. I liked it. I didn't feel as if I was going to be overwhelmed when Thursday came around. I thought, at the very least, I had a chance to play well."

Ben and Candace went sightseeing as planned on Monday, Curtis feeling comfortable already having two practice rounds under his belt. They saw Big Ben, Parliament, and Buckingham Palace, then drove back. Curtis played 18 holes on Tuesday with Cliff Kresge, another American, and a third player Curtis had never met, who was from the European Tour.

"All I remember about the guy is that he hit a spectator in the head on one of the par-fives," Curtis said. "It was a fan. The guy took about three more steps, as if he hadn't even noticed, and then he went down like he'd been shot. Fortunately, he was okay, or it wouldn't have been too funny."

On Wednesday, Chris Smith invited Curtis to play with him and Joe Durant, a veteran who was known as one of the tour's best ball strikers. Smith was Curtis's rookie mentor; every year the tour assigns an older player to each rookie so he has someone to go to with questions or problems. Smith, realizing that Curtis didn't know many tour players, made a point of asking him to play a practice round whenever he could.

Durant had never met Curtis before, but he was impressed with him. "He was very quiet, which isn't that unusual in a young player," Durant said. "But I noticed he looked very comfortable playing the golf course, and he had a very solid golf swing. There was no doubt he was talented."

Did the thought cross Durant's mind that Curtis might contend that week? He smiled. "Absolutely not."

They actually quit after nine holes, in part because the pace of play was so slow—the day before a major is almost impossible because players want to putt from every imaginable angle on each green—and in part because Curtis, having played 63 holes already, felt he knew the golf course as well as he was going to.

"I felt very comfortable," he said. "The golf course wasn't that long, which was good for me. The weather was warmer than usual. I remembered watching at Muirfield the year before when it looked like they were playing in a hurricane a lot of the time. I heard some guys complaining in the locker room about the course and all the blind shots, but it didn't really bother me."

He and Candace had been walking into town for dinner each day since their arrival. On the first night, they both ate Indian food for the first time in their lives, then the next couple of nights they went to a local pub. On Wednesday, though, hoping for an easy way to have dinner and relax before the tournament began, they went to the house that IMG had rented for the week near the golf course.

They each got plates of food and sat down. A moment later,

Mike Weir, then also an IMG client, sat down across from them. As with Durant, Weir had never met Curtis before. Curtis introduced himself and then Candace.

"Congratulations on the Masters," Curtis said. "That was great playing, especially down the stretch."

By now Weir had become accustomed to strangers bringing up the Masters win to him. He laughed, said something about being lucky to pull out the playoff, and thanked Curtis.

"So," Weir said, settling in with his food. "What brings you guys over here? Did you come for the tournament?"

Curtis smiled. "Well, actually," he said, "I'm playing in it."

Weir was mortified. "Oh God, I'm so sorry," he said. "I didn't know..."

Curtis waved a hand. "Don't be sorry. I'm just a rookie. Why should you know?"

Even so, Weir felt bad. "I had no clue at all who he was," he said. "Obviously we'd been in some tournaments together, but I guess I'd never crossed his path because I just didn't know him at all. I honestly figured they were golf fans or something like that."

Weir certainly wasn't the only one who had no idea who Curtis was at that point. "If you had asked me to pick the guy out of a lineup, I never would have had a chance," Jim Furyk said. "I might have vaguely recognized the name as someone new on tour, but I can't guarantee that either."

The PGA Tour is divided into three tiers each week when pairings are made. First, there are what the players call the "TV pairings," threesomes of players who are recent tournament winners, major champions—the big-name stars. They always play in the middle of their wave (there is a morning wave on Thursday–Friday that tees off between 7:15 and 9:15 and an afternoon wave that goes between noon and 2 p.m.), guaranteeing that they will be on the golf course for the bulk of the telecast when they play late. That's why Tiger Woods and Phil Mickelson are almost never in the same Thursday–Friday wave. TV wants to ensure that at least one of them is a part of the broadcast each day.

The second group is made up of players who have had some success on tour—they've made the top 125, won at some point in their careers, or been name players in the past. They get most of the early tee times.

Third is the group of guys who have just made the tour out of Q-School or the Nationwide Tour, and sponsor-exempt players who aren't named John Daly. They get the last of the tee times, often fighting darkness early and late in the year when the days are shorter.

What this means is that a rookie like Curtis might never be in the locker room or on the range or in the players' dining room at the same time as people like Weir, Furyk, and Joe Durant. The only way for a rookie to cross paths with the stars is to play his way into a grouping with them on the weekend.

Curtis had already been paired with Vijay Singh three times, the first at Bay Hill, where Singh complimented his ball striking but suggested Curtis work more on his short game; the most recent at the Western, where Curtis had played his way into the British.

The players Curtis was closest to at that point were other rookies, most notably Andy Miller, the son of Johnny Miller, and Ty Tryon, then a teenage sensation who had made it through Q-School at age seventeen.

"It's funny that Mike [Weir] felt so bad about that," Curtis said, laughing, years later. "If I know half the rookies who come out by the end of a given year, that's pretty good for me. I thought it was cool just to sit and eat dinner with him."

Of course, the really cool stuff had not yet begun. Curtis had a late tee time the next day. Even with a field of 156 players, the British Open still sends everyone off the first tee on Thursday and Friday, which means that tee times begin at 6:30 a.m. and don't finish until 4:15 p.m. The Royal and Ancient can afford to do this because there is so much daylight in July, especially in Scotland, where casual golfers can often be seen finishing rounds at eleven o'clock at night.

Curtis killed time in the morning reading and watching the tournament on TV—coverage of the Open Championship in Great Britain is almost round the clock. His tee time wasn't until 3 p.m., so the day really dragged. By the time he reached the first tee, he had seen Tiger Woods pull his opening tee shot so far left that Woods never found his ball. Curtis was pumping a lot of adrenaline and was extremely nervous. His tee shot on number one also sailed left but not to the point where he was in serious trouble. Still, he started his first major with a bogey five.

The day was breezy—the winds were around twenty miles per hour—but Curtis had caught a break with the late tee time because it had rained all morning. Woods, after his terrible start, had scrambled back to shoot a two-over-par 73. The lead at day's end was held by a Swede named Hennie Otto, who shot a three-under-par 68. In all, only five players broke par. Seven others shot an even-par 71. That meant that Curtis's one-over-par 72 put him in decent position.

"Once I settled down, I was okay," Curtis said. "The wind was about the way it had been during the practice rounds, and I knew no one was going to go very low."

Two players who had won majors in the past—Davis Love III and Greg Norman—were just a shot behind Otto, whom no one expected to be in serious contention by Sunday. They were right: Otto shot 76–75 the next two days, then rallied with a 69 on Sunday to tie for 10th place. Love and Norman were a different story. In fact, the last time the Open had been played at St. George's, Norman had shot 64 on the final day to pass Nick Faldo and win the championship. It was the first and only time that Norman outplayed Faldo on the last day of a major when both were in serious contention. Even at age forty-eight, Norman was still a threat.

Curtis wasn't thinking about any of that. He was thinking that now he had a very good chance to make the cut. He backed up his solid play on Thursday with another 72. At a lot of weekly tournaments on tour, two over par for 36 holes will leave you slamming your trunk in the parking lot and heading for home. Not at the British Open. At 144, Curtis was three shots out of lead, which Love now held. In fact, only two other players—S. K. Ho and Denmark's Thomas Bjorn—were ahead of Curtis, who was tied for fourth with six other players.

Bjorn hadn't won a major, but he had been close. He was thirty-two years old and had played on the European Tour throughout his career. In 1997, he had become the first Danish player to make a Ryder Cup team, and in 2000 he had finished tied for second in the British Open and alone in third at the PGA—tournaments that had been part of Woods's "Tiger Slam," when he won four straight majors beginning with the 2000 U.S. Open.

Bjorn actually had a distinction that was more unusual than winning a major: he had played with Woods in the final group of the 2001 Dubai Classic and had beaten him when Woods—shockingly—dumped a ball in the water on the 18th hole, giving Bjorn a two-shot victory. Bjorn was a highly respected player in Europe, someone well liked by players on both sides of the Atlantic.

"He's just a classy guy," said Love, who had gotten to know Bjorn playing against him in two Ryder Cups. "Obviously he's a good player, but he's also one of those guys who understands that the Ryder Cup is a competition, not life and death. I always enjoyed being on the golf course with him."

In all, Bjorn had three top 10s in British Opens. He was clearly a player who appeared ready to take the next step and become a major champion. Now, after rounds of 73 and 70, he was very much in position to try to take that step.

There were a lot of big names still in contention going into the weekend. Sergio Garcia, who had unofficially taken Furyk's spot in the top-three-players-who-had-never-won-a-major category after Furyk's win at Olympia Fields, was in the group with Curtis at 144. So was Kenny Perry, who had finished 1–1–3–1 in his previous four tournaments. The third-place finish had come at the U.S. Open, and the case could be made that Perry was also one of the best players in the world without a major title.

But that wasn't surprising because majors had never been a priority for Perry. In fact, this was only his third British Open. He was an American player who would often skip the event even though he was exempt. Perry was forty-two and had pieced together a very solid career that was actually getting better as he got older. He'd had one serious chance to win a major at the 1996 PGA Championship in Louisville, Kentucky, not far from his hometown of Franklin.

Since it was a home game for him, Perry had prepared and played hard and finished on Sunday with a one-shot lead on Mark Brooks. Unlike most players who faced the possibility of a playoff, especially in a major, Perry accepted CBS's invitation to sit in the 18th-hole tower with Jim Nantz and Ken Venturi rather than go to the range or putting green to stay loose.

One reason Perry said yes was simple: he's a nice man. But climbing up to the booth and sitting there for twenty minutes was clearly a sign that he just wasn't as focused on winning as he needed to be. Try to imagine Tiger Woods talking to anyone with a possible playoff ahead of him. Nantz even asked Perry during a break if he wanted to go warm up, and Perry said no thanks. Only after Brooks had birdied the 18th hole—a par-five, so it wasn't a huge surprise—did Perry leave the tower to get ready for the playoff. He then hit an awful tee shot on the playoff hole (it was still sudden death back then) that led to a bogey. Perry lost to Brooks's par.

Since then, Perry's tie for third at the U.S. Open — seven shots behind Jim Furyk and never in contention to win — was his best performance in a major.

There were other big names lurking not far behind, especially with 36 holes to play. Woods and Singh were at 145, four shots behind Love and one shot behind Curtis at 144. Ernie Els, the defending champion, was another shot back after recovering from a disastrous opening 78 with a 68. It was a tightly bunched field going into Saturday, which is known on tour as "moving day," because players who are well back can take advantage of the relatively mild conditions early in the day and put up low numbers that move them into contention.

Curtis would again play very late in the day, since he was only two groups from the final twosome of Love and Ho. That meant another long wait, but he had almost become accustomed to it at that point. Saturday was similar to the first two, a breeze freshening as the afternoon wore on. And, sure enough, several players out early in the day put up low numbers, but most not as ably as three-time champion Nick Faldo, who was having a late-career renaissance at age forty-six. The previous year he had needed an exemption from the USGA just to get into the U.S. Open and had backed it up by finishing fifth, all the while wearing an "I Love NY" cap that won over the New York crowds.

Now, after barely making the cut right on the number at 150, Faldo went out early in the morning and shot 67, which put him at four over par for the championship. With only Love beginning the day in red numbers under par, that certainly put Faldo into contention.

Curtis, paired with Hennie Otto, again got off to a nervous

start, missing the fairway at number one and making a bogey. "I just couldn't hit that fairway," Curtis said. "It was as if it was invisible. I couldn't find it."

Once again, though, he settled himself down. Like most links courses, Royal St. George's goes away from the clubhouse for nine holes, then turns and comes back toward it. The model for all British golf courses is St. Andrews, which was 18 holes when it was built all those hundreds of years ago, because when the designers ran out of room after nine holes going in one direction, they turned and built nine more holes heading back toward the town.

"If you're going to get the golf course, you really have to do it in the first seven holes," said Love of Royal St. George's. "There are two very reachable par-fives [the fourth and seventh] and short par-fours. What you really want to do is make sure you par the first, make your birdies on the next six holes, and then hang on for dear life coming in."

Curtis hadn't parred the first, but he did birdie the par-five seventh and steadied himself. While all the attention was focused on the name players around him, he quietly pieced together a third straight solid round, managing to par the almost impossible 18th hole to finish the day with a one-under-par 70. By the time the dust had settled that evening, Curtis was tied for third place at one over par and in very distinguished company.

Bjorn had shot 69, which made him the only player under par for the championship. He was at 212 (one under) and led Love (72) by a shot and five other players by two shots. Those players were Woods, who had finally played like Tiger Woods and shot 69; Singh, who also had shot 69; and Perry (70) and Garcia (70). All four of those players were ranked in the top 20 in the world, led by Woods at number one and Singh at number three. Garcia was 10th and Perry 18th. The fifth player at 214 was Curtis, who had risen to number 496 in the world after his performance at the Western Open.

With so many big names bunched near the top as the sun set that evening, Sunday was shaping up to have a great finish. That was certainly what ABC, which has televised the British Open forever, wanted.

Bjorn and Love would be in the final group or, as they call pairings in Europe, the final game. Woods and Singh would be directly in front of them, with Garcia and Perry teeing off one game before. The fourth-to-last twosome to tee off would be Curtis and Phillip Price, who, like Bjorn, was a European Ryder Cupper, though without Bjorn's résumé. He was a thirty-six-year-old Welshman, who had won three times in Europe. He hadn't played much in the U.S., though he had finished second to Woods in the NEC Invitational in Akron in 2000. If American golf fans knew the name, it was because he had beaten Phil Mickelson three-and-two in a Ryder Cup singles match the previous year at the Belfry, helping the Europeans beat the Americans for the third time in four Ryder Cups.

When Curtis saw that he was paired with Price, he was delighted, even though he didn't know him at all. "I figured if I was with one of the big names, we'd have a lot of people following us, but everyone would be focused on the star—whoever it was," Curtis said. "That can be a problem sometimes when you're the 'other guy,' because people start moving as soon as they hit or putt out, and it can get distracting.

"I really didn't expect a lot of people to be paying much attention to us. The way that golf course is set up and with the way they spread the pairings out [eleven minutes apart even in twosomes], you can get out there and feel almost as if you're out there alone. That was fine with me."

He and Candace went through what had now become their

daily ritual on Saturday night: walking to the local pub for dinner, then making their way back to the room. Candace noticed that Ben was quieter than usual. She wondered if he was nervous about what was to come the next day.

"As we were getting ready for bed, I said to him, trying to almost sound casual, 'So, what do you think is going to happen tomorrow?'" she remembered. "He was sitting on the edge of the bed, and he just looked at me and said, 'I'm going to win.' I had never heard him say anything like that. It really caught me off guard."

Curtis can still remember the look on Candace's face. "I could tell I freaked her out," he said. "I didn't say it for effect or to sound tough or anything; it was just the way I felt at that moment. I knew I was playing well. I'd been very steady and sound the entire week—starting with the practice rounds I played. I liked the golf course. I knew some of the other guys didn't. I just had a feeling I could win if I did one thing."

That one thing was hit the first fairway. He hadn't done it all week. He certainly wasn't alone in that because the fairway was both tight and rolling. If your tee shot went anywhere near the rough, it was bound to end up there. "All I focused on from the time I left the golf course on Saturday was hitting that first fairway," Curtis said. "If you hit the fairway, you've got a wedge or, at most, a nine-iron into the green.

"I'm not someone who sits around doing a lot of visualization. I'm not real good at it anyway. But that night I just kept trying to picture myself on the first fairway with a wedge in my hands. It felt weird trying to do it. Looking back, I probably had no idea what I was doing. But I was in this kind of zone that I guess you get in when you're going through something you've never gone through, and you have no idea what to do or what's going to happen next. I felt like I was floating in a way—just in this place that had nothing to do with where I'd been before or where I was going next. I honestly don't think I snapped out of it until we were back home."

Floating around in his zone, visualizing the first fairway over and over, Curtis slept soundly and packed in the morning. He and Candace planned to stay at a mostly empty IMG house on Sunday night so they could get up early the next morning, drive to London, and catch their flight back to Cleveland. There was a lot to do—their wedding was now less than five weeks away.

They were at the golf course by eleven, which was early for a 1:25 tee time. But they had planned to meet two of Ben's cousins who had flown over from Ohio to watch him play. The four of them had breakfast, then Ben made the short walk over to the locker room to get ready.

"I was really anxious right about then," he said. "Candace had gotten really quiet after I said I was going to win, and walking into the locker room felt strange because it was so empty. The last day of a major, no one hangs out in there. Guys come in and head for the range, or when they're done, they come in, clean out their lockers, and head out—usually in a hurry.

"I saw Phil [Mickelson] in there and realized he was already finished playing, and I hadn't been out to the range to warm up yet. He had a friend with him, and they were planning to take off to fly home by one o'clock, which was before my tee time. That sort of made it hit home just how late I was playing."

Curtis hadn't eaten much at breakfast, so he sat down and ate a little bit more. He was trying to calm himself even before he went out to warm up. "I felt like I needed to slow myself down. I could feel all sorts of adrenaline, and I was more than an hour from my tee time. I didn't want to get to the first tee and be worn out already. There's no doubt the toughest thing about a day like that is waiting around."

He finally went outside and decided to hit a few putts before he went to the range. "I was just trying to get a feel for the environment. I could hear the roars out on the golf course, and I knew how special the day was going to be. When I got to the range, I finally began to calm down a little bit. The range isn't that far from the grandstands that surround the 18th green, and I could see people already piling into the grandstands so they could have a spot when the leaders came up—even though it was four hours away. Those huge grandstands make it feel more like you're in a football stadium than on a golf course when you're walking up 18. There aren't any corporate boxes or anything like at most tournaments, so it's different. While I was on the range, [Greg] Norman was finishing, and the roar for him walking up was really, really loud. I thought that was pretty cool."

Curtis hit a few extra drivers on the range, his focus still being the opening tee shot. He was playing the old mind game with himself, trying to stay in the present, trying not to think about what was going to be at stake as he made his way around the golf course. Even if he didn't win, his life would change with a high finish. He could clinch his exemption for 2004 by finishing in the top three or four, and a top-four finish would get him into the Masters the following year.

"Somewhere in the back of my mind, I'm sure I knew all that," Curtis said. "But I honestly had just one thought: hit the first fairway, then go win the golf tournament."

Bjorn and Love were the last two to arrive on the range, Bjorn dressed in a white shirt and black pants. He had his sports psychologist, Jos Vanstiphout, with him. Vanstiphout, who wasn't actually a psychologist of any kind but had made a reputation for himself by working with Ernie Els, was trying to win his second straight British Open since Els had won the year before. Els himself had dropped back the previous day with a one-over-par 72 and was six shots behind Bjorn—not an impossible mountain to climb, but an unlikely one, especially given the players he'd have to go through to get to Bjorn.

The first thing Curtis noticed when he finally walked on the tee and shook hands with Price was the wind. It wasn't blowing much harder than it had the three previous days, but it was left to right. Curtis, who hits the ball left to right, would have preferred it the other way. Waiting for Ivor Robson, who has been introducing players on the first tee at the British Open for twenty-nine years, to announce him, Curtis could feel his stomach churning.

But seconds after he heard Robson say, "This is game number 34. From the USA, Ben Curtis!" he felt suddenly calm.

"Once I got up and over the ball, I was okay," he said. "The first tee shot of the day is always tough, but I had gotten myself so prepared to hit that one shot, it was almost as if, when I got over it, I had already hit it before, so I was fine. When I took the club back and saw the ball head down the middle, I felt a huge wave of relief come over me. I thought, 'Okay. Here we go. Now let's go play some golf.' I was just really pleased with the idea that I didn't have to hack the ball out of some weeds and try to make a 30-footer for par."

Instead, Curtis found himself with a wedge in his hands, and he hit it to six feet. Several years later, he would remember making a 15-footer for birdie on the first hole. It was, in fact, a six-footer. That it seemed that much longer is evidence of just how unnerving the last round of a major can be, especially for someone going through it for the first time.

"It's hard to describe, but it just feels different when you're out there," he said. "It feels different than a Sunday on tour. It even feels different from Saturday at a major. The pace of play is slower. I noticed that right away. Phillip [Price] is a pretty deliberate player, but when we got to the third hole [a par-three], we had to wait. That told me right away, it was going to be a long day and that I wasn't the only one feeling some nerves."

Price turned out to be about as good a pairing as Curtis could have hoped for under the circumstances. He was friendly and outgoing, asking Curtis questions about his background, how his first year on tour was going—anything, it seemed, to keep his mind off the pressure. "I really think if I had played with Davis or Vijay or Tiger, it would have been a completely different kind of day," he said. "It would have just been so quiet."

There certainly wasn't a lot of chatter in the last three groups as they began their rounds. Perry and Garcia both made bogeys at the first hole, and Woods and Singh missed long birdie putts and settled for pars. Love was in trouble off the first tee and came up short of the green, leading to a bogey. Bjorn was way left off the tee, over the green, and also made bogey. Since Price had also bogeyed the first, that meant that five of the last eight players had bogeyed the hole. Two had made par.

Only one had made birdie. That was the rookie in the orange shirt, most of whose opponents could not, as Furyk said, pick him out of a lineup.

Curtis made routine pars on the next two holes, which meant he was tied for the lead with Bjorn and Singh, who had made a long birdie putt at the second. After Curtis found the fairway off the fourth tee, Curtis Strange, ABC's lead analyst, tried to lend perspective to what it meant for Ben Curtis to be tied for the lead during the last round of the British Open.

"Going from being on the Hooters Tour a year ago to leading the British Open is a lot like going from Class A ball [the lowest level of minor league baseball] to being a star in the major leagues," he said.

To which anchor Mike Tirico added: "And this is just his sixteenth tournament in the big leagues."

For most of the front nine, Curtis was Joe Hardy—the character in *Damn Yankees*, who had been transformed from an old man into a young superstar so he could revive the Washington

Senators. He reached the fourth green in two and made a two-putt birdie to take the lead at one under par. On the fifth, he missed the green left and chipped to six feet.

"This will be our first real chance to see how his nerves are holding up," Strange said as Curtis settled over the putt. When it went into the center of the hole, Strange said, "I'd say they're pretty good right now."

The other leaders were also taking advantage of the early holes, with the exception of Love, who bogeyed three of the first four, including the par-five fourth. Up ahead, Nick Faldo had birdied two of the first seven holes to get to one over par and stir the hearts of the locals. But he missed a short par putt on the eighth and never really made a move after that, eventually finishing tied for eighth.

The wind was picking up as the players moved toward the turn and the most difficult part of the golf course. Curtis made another two-putt birdie at the seventh to get to two under par, which again tied him with Bjorn and Singh for the lead. A few moments later, when Woods, Singh, and then Bjorn birdied the seventh, Singh had a one-shot lead over Woods, Bjorn, and Curtis at three under. No one else was within three shots of those four men.

But now the easy downwind holes were behind them. It was here, as players say, that the golf course really began. "The eighth hole is the hardest on the golf course," Ben Curtis said. "Any par there was a good par."

At that point the ABC producers tracked down Ben's father, Bob, and got him on the phone briefly with Tirico and Strange. "We're all sitting around here at the golf course [Mill Creek]," Bob Curtis said. "We're trying not to think too far ahead."

His son was doing the same thing. At the ninth, a short but tricky par-four with the pin tucked on the right side of a green that tilted from left to right, Curtis stuck a wedge two feet from the hole for a tap-in birdie. Then at the tenth, he rolled in a

20-footer for another birdie. For the first time all day, he showed just a hint of emotion, shaking his fist as the putt went in.

"That was when I think I started to get a little bit excited," he said. "The tenth is a tough second shot. It's an elevated green, and from the fairway it looks like everything just falls off the earth around it. If you miss the green left or right, it's a very hard up and down. I was happy to get it on the green. Making the putt was a huge bonus."

Curtis was now five under on the day and four under for the tournament, and he led Bjorn by one. Singh had bogeyed the eighth, as had Woods —three-putting from 40 feet.

It was at that point that Mike Tirico brought up Francis Ouimet, the only player in history to have won the first major he had ever played in. That was in 1913 and had been the subject of books and a movie. It was fair to say that Curtis was closing in on something historic. Eight holes, though, was a long way to go.

"I really was in the zone by then," Curtis said. "I knew after nine that I'd gone into the lead, but I really wasn't thinking about it much. I just knew I felt great with my putter. I had great feel for the greens, even in the wind, at that point. It seemed as if everything had slowed down. I didn't feel any nerves at all."

The 11th was a downwind, 230-yard par-three. "It played exactly the same every day," Curtis said. "Same wind and I hit the same club—a five-iron."

The shot landed just short of the green and rolled to within 10 feet of the hole. Still confident, Curtis made that one too, for his third straight birdie and his sixth of the day. He was five under par and now had a two-shot lead.

Behind Curtis, only Bjorn was keeping pace. Singh had bogeyed the eighth and the tenth to drop to one under, and Woods had bogeyed the eighth and the 10th and was at even par. Bjorn turned at three under.

On the 12th, Curtis pulled his tee shot a little bit but had 70 yards to the hole with a good angle. "I thought I had a good chance to make another birdie," he said. "But I thinned it and hit it over the green. Right at that moment, for the first time all day, nerves came into play. All of a sudden, I was worried about what would happen if I made a bogey. Sure enough, I made a bogey."

He hit a reasonable chip to five feet but missed the par putt, his first miss inside 10 feet all day.

"I could almost feel the momentum shift right there, even though I still had the lead," Curtis said. "If I had made the putt, my confidence would have come right back, but I didn't. As soon as I missed, it felt as if everything started going fast again."

Curtis snap hooked his drive at 13 but caught a decent lie and managed to gouge his second shot onto the green. His 25-foot birdie putt pulled up just short. "That would have been nice," he said. "The 14th tee is scary, and by then my lead on Bjorn was down to one."

What made the tee shot at 14 tough was that Curtis had to aim the ball at the out-of-bounds markers and try to draw it back into the fairway. Instead, he hit another dead pull—"which I do when I'm nervous," he said—and had no chance to go for the green. He had to lay up well short of the green because there was a creek running through the fairway that he couldn't carry. He hit what he thought was a great shot with a four-iron and watched it roll through the green, the ball coming to rest in the rough to the left.

His lie was okay, but the green ran straight downhill from where he was, and it was almost impossible to stop the ball. His chip went to the other side of the green—dangerously close to the out-of-bounds stakes—and he missed the 12-foot par putt coming back. Now he was three under for the tournament and tied with Bjorn, who had missed the green at 12 after his drive found a pot bunker but then saved par by making a 10-footer. Singh and Woods were both three shots back.

Curtis was trying to stop the bleeding. He hit a good drive at 15 but got another case of the pulls on his second shot and missed the green way left, leading to his third bogey in four holes. Bjorn now had the lead, and Woods and Singh, after making birdie at the par-five 14th that Curtis had bogeyed, were one shot back of Curtis and two behind Bjorn. When Bjorn also birdied the 14th, hitting a wedge to three feet on his third shot, he was at four under and appeared to be in control. Love, who had made three birdies in four holes to pull back into the fringes of contention, missed an opportunity to get close when he didn't make his birdie putt at 14, leaving him at even par.

At that moment, it was Bjorn's tournament to lose. He had a two-shot lead with four holes to play, and his nearest competitor—Curtis—had only two holes to play since he had just parred the par-three 16th, missing his 30-foot birdie putt by about six inches.

When Woods bogeyed 15 to drop back to even par, Bjorn's path appeared even clearer. But Bjorn himself found a pot bunker at the 15th and also made bogey, dropping to three under.

Up ahead of Bjorn, Curtis believed if he could par 17 and 18, he still had a chance to win. He'd had trouble driving the ball at 17 all week. "It's a weird-shaped fairway," he said. "You hit your drive right down the middle, and you would end up in the first cut. It seemed like you couldn't find the fairway from the tee no matter what you did. It was one of those holes the guys complained about."

Despite having again found the first cut, Curtis had a good lie. Sutton suggested he hit a five-iron, aim it left of the flag, and let the wind drift the ball back in the direction of the hole. As Curtis stood over the shot, Bob Rosburg, the ex-PGA champion who had been working for ABC forever as an on-course commentator, told the audience, "This is a sucker pin. You come up short at all, the ball will roll back and you'll be way short."

He was prescient. Curtis hit the shot exactly the way he wanted to, but the ball landed about 20 feet short of the flag and never made it over the ridge in the middle of the green. It rolled back to about 35 feet short of the hole. "It was close to being perfect," Curtis said. "I told myself, 'Well, at least you're uphill.' But I gunned the putt trying not to leave it short and went about eight feet by the hole. Then, I got nervous on the par putt. I really hit it badly. It never had a chance."

Another bogey. That was four in six holes. Few people were surprised. After all, it was the British Open. It was his first major. Kids playing their sixteenth tournament on tour don't win the British Open.

The person who may have been suffering the most at that stage was Candace. She had been walking along outside the ropes most of the day, listening to the BBC feed on a little transistor radio that she had rented. As the hour grew late and Ben hung in contention, her nerves got worse and worse.

"It's the only day I can remember where I really wanted a shot and a beer while I was on a golf course," she said later. "By the time he got to the last few holes, I was a complete wreck."

The crowds following Curtis and Price had grown as the day wore on. By the 16th hole, Candace had no view from outside the ropes, and one of the officials got her under the ropes so she could see. "Being able to see," she said laughing, "wasn't necessarily a good thing."

As Curtis walked onto the 18th tee, Woods and Singh, both at even par and one shot behind him, were walking off the 16th green. Bjorn, at three under, and Love, also at even par, were waiting for Woods and Singh to finish on the 16th green. All Curtis wanted to do was finish with a par and then let the chips fall where they may.

"I wasn't angry," Curtis said. "I never got angry or down the whole day. To be honest, if someone had told me starting the day

I'd finish in the top five, I would have been thrilled. Sure, for a little while it had looked as if I had a chance to win. But then it looked like, 'Oh well, I didn't pull it off.' But I was thinking I'd have other chances to win, and this wouldn't be the last time I'd blow a lead. I knew I'd learn from it because it's harder to learn from winning than from losing. All I wanted to do on 18 was make par. I knew that wouldn't be easy, but I knew if I did, I'd finish in the top four. I'd looked at the board walking off 17 and saw Thomas [Bjorn] was ahead by a couple."

The 18th was probably the most difficult driving hole on the golf course. For the day, only 10 percent of the players in the field would find the fairway. Thirty-one of 72 would make bogey, and another one would make a double bogey. There had been one birdie. Curtis missed the fairway left but drew a reasonable lie. His second shot, a six-iron, rolled through the green to the back fringe.

Back on 16, Love, hitting first, had hit a gorgeous six-iron that landed 10 feet to the left of the flag and stopped. Bjorn also selected a six-iron. The ball was right of the flag all the way. It took one hard bounce on the green and hopped into an adjacent bunker.

Judy Rankin, who had been walking with the final twosome all day for ABC, went over and got a good look at the ball. "It's a good lie," she said, "but the sand is a little bit soft."

Soft sand means a player can't afford to play a shot too delicately. Bjorn was no more than 25 feet from the hole, but there was an upslope just outside the bunker. That meant he had to be careful not to take too much sand and come up short, because the ball might roll backward if it didn't make it past the upslope.

Standing on the other side of the green, Love assumed that Bjorn would make sure to get the ball past the pin. "He had a two-shot lead," he said. "I knew that wasn't a bunker you wanted to mess around with. I figured he'd hit it past the hole, try to get it inside 10 feet, and if he missed the par putt he'd still be in the lead."

Bjorn got over the ball, blasted it out, and then watched helplessly as it landed on the upslope, teetered for a moment, and then rolled backward. It ended up back in the bunker, no more than a foot from where it had been before he had played the shot. Bjorn glanced down at the ball in disgust and then, much like a Sunday hacker who was upset with himself, took almost no time before he hit the ball again.

This time, the result was even worse. The ball again rolled back into the bunker, but it plugged. "I can't believe it," Strange said. "He took almost no time over that shot. This is unbelievable."

Across the green, Love was still leaning on his putter trying to look casual, but his heart was going a million miles an hour. "On the one hand, I felt terrible for Thomas. He had played so well. It seemed like it was his tournament, his championship to win. I felt a little bit sick watching those two shots, and I was completely baffled by what he was doing. Then it occurred to me that if I made my putt, I could be tied for the lead in spite of my terrible start. That got my attention."

Bjorn finally got his third bunker shot—by far the toughest one he'd had—out of the bunker and onto the green, the ball stopping four feet past the hole. From there he managed to make the putt for double bogey to drop back to one under. Love then left his birdie putt short, making Strange distraught. "Come on, Davis," he said on air. "You cannot leave that putt short. You have to give it a chance at this point in the day."

At that point in the day, there were, suddenly, five players with a chance to win the Claret Jug. Bjorn and Curtis were one under par. Woods and Singh—both on 17—were at even par, as was Love. Everything had changed in the blink of two poorly thought-out swings by Bjorn.

Curtis knew none of this as he prepared to play his third shot at 18. Moments earlier, just before Bjorn stepped into the bunker at 16, Curtis had received a huge ovation from the crowd as he walked between the massive, now-packed grandstands. "He's not going to win," Strange said as the cheers rained down. "But this is a moment he'll remember the rest of his life."

Curtis's ball had stopped in the back fringe, and he opted to chip it from there. "It wasn't that hard a shot," he said. "I thought, 'Why not try to make it, because if I do, I might still have an outside shot to win?'" He caught a little too much of the ball, and it skittered about 12 feet past the hole. As Curtis stood waiting for Price to putt, his glance happened to fall upon the clock behind the green.

"Hey, Andy," he said to Sutton. "Take a look at that."

Sutton looked and then smiled. The clock said 5:15, the precise time the two men had walked onto the completely empty green just a week earlier, hoping for this very result.

"Here we were," Curtis said. "I just had to make that putt for par. I actually took four or five deep breaths before I putted. I really wanted to make the putt, and I just felt like a lot was at stake and that I had to find a way to get it in the hole."

It had been a while since he had made a putt that wasn't a tap-in, but this one was dead center the minute he hit it. As soon as it dropped in the hole, Curtis was shaking his fist, delighted to have made par because he figured he had clinched a top-four finish, a spot in the Masters, and probably his tour card for 2004.

"As I went to pick my ball up out of the cup, I heard someone in the crowd yell, 'You're tied for the lead!'" Curtis said. "Nothing had changed on the scoreboard, but I knew there were people listening on the radio to the BBC feed. I wasn't sure if it was true or if I had heard wrong. But as soon as I walked into the scoring trailer, I found out it was true."

Woods and Singh, walking on the 17th green, had also seen what had happened because there was a scoreboard nearby. Each had suddenly gone from three shots out of the lead to one shot out of the lead. At that moment, neither knew that Curtis had parred the 18th, meaning that both of them would need a birdie to tie him. In fact, each would say later that it had occurred to them that two pars — since both were even par at the moment — might very well land them in a playoff since Bjorn still had two tough holes to play and had to be shaken by what had happened at 16.

Woods would later lament the fact that, given a second chance to win the tournament, he hadn't been able to take advantage. "When we walked on the 17th and saw the scoreboard, I was surprised, obviously," he said. "I told myself, 'Just make par here, and you've got a real chance to win.'"

Woods's second shot had come up short of the green. Like Curtis on his second shot, Woods was done in by the "sucker pin," leaving his chip about 10 feet short. When the putt for par slid just below the hole, the look on Woods's face made it clear that he had blown his chance to steal the tournament late. Singh, on the other hand, made his 10-footer for par to keep his hopes alive. It was impossible to miss the irony: Singh, who might very well have doubled the major titles he had won if he had putted even reasonably well, making a clutch putt. Woods, arguably the greatest clutch putter in history, was unable to make any putts on the final day of a major when he most needed to make them.

While they walked to 18, Woods's body language revealing how disgusted he was, Bjorn was walking to his ball in the right rough back on 17. He had taken driver off the tee, no doubt hoping to use his anger to launch a big drive. Instead, he had pushed it and had a gnarly lie in the rough.

Sitting in the scoring trailer, Curtis watched Woods miss his putt and then saw Bjorn's drive. He could feel his heart pounding.

"When I walked off the green, I still wasn't sure if what the guy had said about Bjorn was true," he said. "I was thinking, 'Well, if you make top four, you'll make the Masters and the PGA and probably clinch your card. That's a pretty good effort for a first major.'

"I saw Candace as I was walking in. She was in tears, just completely drained by the whole thing. When I got inside, they confirmed Bjorn's double bogey, and my heart started racing. All of a sudden, winning was a real thing. I knew it would be tough for Vijay or Tiger to make a birdie on the 18th and that Bjorn had two very tough holes to play."

Bjorn hit a reasonably good shot from the rough, punching the ball out to just short of the green. His pitch shot from there was right on line and actually hit the hole. But it was going too fast and rolled six feet past the cup. Bjorn had been putting confidently all day—in fact, he'd made a tricky four-footer at 16 to make the double bogey. But now he was shaken by what had happened.

"You could see it in the way he was walking," Love said. "All day, he'd been really confident, kind of firing the ball when he stood over it, stepping up to putts with a lot of confidence, not really taking that much time. But the last two holes, you could tell he was shaken up. You could almost hear him thinking, 'What did I just do?'"

Bjorn's par putt looked for a brief instant as if it would go in. But it swerved left just before it got to the hole and stopped an inch to the left of the cup. Curtis was now in the lead by one over Bjorn and Singh.

He decided at that point that he simply couldn't watch anymore.

"I asked them [the Royal and Ancient officials in the scoring trailer] what would happen if there was a playoff," Curtis said. "I wondered if there was any break, and they told me no, that as soon as the last guy had signed his card, anyone in the playoff would be carted out to the 15th tee. [The playoff would be four holes.]

"I decided to go out to the range and hit some balls, in part to stay loose but also to keep my mind off what was going on. I remembered that when guys thought they were going to be in a playoff, I'd see them hitting balls on the range. I remembered what had happened to Kenny Perry at the PGA in '96. The only thing I knew for sure was that I really didn't want to watch. I had some fruit, drank a couple of Gatorades, and asked them to take me to the range. By the time I got out there, it felt like everything was spinning. I was a lot more nervous at that moment than I'd been on the golf course."

He wanted Candace to go with him to the range, but she had been taken to a separate trailer to watch the last groups finish. In a technical sense, Curtis's round wasn't over since he might have to play off, so, other than a brief hug, he really wasn't allowed contact with the outside world other than his caddy.

"There really wasn't any choice," Candace said later. "They just said, 'Go here, go there, sit here.' I wasn't in any shape to argue with anyone. A lot of people were coming at me to try to interview me while he was on the range. I was a newbie. I had no idea what was going on or how to handle it."

Few things are eerier than a driving range late on Sunday afternoon at a golf tournament. There were a couple of security guards there and a couple of camera crews hanging back just in case they needed to get a shot of the new Open champion, but that was about it. There wasn't another player or caddy in sight.

Woods and Singh were playing 18. The only way Woods could tie would be to hole out from the fairway—or, more accurately, from the rough, since both he and Singh, like almost everyone else, had missed the fairway from the tee. Woods hit one of the better shots of the day, finding the green, but coming up about 20 feet short of the hole. He was officially eliminated.

Singh had caught a perfect lie and had 161 yards to the hole. But he popped the shot up, and it landed in the front bunker, meaning he would have to hole out to tie. He actually hit a superb shot, the ball spinning just to the right of the flag, stopping inside two feet. It was a great up and down, but it wasn't good enough.

Curtis was busy hitting wedge shots on the range when he heard the "just missed" sigh after Singh's bunker shot. Sutton had walked over to an equipment trailer on the side of the range where there was a TV set and was standing in the doorway doing play-by-play as Curtis tried to remain calm and focus on his golf swing, which was completely impossible.

"Singh missed from the bunker," Sutton called out. "Bjorn is the only one left now."

Love had also bogeyed 17 — meaning that among the five contenders, only Singh had parred the hole — so he was in the same situation as Woods, needing to hole out his second shot on 18 to tie. Bjorn needed a birdie.

Love's second shot landed on the front of the green but was nowhere near the hole. Now, officially, there was only one player left who could tie Curtis. Bjorn had found the right rough with his drive but had a good lie and was 168 yards from the hole. The swirling winds and the pressure and the hole location — front left, behind the bunker that Singh had found — were making everyone's second shot difficult.

Bjorn had a good angle to the hole, but his shot checked up just short of the green. He was about 30 feet from the flag and needed to hole out from there to force a playoff. As Bjorn was hitting his second shot, Curtis had walked over to the trailer and leaned over Sutton's shoulder for a moment. When he saw the ball land, he returned to the range.

"I couldn't look," he said. "My stomach was a mess. I felt as if the shock of the whole thing was starting to set in."

He picked up his wedge again and thought about trying to hit a few more shots. But there was no point. Instead, he just stood there and listened to Sutton.

"He's going to chip it," Sutton said, as Bjorn took out his wedge and studied the shot.

"He's over the ball now..."

Curtis was completely frozen as he waited. He heard the crowd go "Ooh" and then thought he heard the "Aah" that usually accompanies a close miss.

Then he heard Sutton's voice. It was very measured and calm. "Ben," he said, "you've just won the Open championship."

Bjorn had hit a wonderful shot, the ball heading straight at the flag before slipping to the right at the last possible moment. The 12 inches remaining were the difference between a playoff and Curtis being the champion.

Curtis didn't have even a second to let what Sutton had said sink in, because the camera crews—led by the BBC and ABC—were now coming at him. What he really wanted to do at that moment was hug Candace, or at least Sutton. But Candace was back behind the 18th green, and Sutton was several yards away.

"It was a little bit weird," he said, laughing. "I was thinking, 'Should I hug one of the camera guys? Should I kiss the camera?' I wanted to do something, but there was no one around that I knew."

Candace, at least, had Ben's cousins to hug when Bjorn's shot missed the hole. Even so, she also regretted not being with Ben at that moment of victory. "I just wanted to be with him right then," she said. "That's probably my only regret about that entire week, that we weren't together when he realized he'd won."

They took Curtis back to the scoring area, fans clapping for him as the cart went by. Candace was waiting, tears streaming down her face. "When I hugged her, that's when I completely lost it," he said. "It really was surreal."

There was no sign of Woods, who had signed his card after finishing tied with Love for fourth place and left, but Love stopped to offer congratulations as he came out of the trailer, as did Singh, who as co-runner-up had to stay for the awards ceremony. Bjorn was still inside the scoring trailer, apparently trying to gather himself before coming out for the ceremony.

Curtis was being bombarded with questions, most of them the same: how in the world did you pull this off? He had shot a two-under-par 69, making him the only player in the last four groups who had broken 70 on the day. Singh had shot 70, Woods 71, Bjorn and Love 72, Perry and Price 73, and Sergio Garcia 74. With the exception of Price, all had won or seriously contended in majors in the past. Curtis had outplayed them all.

The players were taken to the back of the green while the officials gathered for the awards ceremony. As Curtis stood with Candace waiting for his name to be called, he felt a tap on his shoulder. He looked up and saw Bjorn, still apparently in shock.

"Great playing," he said. "Congratulations."

"All I could think to say was, 'Thanks,'" Curtis said. "By then I'd heard what had happened at 16, and I really didn't know what to say to him. I thought it was pretty classy for him to come find me like that."

When they gave Curtis the Claret Jug, he handled the victory speech like an old pro, except when his voice caught as he tried to thank his family watching back home at the golf club.

"I thought about my grandfather right then," he said. "My only regret was that he didn't live to see that moment."

The rest of the evening was a nonstop whirlwind. As ABC was going off the air, it showed a replay of Bjorn missing the last chip and Curtis reacting to the news that he was the Open champion.

"That happened at 6:06 p.m.," Curtis Strange said. "That young man has no idea how his life changed at that moment."

Strange was right. Ben Curtis had no idea how much his life had changed. It would not take him long, though, to find out.

———

THE SIGHT OF BEN CURTIS holding the Claret Jug stunned most of the golf world.

It was one thing for a relative unknown to win a major. Golf fans had known who Mike Weir was before the Masters, but the average sports fan, the kind who tuned in to golf only when Tiger Woods was in contention, had no idea who Weir was. Jim Furyk was certainly well known before winning the U.S. Open, but his name often appeared next to Phil Mickelson's at the top of the Best Player to Have Never Won a Major list.

It also was not completely unheard of for a player to win his first tournament at a major, though it was rare. Eight players had done it in the game's history, the most recent having been John Daly at the 1991 PGA.

But this was at a completely different level. There was now a new list in golf: all the players who had won majors in their first appearance in one: Francis Ouimet and Ben Curtis.

Even those who knew Curtis were stunned by his victory. Zach Johnson, who had made it to Q-School finals in 2002 but had not made the PGA Tour, was playing on that Sunday in the Nationwide Tour event in Richmond, Virginia. As he came off the ninth green, not seriously in contention, but having a good week, he spotted his wife, Kim, standing behind the green.

Johnson had been following his old Hooters Tour buddy throughout the week and had been hoping he could hang on against all the big stars and pull off a top-five finish on Sunday. Kim had gone into the clubhouse to see how Curtis was doing.

Walking off the green, Johnson said to his wife, "How'd Ben do?"

"He won," she said.

Johnson stared at his wife in disbelief for a moment. "He won? He won the British Open?"

She nodded. "Yes. He won."

Johnson was completely shocked. "It literally knocked me to my knees," he said. "I mean, I always knew Ben was talented; I could see that playing with him on the Hooters. But talented is one thing, winning a major in your first year on tour is another. I almost couldn't believe it.

"But when I realized it was true, that it had happened, I felt inspired. I just thought, 'If Ben can do that, why can't I win this tournament?' I played great on the back nine, thinking about Ben, and got myself into a playoff."

He lost the playoff, but even so the point had been made. Believe in yourself — as Curtis clearly had done — and just about anything can happen.

While the golf world and the nongolf world were trying to figure out how Ben Curtis had held off Tiger Woods, Vijay Singh, Davis Love III, Kenny Perry, and Sergio Garcia, not to mention Thomas Bjorn, Ben Curtis was beginning to live out Curtis Strange's prediction.

And there was one other remarkable twist to an already remarkable story. Unlike Mike Weir and Jim Furyk, Curtis had *not* been born on May 12, 1970. His birthday is May 26, 1977. But Andrew Coltart, the European Tour player whom caddy Andy Sutton would have normally worked for during the British Open, had been born on — you guessed it — May 12, 1970.

Ben and Candace got very little sleep before driving to London to catch their plane home. When they landed in Cleveland, there was a horde of media waiting, in addition to friends and family.

"I guess it wasn't too tough for anyone to figure out when we were landing," he said. "There's one flight a day from London to Cleveland."

There wasn't much rest for the weary over the next few days. After spending one night at home, Ben and Candace flew to New York to make the media rounds. There were the usual interviews with ESPN TV and radio, the *Paula Zahn Now* show on CNN, interviews with Fox and MSNBC, and various radio interviews around the country that neither Ben nor Candace can remember.

"I'm not sure I knew who I was on with when it was happening," Ben said. "Between the shock of winning, the jet lag, the exhaustion, and the whirlwind, I was lost."

The capper interview was to be with David Letterman. Before going to the studio, Ben and Candace and IMG agent Jay Danzi went to one of IMG's New York offices to go over some plans for the coming weeks. Ben had gone into another room to do another radio interview, and Candace found herself alone with Danzi.

"He was talking about all these different 'opportunities' Ben was going to have right away and in the future," she said. "I got that. But I'm not sure I was listening all that closely. This wasn't the time or the day to make any decisions when we were both so tired. Then I heard him say, 'And of course we're going to need to think about changing the wedding.'

"I looked at him and said, 'What?' And he went on about needing to push the wedding back because there was going to be so much for Ben to do and he was going to be playing that weekend [in the World Golf Championships in Akron, not far from where the wedding was to be held], and we were just going to have to think about picking a new date.

"I was so tired and so stunned that I just started to cry. I kept looking at him and saying, 'Are you kidding me? I've been planning this for a year.' A lot had been running through my mind about all the life changes we were going through almost from the minute he finished on 18 and they separated us. It was as if we'd lost control all of a sudden.

"Now I was being told I had to reschedule my wedding? I just lost it right there."

Ben walked in moments later and found his fiancée in tears. "What happened?" he asked, looking at Candace and then at Danzi.

"Jay wants us to change the wedding date."

"We aren't going to do that," Ben said, looking at Danzi. "We're getting married on August 23rd. That's the end of the discussion on that topic."

Candace was relieved. "He's such a nice guy; he doesn't like to disappoint people," she said. "He did exactly what I wanted him to do when he walked into the room—just said, 'No way; this is not an option.' If he hadn't reacted that way, I think I really would have lost it right there."

It was a seminal moment for both Ben and Candace. Even though the wedding date would not change, they both realized that nothing was the same anymore. Candace later remembered something that Peter Jacobsen said to the two of them in a family dining area at a tournament: "Don't think anyone is looking out for you out here, because they're not," he said. "You have to look out for one another, because no one else is going to do that."

Almost at that moment, Candace made a decision. "I had to be the one to look out for us," she said. "Ben's job was to play golf. I didn't want him to have to worry about the outside stuff anymore than he absolutely had to. I had to be more protective of him, of his time, and of our lives. I had to make sure people didn't walk all over him, because he's so gentle by nature. We were starting a new life before St. George's happened. Now we were starting a new life in every possible way."

The Letterman appearance went well. The plan had been for Ben to hit chip shots off a New York City rooftop. That went fine, but then Letterman decided to ask a few questions, and Ben, who was clearly a little bit nervous, was asked (naturally) about Woods. Wanting to say that Woods had "an aura" about him, Ben instead said he had "an aroma" about him. If nothing else, that gave his buddies something to tease him about, British Open champion or not.

After New York came a trip to Washington and a visit to the White House. Then it was time to play golf again. Getting back to playing was good for him. The congratulations from everyone in the locker room at the Buick Open were fun. He didn't mind being asked, for the first time in his life, to come into the interview room to talk to the media before the tournament began. It was all good.

Even so, it was still a bit of a shock when he stepped onto the tee on Thursday morning and heard the starter introducing, "The 2003 British Open champion..."

Curtis looked around at the packed gallery. Then it occurred to him: the applause was for him. *He* was the 2003 British Open champion.

As he stepped onto the tee, realizing that all eyes were on him, he knew that Curtis Strange had been right. His life had indeed changed forever. And there was no going back.

13

Glory's Last Shot

THERE WAS ONE MAJOR championship left in 2003. It would be played three weeks after the British Open, with the tour making stops in Hartford, Connecticut (Greater Hartford Open), Grand Blanc, Michigan (Buick Open), and Castle Rock (outside Denver; the International) before almost all of the top 136 players in the world headed for Oak Hill Country Club in Rochester, New York, for the PGA Championship.

The reason that most of the top 136 players were in the field and not 156 was because the PGA of America, which runs the championship, still reserves twenty spots for club pros—men who spend much of the year giving hackers lessons and selling clothing and golf equipment out of their pro shops. When someone in golf wants to put down a club pro, the phrase frequently used is "sweater stacker."

Once upon a time, all golf pros were club pros in some way, shape, or form. Not until Arnold Palmer brought big money into the game in the 1960s did those good enough to play on tour no longer feel the need to work as a club pro part of the year. The PGA Tour's qualifying tournament is still referred to as "Q-School" because when it first began there was a classroom element to the event, as those training to play golf for a living also needed to train to run a small business.

It was the PGA of America that ran the tour until 1968, when the touring pros broke off and formed the PGA Tour. To this day, many people do not understand how different the two organizations are. Members of the PGA Tour are focused on one thing almost all the time: improving their golf games. Members of the PGA of America almost never get the chance to work on their golf games because they spend so much time working on the golf games of those who aspire to someday break 100.

But the PGA of America still controls one of the four major championships (and the Ryder Cup), and that's why twenty club pros get to tee it up with the stars once a year. This galls many tour players because, inevitably, a number of good players don't get to play in the PGA Championship.

For a long time the presence of the club pros was the least of the PGA Championship's ongoing issues. Even though it had a glamorous list of past champions, from Walter Hagen and Gene Sarazen and Byron Nelson and Sam Snead to Ben Hogan and Jack Nicklaus and Gary Player and Tiger Woods, it had always been the fourth of the four majors.

"Hey, that's life," David Duval once said. "If you've got four majors, one of them has to be number four."

Unless you are in danger of no longer being number four. During the 1980s, there was actually talk that the PGA Championship might cease to be a major. Those running the tour were constantly insisting that the Players Championship had become more important than the PGA because it "belonged" to the players and had a stronger field. When Jack Nicklaus launched the Memorial Tournament in 1970, it was clear that he intended it to be considered a major championship eventually. That was why he modeled so much of the tournament and its trappings on the Masters.

As recently as 1990, the possibility that the PGA Championship might cease to be a major lingered. In 1987, the tournament was played at PGA National in Palm Beach in brutally hot conditions on greens that completely baked out in the heat and the humidity. Jim Awtrey, who was then the PGA of America's CEO, frequently told the story about standing near the 18th green and seeing someone rowing a woman in a raincoat out to the scoreboard that floated in the lake to the right of the 18th green. As soon as the woman got out of the boat, Awtrey understood what was going on: one of the local sponsors had hired her to put up scores—in a bikini.

"I knew at that moment," Awtrey said, "that this was a championship that was in trouble."

It got worse three years later when the PGA Championship was scheduled to be played at Shoal Creek Country Club in Birmingham, Alabama. The PGA was always searching for new and different venues because it didn't want to copycat sites chosen by the USGA for the U.S. Open. Shoal Creek was one of those relatively new courses. The golf course had gotten good reviews when it had hosted the event in 1984—helped by the fact that Lee Trevino won—so the PGA decided to go back just six years later.

Not long before the tournament, Hall Thompson, the club president, was asked in an interview what would happen if an African American ever applied for membership at Shoal Creek. That would never happen in Birmingham, Thompson responded.

A firestorm ensued. There was talk of boycotts, of moving the championship, even of canceling it. Eventually, a local African American businessman was recruited to become an instant member at Shoal Creek, and the tournament was held, but the memories lingered.

As it turned out, Shoal Creek was a turning point for the PGA. A decision had been made after 1987 to seek out more classic venues. In 1991, John Daly made his Cinderella out-of-nowhere run from ninth alternate to PGA champion at Crooked Stick. Two years later, playing at Inverness—a past U.S. Open venue—Paul

Azinger outdueled Nick Faldo and Greg Norman down the stretch, beating Norman in a playoff to win his long overdue first major title.

Nick Price won at Southern Hills a year later, and Davis Love III won at Winged Foot in 1997—both had been U.S. Open courses. Woods won dramatically in 1999 and 2000. By then, all the talk about the PGA Championship being supplanted as a major had quieted down. It was still number four, but it was, without doubt, number four. The PGA Tour began trying to sell the notion that the Players Championship was now the "fifth major."

This led to a classic quote from 1988 PGA champion Jeff Sluman: "There are only four items on the Grand Slam breakfast at Denny's," he said. "Not five."

Oak Hill was where Sluman, a Rochester, New York, native, had grown up and had learned the game. His pro then and the pro at Oak Hill in 2003 was Craig Harmon, one of the four teaching Harmon brothers who were the sons of Claude Harmon, the pro at Winged Foot in 1948—the year he won the Masters.

Oak Hill had plenty of history. It was designed by the Scottish master designer Donald Ross and was usually talked about in hushed, reverential tones by those in golf. It had hosted three U.S. Opens (1956, 1968, and 1989) and a PGA—1980 when Jack Nicklaus won the last of his five championships. It had also hosted the Ryder Cup in 1995. It was considered a classic golf course, greatly respected by the pros and, in a sense, a respite from two relatively untraditional sites: Olympia Fields, which had produced almost embarrassingly low scores for three rounds during the Open in June, and Royal St. George's, one of the least popular British Open sites among the players.

Oak Hill was not a golf course anyone was likely to complain about, although in 2003 the weather was surprisingly hot and humid in mid-August when the players began arriving to play practice rounds and get ready for their last major of the year—or,

as the CBS marketing people had come to call it, "Glory's
Last Shot."

It was, without question, Tiger Woods's last chance to salvage
his year. He had finished tied for fourth at the British Open, easily his best performance in a major championship in 2003. He
was still in the midst of his swing change and was working more
and more with Hank Haney. There hadn't yet been a formal
announcement, but everyone in golf, including Butch Harmon,
knew the two were working together.

"I knew they'd been working together when Tiger told me we
were done at Muirfield in '02," Harmon said. "I could tell just by
looking at his swing."

In his previous six years on tour, Woods had failed to win at
least one major only once — in 1998 when he was going through
his first major swing change while still working with Harmon. He
then had won the PGA in 1999; the U.S. Open (by 15 shots); the
British Open (by eight); and the PGA again in 2000. He had
started 2001 by winning the Masters, and then had started 2002
by winning the Masters and the U.S. Open.

Going into the 2003 PGA, Woods had gone five straight majors
without a win. The only "drought" he'd had that had lasted longer
had been after his win at the '97 Masters, when he had gone ten
straight majors without a win.

Because Woods had played well at Royal St. George's, the con-
sensus during the pretournament run-up was that he was now
ready to win again. He had finished second to Rich Beem in the
2002 PGA, and most people believed he would turn a bad year
(for him — he had still won four tournaments) into a good one by
winning the PGA.

One person who arrived in Rochester without any such expec-
tation was Shaun Micheel. He was, as the cliché goes, just happy
to be there. He was thirty-four years old and had been on and off
the tour since first getting through Q-School in 1993. His two

biggest wins at that moment were the 1998 Singapore Open and the 1999 Nike Greensboro Open. He had played in exactly two major championships in his life: the 1999 U.S. Open at Pinehurst, where he had missed the cut, and the 2001 Open at Southern Hills, where he had tied for 40th place. His highest finish on the PGA Tour had been a tie for third in 2002 at the B.C. Open.

"Should have won that," Micheel said. "I had a three-shot lead on Sunday and finished bogey-bogey. That hurt."

If Micheel hadn't been a golfer, he probably would have been a pilot like his dad, Buck. Many of his boyhood memories are of his father leaving on trips that would take him to three continents in a week.

"The good news was that when he was home, it was usually for a long time," he said. "That gave us a chance to spend time together."

A lot of that time was spent on the golf course. The Micheels lived near the fourth hole of the Colonial Country Club, which in those days was the host course for the annual PGA Tour event played in Memphis. "I grew up with the PGA Tour literally in my backyard once a year," Micheel said. "I couldn't get enough of hanging around during tournament week. I was never into autographs; I just wanted to be around for the golf."

Micheel's parents had grown up in Nebraska, and his father had been in the Air Force as a code breaker. "I like to tell people he was a spy," Micheel said, laughing.

After retiring from the air force, Buck Micheel worked first for a company that flew in and out of places like Vietnam and Laos — during the Vietnam War. He moved to a company called Shawnee Air and settled in Orlando in the late 1960s.

That was where Shaun was born, in 1969. His sister, Shannon, came along two years later. Not long after that, a new company called Federal Express, which had a start-up fleet of three airplanes, was looking for pilots. Buck Micheel was hired as one of the company's first pilots. Soon after that, the family moved to Memphis, and Buck and Donna Micheel bought the house at Colonial and settled in with their two young children. In those days, the tour stop in Memphis was known as the Danny Thomas Memphis Classic. Although the Micheels didn't belong to Colonial, Shaun played part of the course almost every evening once he got hooked on golf.

"When I was little, my dad would take me with him a lot when he went to play," he said. "I always thought he did it because he felt bad about being on the road so much flying. Now that I have my own kids, I know he did it because he liked the time with me. I loved being there right away, although when I was little it was mostly about driving the cart."

Buck Micheel was a very good player, a low single-digit handicapper, and he won a membership in a club across the street from Colonial during a member-guest tournament drawing. Later he joined a club in nearby Germantown because a lot of his pilot buddies lived up there and were members. Often, he would take Shaun to play with them.

"I loved that," he said. "I probably played more with my dad and his friends when I was young than with other kids because not that many of my friends played. I'd play with him when he was home, but when he wasn't I'd go out on the course at Colonial late in the day and play my own little course. I'd start on the fifth tee and then play two, three, and four. That way I never encountered any members because no one teed off that late, and I never got hassled about being out there. I'd usually come in at dark when my mom or my dad came out in the backyard and called for me."

By the time he was thirteen, Micheel was becoming a very good junior player. His handicap dropped nine strokes that summer. "I can't remember if it was from 12 to three or from 10 to one," he said, laughing. "But I do remember I became a good player."

At fifteen, he gave up playing high school basketball, even though he loved it, because he knew golf was what he wanted to do, in terms of both college and a career. He enjoyed competing, and he also enjoyed playing on his own at Colonial. "I liked playing in competition a lot," he said. "But I also enjoyed being off by myself and playing or practicing. I liked the solitude.

"Once I got a good look at the pros and what they could do, I was hooked. Every year I'd spend the week of the tournament hanging around at the club, watching everything the pros did. I knew then I wanted to be a part of what they were doing, even though it seemed like a million miles away from me at that point. I'd like to think that I had other interests then and I have other interests now, but golf is what I've loved doing and being a part of for as long as I can remember."

He was an outstanding junior player while in high school and was recruited by many of the top college programs. He almost went to Kentucky because he enjoyed his visit to the school so much. Steve Flesch, to this day a good friend on tour, was his host and took Micheel to a basketball game between Kentucky and then top-ranked University of Nevada, Las Vegas.

"I thought the whole thing was great," he said. "I knew that was where I wanted to go, and they were offering me a full ride. So, I committed. A few months later, I got a call from the coach saying that a player on the team who he had thought was going to flunk out had actually stayed eligible. He didn't have a full scholarship to offer. So, he offered me a half ride instead."

That spring Micheel was playing in a local tournament in Memphis the same week that a major college tournament was being played nearby. Indiana was in the tournament, and IU Coach Bob Fitch came over to watch the juniors. After seeing Micheel play, he invited him to visit Indiana.

Micheel agreed. There were no basketball games being played, but he loved the school anyway. And he knew Indiana played pretty good basketball too since the Hoosiers had beaten the UNLV team he had seen on his winter visit to Kentucky and had gone on to win the 1987 national championship.

"The only reason I hesitated at all was that I was really interested in aviation, in flying," Micheel said. "I had already gotten my pilot's license my senior year in high school, and I knew Illinois had a really good golf team too, and they had an aviation major. I asked Coach Fitch about it, and he said, 'Oh, well we have aviation here too.' 'Perfect,' I thought. So I signed to go there."

As it turned out, Indiana did have an aviation program: it was called ROTC. That summer, Micheel won a major national junior tournament. His phone started ringing off the hook with scholarship offers. But he had already signed with Indiana and had no intention of reneging on that commitment.

"Going to IU was one of the best decisions I ever made," he said. "It wasn't all smooth sailing, but it was definitely a great experience."

He was good enough to play right away, and he did well academically, although finding a major wasn't easy. At first he wanted economics but ran into a problem many athletes run into: a professor who wouldn't reschedule tests that were missed to travel to an away game or, in this case, a golf tournament. The same thing happened in biology, so he finally settled on general studies, where he could pick and choose courses that fit with his golf schedule.

"It was important to me to get my degree," he said. "That's why I went back in the fall of '91 to finish up. I knew I wanted to play golf for a living, but I had no idea if I would be good enough. Doing well in college is a lot different than doing well on tour or even making it to the tour. A lot of very successful college golfers never even make it to the tour."

Fitch retired after Micheel's sophomore year and was replaced by Sam Carmichael, who was the Indiana women's coach and a good friend of Bob Knight. Carmichael brought a lot of Knight's intensity to his coaching, which was a lot different from Fitch, who often sent the players out in carts to practice and figured those who wanted to play would be those who put in the most time.

"Sam was a *lot* like Coach Knight," Micheel said. "It was his way or the highway, no doubt about that. He knew what he was doing, and we eventually became good friends. But it wasn't easy at the start."

In fact, Micheel came very close to quitting the team his junior year. Indiana was playing in a tournament outside Baton Rouge, and Micheel called Stephanie Abbott to see if she wanted to come to have dinner before the tournament began. Abbott had also grown up in a house at Colonial (her family lived on the 16th hole), and she and Shaun had known each other as kids. She was now a freshman at LSU, and she and Shaun dated occasionally. This seemed like a good chance to spend some time together.

Stephanie drove up with one of her friends and arrived at the team's hotel a little earlier than expected. "I was in the shower getting ready," Micheel remembered. "So the guys let her and her friend in so they could wait until I was ready. They were sitting there, and Sam walked by. The curtains were open—no one was trying to hide anything—and he saw these two girls sitting in the room.

"He went ballistic. He came in and started screaming at Stephanie and her friend for being in the room. Then he screamed at me, basically accused me of trying to sneak girls into the room. I said to him, 'Coach, you don't know me very well if you think I'd do that,' and we really went at it. I was angry because he was questioning my integrity. He was just angry."

Micheel's teammates talked him out of doing anything rash, and he figured out how to deal with Carmichael's intensity and temper. "The problem was I had a temper too," Micheel said.

"Sometimes it was an oil and water mix. But I did play well those two years."

He was the Big Ten champion as a senior and a first-team All American. He got his degree in December 1991 and headed straight to South Africa to play for a couple of months. "Fascinating trip," he said. "Talk about a culture shock. It was right at the end of apartheid, but the way they still treated blacks at times was just awful.

"I remember we went to one club to play, and we asked about getting caddies. They took us over to a pen where they had them all locked up and let a couple of them out to work for us that day. I almost got sick when I saw that."

He came home and played minitours in Florida for the rest of 1992, rooming with Doug Barron, a boyhood friend, who would also make it to the tour. Micheel won his first tournament by winning a nine-hole playoff. "I remember it was just about pitch dark when we finished," he said. "They'd already told us this would be the last hole we played. I won $3,000. Felt like I'd struck it rich."

His first chance at Q-School came that fall when he went to the Country Club of Indiana for first stage.

"I don't remember the exact details because I've blocked it from my mind," Micheel said. "But I think I bogeyed the last three holes to miss by one. That really hurt. Up until then, I still felt invulnerable. I was just climbing up this ladder step-by-step to get where I wanted to go, and then all of a sudden I took a hard fall. It took me a little while to get over that one."

The following year he decided to play on what was then the T.C. Jordan Tour. (Today it is the Hooters Tour.) The money wasn't much, but the T.C. Jordan did have the advantage of feeling like a real golf tour. The events were 72 holes, and the players traveled — almost always by car — from small town to small town, learning about life on the road and how to prepare to tee it up every Thursday.

Micheel's dad had put together a group of sponsors for his son among his pilot friends in Memphis; they were floating about $25,000 for Shaun to live on, which made another year of playing for relatively small purses both possible and bearable.

The highlight of that year had nothing to do with golf. Micheel and Barron were playing in a tournament in New Bern, North Carolina. On Tuesday morning, they were walking to their cars in the hotel parking lot, when they became aware of an out-of-control car hurtling past them on the road near the hotel.

"I'm not sure what drew our attention to it, but there was this loud noise," Micheel said. "I looked up and saw this car go by and then literally become airborne. I knew that the road there dead-ended at the Neuse River, so I took off running right away. I'm not sure if I heard the splash or not, but when I got there, the car was in the water and clearly starting to sink.

"Someone else who worked at a gas station that was right there had either heard the noise or seen the car and had come running too. We both just looked at each other for a second and then started to take off our clothes. I took off everything but my boxers and dove in. It wasn't something I thought about; it was just something I did.

"We got to the car and the windows were open — I guess they didn't have air conditioning; it was August and very hot. There was a woman in the front seat and a man in the backseat. The other guy started working to get the woman out, and I went to get the man.

"I remember that he couldn't swim and he was panicked, so I kind of had to fight him at first. Fortunately, the water wasn't very deep — maybe six feet — so once I got him out of the car, I was pretty sure we were going to be okay. By the time we got to shore, a bunch of people were there to help."

The two people in the car were an elderly couple who had apparently been on the way home from the grocery store. Micheel never actually spoke to them because they were both taken away in an ambulance even though they checked out just fine.

"From what I gathered later, they were on their way back from the grocery store and missed the turn just before the dead end. I guess when the lady who was driving saw the barrier, she tried to hit the brake but somehow hit the accelerator, and that's why they were going so fast when they got to the water."

When the story made the local paper in New Bern, Micheel instantly became a local hero. The T.C. Jordan Tour didn't draw big galleries, but many of those who did come out made a point of finding him to tell him how proud he should be of what he had done.

"I remember playing well that week," he said. "I had a chance to win on Sunday but didn't. I never thought of myself as heroic. I'm proud that at a moment like that, I responded in what turned out to be the correct way. I didn't panic, and I didn't freeze. I think most people would want to do the right thing at a moment like that, and I'm glad that I did. But I never thought of myself as a hero."

The local branch of the Sons of Confederate Veterans felt differently. The following year, they awarded Micheel their Award for Bravery at their annual dinner. "All I remember about that night is that they all showed up in their uniforms," Stephanie Micheel recalled. "I was proud of Shaun for what he did, but that night was, let's say, different."

Shaun and Stephanie still joke about the episode and the dinner. "Like I said, I'm very proud of what Shaun did," Stephanie said. "But it does crack me up sometimes when they put his name up on the scoreboard. Today [the Honda Classic in 2009] he's playing with Joe Ogilvie and Jonathan Byrd. Joe's name comes up and his bio says, 'Won his first tour event in Milwaukee in 2007.' Then for Jonathan it says, 'Three-time winner on tour, three-time All American at Clemson.' Up comes Shaun, and it says, 'Winner of 1994 Sons of Confederate Veterans Award for Bravery.' It's as if he never played golf. I don't mind it; I just find it kind of funny."

Shaun and Stephanie started dating again in the fall of 1993, soon after Shaun's heroics in New Bern, this time on a serious basis. "We'd known each other so long and we'd dated on and off, but it had never been serious because it had always been long distance," he said. "But at some point, I guess we decided we really liked each other."

He made it through the first two stages of Q-School that fall, meaning he would at the very least have a chance to play on the Nike Tour in 1994. The Q-School finals were in Palm Springs that December. His parents and sister came to watch him play. On the sixth and final day, Micheel played his best round of the week and shot 67 to move up from well outside to right on the qualifying number.

When his score went up, people came up and congratulated him. Micheel knew that the low 40 players and ties made it to the PGA Tour. He had moved into a tie for 37th place with nine other golfers. "I was so excited because I'd made it," he said. "Then I heard someone say, 'The playoff for all players tied for 37th place will begin on the 10th tee in fifteen minutes.' I was like, 'Playoff, *playoff*? I thought I was in, I thought I'd made the tour. We have to play off?'"

He was working himself into a panic when someone told him the playoff was just to determine the players' rankings. They were all on the tour, but as the last guys in from Q-School, they wouldn't know week to week (especially on the West Coast) if they were high enough on the exempt list to get into tournaments. Thus, figuring out who was number 37 as opposed to who was number 46 was significant.

"At that moment, it didn't matter to me at all," Micheel said. "All I knew was I had made the PGA Tour. I was so loose when we played the 10th hole that I hit two perfect shots, made the putt for birdie, and got the 37th spot. After everything I'd been through, that seemed easy."

The family was so exhausted and drained that the postround victory celebration took place at a Wendy's. "None of us had the strength to do anything else," Micheel said.

Back home, Stephanie was just starting law school and told her friends that the guy she was dating had made it to the PGA Tour. "A few months into the season, some of my friends told me that everyone thought I was lying because no one could find his name in the results," she said. "No one knew how to spell Micheel."

The results they would have found had they known how to spell Micheel were not especially encouraging. Like a lot of tour rookies, Micheel was completely overwhelmed by life on the tour.

"I think it's something almost every young guy goes through," he said. "I wasn't yet twenty-five when I got out there, and I knew absolutely no one. I never felt like I belonged. I can remember walking onto the range and seeing Nick Price and Greg Norman and thinking, 'What in the world am I doing out here with these guys?' I remember I hit the ball pretty well at times that year, but I could never make anything happen scoringwise. I just felt as if I was out of my league."

One reason Micheel didn't know anyone was that very few of the players with whom he had played junior golf, college golf, or minitour golf had made it to the tour. "Phil [Mickelson] was there, but I barely knew him. We had roomed together once at an event, but we just didn't travel in the same circles. When he came on the tour, he had already won an event while he was in college, so he was playing in the tournament winners category right from the beginning. I played in the last group of the day a lot.

"It wasn't as if people weren't nice to me; they were. I'm just not the kind of guy who can walk into a room and start making friends. I've always been more of an observer: walk into a room and watch people. That's just me. If I'd been more outgoing, it might have been easier."

From his spot as the number 37 player coming out of Q-School, Micheel ended up getting into nineteen tournaments that year. He made only four cuts, and his highest finish was a tie for 26th at the Deposit Guaranty Classic, an event that was held opposite the British Open back then, meaning that most of the top players weren't entered. Of the last eleven tournaments he played, that was the only one in which he made it to the weekend. His highest finish in a full-field tournament was in Houston, where he ended up tied for 55th.

"I remember when I made it through Q-School, my dad saying to me that as excited as he was and as proud as he was, he wasn't sure that a year on the Nike Tour to get experience wouldn't be better for me at that point. I remember that same year David Duval didn't make it through Q-School, and he went on and had a great year on the Nike and later said it was an important learning experience for him at that point in his career.

"My attitude then was that I wanted to play against the best, and I thought the best way to learn was by being up close with the best, week in and week out. But after a while, when you just feel overwhelmed, I'm not so sure it's still a learning experience."

Micheel ended up making $12,252 in prize money that year, which landed him in 247th place on the money list, a long way from the top 125. He went back to the second stage of Q-School and, still staggered by what had happened during the year, didn't make it to the finals. That sent him back to the minitours for 1995.

"That may have been the most discouraging year of my golf career," Micheel said. "Those first couple of years playing on the minitours, it was all fun. I was up and coming and still learning. But the old saying about, 'You don't know what you've got till it's gone,' is true. It was very hard to be back playing on that level after I'd been on the PGA Tour, regardless of how I'd done when I was on the tour. You get used to that lifestyle pretty fast. One minute I'm teeing it up against the best guys on the best golf courses, the next I'm back playing minitour events, driving from place to place in a Honda Accord my parents had bought for me.

"It was tough. I was down on myself. It didn't get to a point where I thought about quitting, but I remember thinking, 'This isn't what I signed up for when I turned pro.'"

He managed to make it back to the Q-School finals at the end of that year, and, even though he didn't make it back to the tour, he did secure a spot on the Nike Tour. "That was important," Micheel said. "I needed to at least feel like I was making progress. And, even though I didn't exactly tear it up out there the next year, at least I felt as if I could compete."

He finished 82nd on the Nike money list that year, went back to Q-School, and this time cruised back to the tour. That was the year the sixth round was rained out in California, leaving a lot of players angry and upset because they didn't get a chance to play their way inside the number on that final day.

"I remember one of the guys who was outside the number sitting around while it rained, saying how unfair it was because he had worked so hard to get to where he was," Micheel said. "I understood his frustration. But all of us who were inside the number at that point had probably worked just as hard. The rain wasn't anyone's fault."

Micheel went back to the tour in 1997 convinced that things would be different than in '94, that he was more mature and more experienced and, as a result, a better player. He knew more guys than the first time around, and he did feel more comfortable. But he didn't play that much better. He made five cuts in twenty-one tournaments, his highest finish a tie for 49th place at the Buick Open. Even though he made a little more money than in '94

($14,519), he actually finished three spots lower on the money list. Then, to make sure the year ended on the same down note as '94, he again failed to make it through the second stage of Q-School.

He was beginning to feel like a hamster on a wheel, going round and round and always ending up back in the same place—a place he didn't want to be.

He and Stephanie had been living together for a couple of years by then and had made the decision to get married in November 1998. She had graduated from law school and was practicing law in Memphis, and they agreed it was time to take the next step.

"I could have gone back to [what had become] the Hooters, I suppose," Micheel said. "But I didn't want to do that. Even though it was a tough time to do it, I decided to take a shot and go to Asia. I knew the competition was decent over there, and the money was better than the Hooters. I just wanted to try something different."

He actually had to go to Q-School to get on the Asian Tour because the tour allowed only twenty non-Asians to be full-time players each year. "Had to go through two stages," Micheel said, laughing. "I was stunned when I found out, but I had already committed to it mentally so I just went."

He got through Q-School and played decently until the tour took its annual monsoon-season break. He flew home during the break to play some golf and to get married. While he was home, he played a round of golf with his dad and some buddies and shot 58.

"It wasn't like I was playing a PGA Tour golf course," Micheel said. "But it was a 58. That's a pretty good round of golf under any circumstances. It gave me some confidence when I went back."

The first tournament back after the break was the Omega PGA Championship in Hong Kong, which was a major on the Asian Tour.

During the pro-am, his first round of golf as a new husband, Micheel started out wearing his wedding band. "It felt really uncomfortable though, so I took it off after a few holes." He smiled. "Once I took it off, I couldn't stop making birdies. That was the last time I played with it on." He ended up shooting another 58. All of a sudden he was making putts, something he had struggled to do throughout his pro career. With another confidence boost, he went out and won the tournament—his first win other than on minitours as a pro. Most important, he won $80,000. That windfall allowed him to finally pay off his sponsors and feel as if he could go forward as a pro without any help. By the end of the year he had finished third in the Asian Order of Merit and, for the first time in his career, had made some serious money, about $125,000 in all.

In 1999, Micheel made it back to the Nike Tour and continued to play solid golf. He won for the first time on that tour in Greensboro and made $173,411 to finish ninth on the money list. That provided him with an instant spot back on the PGA Tour because the top-15 money winners on the tour advanced past Q-School and past go to collect not $200 but their exemption.

"I remember Commissioner [Tim] Finchem giving us all our [tour] cards on the 18th green after the [Nike] Tour Championship," Micheel said. "It obviously wasn't the first time I'd made it to the tour, but this felt special because I'd worked all year as opposed to one week to earn it. I think playing well on the Nike also made me feel like I was finally a good enough player to go out and have a chance to succeed against the big boys."

The first half of the year didn't go a lot better than his two previous years on tour had gone. He missed seven of nine cuts to start the year, his best finish a tie for 40th in Tucson. But things began to pick up slowly. He made five cuts in a row—by far his best streak ever on tour—even though he didn't finish higher than 37th.

The breakthrough came in the searing late July heat at the John Deere Classic. On Sunday, Micheel played perhaps his best round of golf since his final round at the '93 Q-School, shooting a 65 to rocket up to a tie for fifth place. Given that he had never before finished in the top 25 in a tour event, it was a massive confidence boost.

"I had been in position going into Sundays before, where a good round might not win the tournament for me but would get me a big check, and I'd never been able to do it," he said. "Finally doing it helped a lot. After a while, you do begin to question yourself. Am I just not good enough to play with these guys? That week told me the answer was at least maybe."

He went to Canada in late August and came back with a tie for 13th in Vancouver and a tie for 10th at the Canadian Open. That put him in position to retain his card if he could finish strong. He did—most notably with another tie for fifth, this one in Las Vegas. That check vaulted him comfortably inside the top 125 on the money list. He finished the year with $467,431 in earnings, good enough for 104th.

"At that point, my attitude was, 'Okay, I know I can do it. No more going back to Q-School,'" he said.

It didn't quite turn out that way. Micheel didn't play poorly in 2001, but there was a distraction that was beyond his control. His mom had dealt with bipolar disease most of her life, and her meds simply weren't working as well that year as they had in the past. Buck Micheel was winding down his career with FedEx but was still away for long stretches. Often the calls from Donna Micheel were made to Shaun, who would try to track his dad down through a special system FedEx had for emergencies.

"I'm not going to use that as an excuse," Micheel said. "Everyone has family issues. But it was difficult at times. The next year my mom started doing a lot better, and my dad had retired and was home, and, coincidence or not, I played a good deal better."

Micheel dropped to 136th on the money list at the end of '01, meaning he would have partially exempt status the next year. He decided to suck it up and go back to Q-School to improve his position, and did so, finishing in a tie for 13th place. That meant he would get to play most weeks without hanging around hoping for withdrawals, which is the lot of most players in the 126 to 150 category. "It definitely turned out to be a good move going back," Micheel said. "I didn't enjoy it, but by then I was used to it. Plus, being in the top 150 meant I went straight to the finals and knew, even if I didn't make it, I had some status on tour the next year. I think that relaxed me a lot."

In 2002, Micheel had his first real chance to win a tournament—the B.C. Open. He led after 54 holes and was within a couple of shots of Jeff Sluman's all-time scoring record for the event. But, as often happens to first-time contenders, he slipped on Sunday, bogeying the last two holes to finish tied for third. It was his highest finish on tour but disappointing nonetheless.

"There's a difference between having a chance to win a tournament and being in position where you should win a tournament," Micheel said. "I'd had chances before, times when if I had a good round on Sunday I could have come from behind to win. But this was different. I was in the last group, and I had a three-shot lead. I should have won."

Still, the finish at B.C., along with a tie for fifth in Texas, wrapped up his card for 2003, allowing him to finish 105th on the money list. His goal going into 2003 was simple: keep your card two years in a row, and crack the top 100 on the money list.

Winning a tournament, which he believed he was capable of doing, would be a bonus.

14

Moving On Up . . . to a Major

At the start of 2003, Shaun Micheel did something he had never done before to begin a year on the PGA Tour: he played good golf. In his five previous years on tour, he had never had a top-10 finish before July. By early March, he had two: a tie for 10th in Los Angeles and a tie for eighth at Doral. The money for those two weeks got him off to the fastest start of his career by far, but they also made him feel good about his game, because both events are played on high-quality golf courses.

"Riviera [Los Angeles] is obviously one of the better courses we play," Micheel said. "There have been U.S. Opens and a PGA there. Doral may not have quite the reputation it did twenty years ago, but it is still a place where you have to hit good shots in order to compete."

The timing for an early hot streak could not have been better. Stephanie was pregnant and due in November, which meant she would have to give up practicing law at least for a while. Job security for Shaun was clearly a good thing, and the fast start meant not having to spend the summer and fall worrying about another trip to Q-School.

"I had become a better player and maybe more important a better putter," Micheel said. "My first few years on tour, there were times I hit the ball well enough to really compete, even to win, but I never did. Every player will tell you the same thing: when you putt well, everything else in your game seems to go better, because you feel less pressure to get the ball close on every hole. Once I started to make putts with some consistency, I felt a lot more relaxed on the golf course."

He began the year by making eleven of twelve cuts, a far cry from his first two years on tour when he had made nine cuts total — in forty starts. When he finished 13th in Washington and 10th in Hartford, Micheel did two things: wrapped up his card for 2004 and earned a spot in the PGA Championship. That was a big deal.

"One thing people don't understand is that it's hard to get into major championships even if you're playing on the tour," he said. "The Masters takes about ninety players, so essentially you have to have won a tournament or be in the top 50 in the world to have a chance to get in. The U.S. Open and the British Open only have a handful of players who are exempt, and everyone else has to play a 36-hole qualifier, which is a crapshoot. That's why every year, you see club pros and amateurs making it into those events while established tour players don't. I'm not saying that's wrong; that's what makes them *open* championships. It just means that being on the tour, unless you are one of the top guys, doesn't guarantee you anything."

The PGA Championship is the most accessible of the four majors to those who play the U.S. Tour. Micheel just about clinched his spot with his performance in Hartford, because it put him in the top 70 on the money list for the twelve months that ran from the end of the Buick Open in 2002 to the end of the Buick Open in 2003. He was 68th on that list and sweating just a little bit when he finished tied for 24th at the Buick. That allowed him to hang on to his spot. Just making the field meant a lot to him. He had never before played in the PGA, just two U.S. Opens.

After Buick, he played at the International outside Denver. He finished tied for 60th and flew directly into Rochester to begin preparing for the PGA. Stephanie, who was by then six months pregnant, was going to work on Monday and Tuesday and planned to fly in on Wednesday to be there when the championship began.

Micheel liked the golf course right from the start. He knew it was going to be a week that put a premium on driving the ball in the fairway, because the rough was cut high, and a missed fairway was likely to mean a lost shot. That was fine with him. He was driving the ball well and felt good about the way he was putting.

What's more, it was hot. In fact, on Wednesday, there was a power outage that left a lot of the city without electricity. Micheel was concerned about Stephanie having to sleep in an un-air-conditioned room, but the hotel never lost power. On the golf course, the heat didn't really bother him. "When you're from Memphis," he said, "you get used to playing in the heat."

Micheel was paired on Thursday morning with Kevin Sutherland and Jeffrey Lankford, one of the club pros, a comfortable pairing for him. The weather was still sticky and humid, with temperatures approaching ninety degrees. He was very happy to piece together a solid round of one-under-par 69. That put Micheel in a tie for sixth place. Rod Pampling and Phil Mickelson had opened with 66s, and Billy Andrade, who had gotten into the field at the last possible moment as the fifth alternate, had shot 67. Two major champions, Mike Weir and two-time U.S. Open champion Lee Janzen, were one shot further back.

Micheel was one of seven players at 69. The group also included Vijay Singh and Chad Campbell, who, in a poll of PGA Tour players done by *Sports Illustrated* a few weeks earlier, had been chosen as the next player expected to win his first major title. Campbell was twenty-nine and, like Micheel, had never won on tour and had never contended in a major, his best finish being a tie for 15th at the British Open a month earlier.

But Campbell had been a hot player all year, having finished second twice, with four other top-10 finishes, including a sixth at the Players Championship. A Texan who was very comfortable playing in heat, humidity, and wind, Campbell was clearly considered an up-and-comer by other players on the tour. Micheel wasn't mentioned in the poll.

Micheel's 69 was satisfying because it was a long, tough day on a difficult golf course. "The one thing you learn out here is that the only thing you can do on Thursday for sure is knock yourself out of a golf tournament with a bad round. A good round assures you of nothing, not even making the cut. Still, I felt as if I was playing well, and, if nothing else, I was in good position to make the cut.

"That was my goal coming into the week: make the cut. After all, I'd only made one in a major, and then see what happened on the weekend. I was at the point where I really wanted to win a golf tournament—any golf tournament—but the thought of winning a major had never crossed my mind. After all, I'd only played in two of them at that point."

By the time he teed it up on Friday afternoon, it was apparent that the cut number was going to be high. There was just enough of a hot breeze blowing through the golf course that the greens had gotten dry and hard, and absolutely no one was going low.

The two Thursday leaders, Mickelson and Pampling, were both struggling. Pampling would shoot a 74 to finish at even par, Mickelson one shot higher than that. Weir managed a one-over-par 71, while Janzen shot 74. Andrade shot a solid 72, which meant he and Weir were the only players in the field under par as the afternoon wave moved around the golf course. Tiger Woods, who had opened with a 74, made no move at all, shooting a 72 that left him two shots inside the cut line (eight-over-par 148) and nine shots behind the leader.

That leader was Micheel. With his putter working well all day and with the help of a number of excellent up and downs after missing greens, he worked his way around the golf course in one shot less than he had needed on Thursday. The two-under-par 68 put him at three under for 36 holes and gave him a two-shot lead on Andrade and Weir. Pampling was at even-par 140, and a host of players, including Mickelson, Ernie Els, and Chad Campbell, were a shot further back.

Being in the lead meant that Micheel was invited into the interview room. The only other time he had been in an interview room had been at the 2002 B.C. Open. This was a little different.

"I remember it was huge; that was my first impression," he said. "There were a lot of guys there. They sort of wanted to know my life story in twenty minutes." He smiled. "I'm generally shy. But once I get going on something, I can't tell you what I had for dinner in under twenty minutes."

Being in the interview room made Micheel keenly aware of where he was and what was at stake. Still, he wasn't about to get carried away after 36 holes. If nothing else, the way he spent the evening brought him back to earth if he needed to be brought back to earth.

"Steph needed a prescription filled," he said, laughing. "We ordered room service for dinner, and then I went out to find a drugstore to get the prescription. There wasn't a lot open. It took a while. I remember thinking, 'Well, Mr. Glamour, here you are leading the PGA, and look at you.' I was tired by the time I went to bed. Fortunately, I could sleep in since my tee time was so late."

Micheel's tee time was 2:50 in the afternoon, so he had plenty of time. He spent that morning watching golf on TV before leaving for the course. As soon as he and Stephanie got out of the car, he noticed a half-dozen camera crews in the parking lot waiting to record his "walk" into the clubhouse.

"I felt kind of silly, to be honest," he said. "I told Steph that I figured this was the opposite of a perp walk."

His nerves were churning as he warmed up, but once he got on the golf course he was just fine. Andrade was a good pairing for him. Although he was a very good player who had won four times on tour, Andrade wasn't a superstar like Woods or Mickelson or Els.

"I think if I'd played with one of those guys, I'd have been really nervous," Micheel said. "I knew Billy was a good player and his rep was as a good guy to play with. That helped relax me."

Andrade is, in fact, one of the friendlier, more outgoing players on the tour, and his small talk and one-liners were the perfect salve for Micheel. "Billy was great the whole day," he said. "Even when he struggled that day [shooting 72], he never lost his sense of humor, never got tense—or at least didn't seem to me to be tense. I think his attitude helped me a lot because I had certainly never been in that position before."

In fact, Andrade knew very little about Micheel and didn't consider him a serious contender to win the tournament. "I knew of him a lot more than I knew him," Andrade said. "I knew he'd been on tour for a while, and I had heard he was a solid player. But I also knew he had never been anywhere close to contention in a major before, and history says that guys who lead majors after 36 holes who have never contended before tend to fade.

"Honestly, I thought of myself, not Shaun, as the leader, and guys like Els, Weir, Mickelson, and Woods—the name guys—were the ones I had to try to stay ahead of to win."

Micheel had been in one weekend final group—on Sunday at the B.C. Open a year earlier. But this was a lot different: much bigger crowds, a sense that he was playing for history, and the knowledge that every swing he took was being seen on national TV.

Fortunately, he got off to a good start, bouncing back from an opening bogey to get on a roll and make birdies at seven, eight, and nine, finishing at five under for the championship. Another birdie at 12, a long par save from 20 feet at 13—after his third shot flew the green and he appeared to be dead—and one more birdie at 15, and he was at seven under par and had a four-shot lead on the field.

Everyone kept waiting for someone else to make a move, but no one did—except for Chad Campbell who was piecing together the best round of the tournament three groups ahead of Micheel and Andrade. By the time they reached the 16th hole, Campbell was in the clubhouse, having shot a five-under-par 65 that put him four under par for 54 holes. Campbell had birdied the 15th and then made a long birdie putt at the difficult 18th. Still, Micheel had a three-shot lead, and Mike Weir, at one under, was the only other player in the field who was under par. By now, Micheel was fully aware that he was not only leading the PGA but that there really weren't very many players close to him.

Whether it was a glance at the scoreboard that showed only two players within seven shots of his lead or just being tired, Micheel stumbled for the first time all week on the finishing holes, making three straight bogeys. The last one dropped him back to four under par and into a tie for the lead with Campbell. Even so, he had shot a solid one-under-par 69, a pretty good day of golf given that he had never been in contention in a major or even an important tour event.

"The finish was disappointing," Micheel said. "It wasn't so much that I gave up the lead as the fact that I just didn't play those holes very well, and I didn't feel like there was any reason or any excuse not to. It was hot and I was tired but so was everyone else out there. Still, I walked off the golf course thinking I was tied for the lead, and Mike [Weir] was the only player within three shots of us. I knew, even though Chad had shot the 65, that going really low on the last round of the PGA on this golf course would be tough, so there really weren't that many players in a position to catch us. My feeling was if somebody did that, well, good for them. My job was to keep playing well and just let the chips fall."

One person who felt that Micheel had done his job well that day was Andrade. "He was a better player than I expected," Andrade said. "A very good ball striker, and he did a great job getting it up and down when he had to. I know he was disappointed the way he finished, but those last two holes were so tough that a bogey was almost like a par."

The irony in Micheel and Campbell being in the last group on Sunday went beyond the fact that neither had won a tournament yet. They were often mistaken for each other because they looked very much alike, though Campbell was taller and huskier than Micheel.

"When Chad was playing well in the spring, I had people come up to me and say, 'Nice playing last week,' on a couple of occasions, when I hadn't played well or hadn't played at all," Micheel said, laughing, after the round was over.

He went straight from the interview room back to the range and hit balls until dark. It was after nine o'clock by the time he and Stephanie made it back to their room. Once again they ordered room service. "I got the same guy on the phone every night," Micheel said. "He was very nice, but I'm sure he must have thought we were weirdos or something, never going out to dinner."

In fact, since Micheel had been asked where he had been eating and had answered "room service" and had told the story about his friend who answered the phone, several media outlets tracked the guy down the following day to get him to talk about his new friend who was tied for the lead in the PGA. He reported that Mr. Micheel was a very nice guy. Film at eleven.

Saturday night wasn't a lot different from Friday, except that Micheel didn't have to tour Rochester looking for a drugstore.

Much like Ben Curtis a month earlier, a lot of his focus as he went to bed that night was on the first shot he would hit the next afternoon.

"I knew I was going to be nervous standing on that tee," Micheel said. "But I knew Chad would be nervous too. He hadn't won a tournament either. In fact, the only person who was close to us who had any experience contending in a major was Mike [Weir], although I guess Ernie [Els] was only five shots back. Still, he was going to have to go low to catch us, unless Chad and I both blew up. I just had this idea that if I could get that first shot in the fairway, my nerves would clear and would turn into adrenaline instead. That was what had happened Saturday. I knew I'd be more nervous on Sunday, which made the first tee shot that much more important."

Micheel had actually killed time on Saturday by watching the classic golf movie *Caddy Shack*. On Sunday, with a 3:05 tee time, he and Stephanie left for the golf course a little earlier, and again the TV crews were there waiting for them. CBS actually showed them walking through the parking lot in slow-mo. "It was a long walk," Micheel said, laughing. "We were the last ones to get there, so we had to park at the far end of the lot."

While Micheel and Campbell went through their warm-up paces, Stephanie chatted briefly with Pam Campbell, who had flown in the night before to be with her husband on what might be a life-changing day.

Because the two players leading the tournament were virtual unknowns, CBS played up two major themes in the hour before the final tee time. First, someone making a move from behind: perhaps Weir, maybe Els or Vijay Singh (six shots back) or Phil Mickelson (seven back). When Mickelson drained a 45-foot birdie putt on number one, Jim Nantz immediately compared it to the 80-footer he had made at Augusta on number two back in April and wondered if this would launch a Mickelson rally. Bogeys at number three and number four quickly quelled that talk, and Mickelson limped home with a 75. His only move was backward.

CBS's second theme was history. Certainly Oak Hill and Rochester had both. Rochester had been the home of many famous Americans, including Frederick Douglass, Susan B. Anthony, and George Eastman (the founder of Eastman Kodak). It had also been home to Walter Hagen, the first truly great golf pro. The Haig had won five PGA Championships among his eleven major titles.

There was more: Lee Trevino, a Texan like Campbell, had burst onto the golf scene by winning the U.S. Open at Oak Hill in 1968. Cary Middlecoff, from Memphis like Micheel, had won the Open at Oak Hill in 1956, beating Ben Hogan, another Texan, by one shot. Hogan had called Oak Hill's first hole the most difficult opening hole he had ever played. He had bogeyed it on the final day in '56, although most people remembered the two and a half foot putt he had missed on 17 as the difference.

While CBS killed time waiting for the leaders to tee off with a tribute to Hagen and the obligatory preround interviews with the leaders, Tiger Woods was doing his very best to get out of town — no matter its history — as fast as he possibly could. He was, truth be told, simply playing out the string on Sunday, having never even sniffed contention the entire week.

"The first couple of days, you sort of kept waiting for his name to pop onto a leaderboard," Micheel said. "By Saturday night, it was pretty apparent it wasn't going to happen."

No one knew that better than Woods. He started the final day at nine over par with the usual talk swirling: "If he could shoot 61 and get to even par and the leaders went backward..."

And if cows had wings, they could fly.

Woods's game was a mess. His swing was, to put it politely, a work in progress. He had no confidence in his putting. His game was so far out of kilter that the best thing he could say about the weekend after he had birdied the 18th hole was "I'm finished."

To his credit, he kept his sense of humor. When he finally made a birdie on the 16th hole—only his sixth of the entire week—he did a fake fist pump. The two birdies on the last three holes allowed him to finish with a 73, meaning he had shot 74–72–73–73 for the week, 12 over par. That put him in a tie for 39th place, by far his worst finish as a pro in a major. He had never before finished outside the top 30.

"I made eighteen bogeys—exactly one quarter of my holes," Woods said, shaking his head when it was finally over. "Basically I spent the entire week making 10-footers for par, or, if I didn't make them, making bogey. That was pretty much the story."

One statistic the CBS people dug out was telling. In 2000, the year he had won three of four majors en route to his "Tiger Slam," which he wrapped up at the 2001 Masters, Woods had played his sixteen rounds in the four majors in a staggering 53 under par. In his six previous years as a pro, he had been over par for the year in the four majors just once: 1998, when he was going through Major Swing Change Number One and had failed to win a major. That year he was a combined seven over par in the majors. In 2003, in the midst of Swing Change Number Two, he was 18 over par in the four majors.

Woods was off the golf course, done with his interviews, and in the process of putting Oak Hill and Rochester in his rearview (airplane) mirror long before Micheel and Campbell walked onto the first tee. Other than Mickelson, just one player among those chasing had birdied the first hole—Tim Clark, another player without a tour win, who had stuffed a seven-iron to within two feet. Singh and Weir had both made bogey, and Els had made par only because his wayward drive kicked off a tree into the fairway.

Micheel could feel his heart pounding as he and Stephanie walked hand-in-hand to the tee, Stephanie peeling off to join the gallery, as he stepped inside the ropes. Campbell was up first, and his drive found the right rough. It wasn't an awful shot, but Micheel knew any shot that made it to the thick stuff about five yards off the fairway was trouble. He also knew once he saw Campbell's ball in the air that he wasn't the only person feeling Sunday nerves at a major for the first time.

Micheel stood behind his ball while he was being introduced, and when his name was announced he took a deep breath, almost like a swimmer about to enter the pool. Like most of the players, Micheel used a three-wood off the first tee. The hole is a 460-yard dogleg left. It plays shorter if you can cut the corner, but there was risk involved in that, as Weir had discovered when his tee shot ended up in the trees.

The wind had changed overnight. A cold front had blown in, dropping the temperature into the seventies, with wind gusts up to twenty miles per hour. Everyone seemed to think that a blustery day favored Campbell, who had grown up playing in the winds of west Texas. The early advantage, though, went to Micheel, whose three-wood found the left side of the fairway, leaving him with a good angle to a back right pin.

"That was a big relief, finding that fairway, because it got a lot of my nerves out right away," Micheel said. "After I hit that shot, it was like, 'Okay, let's just go play golf.' All the waiting and the talking was over. Now it was time to just go and do my job as best I possibly could."

15

The Master of Oak Hill

As it turned out, Chad Campbell's lie in the rough was so poor that he had to punch out to the fairway and still had 118 yards left to the flag for his third shot. He hit a nice wedge shot in to about 10 feet. Shaun Micheel hit an eight-iron for his second but came up a good 30 feet short.

Micheel wasn't thrilled with the shot but realized he was still off to a reasonably good start. When his birdie putt dove into the middle of the hole, he was off to a great start. Campbell missed his par putt, and in one hole Micheel had grabbed a two-shot lead. Up ahead, Tim Clark had made a second birdie at number two to get to two under, but no one else in the field was in red numbers.

In fact, the experienced players all seemed to be going the wrong way. Most surprising was Mike Weir, who had become a popular overnight pick given who was ahead of him and his Sunday play at the Masters. He began the day with five straight bogeys. By the time he finally righted himself and made a couple of birdies, it was too little, too late to make any kind of serious run.

"I hit a bad tee shot at number one and couldn't seem to get things turned around for the next hour," Weir said later. "It was a day you had to be patient, because it was a very tough golf course in the wind, and I just didn't get it done. It was disappointing because I thought I had a real opportunity."

So did Ernie Els, who made two early bogeys but then bounced back to birdie eight and nine and get to even par. But he bogeyed 10 and 12—both times from the middle of the fairway—and that about ended his chances.

As it turned out, none of the stars ever got close. The only name player to shoot the kind of subpar round the CBS announcers were practically pleading for was Jay Haas, who shot 69. But Haas had started the day seven shots back, and his sterling round simply moved him into a tie for fifth with Els, who managed a 71.

By the midway point of the round, CBS had pretty much given up on any Tiger 61s or Phil 65s or Ernie or Vijay 67s and was pumping the fact that one of four players was going to win his first major: Micheel, Campbell, Clark, or Czechoslovakian Alex Cejka, a veteran of the European Tour who the year before had decided to try his luck on the PGA Tour and had made it through Q-School at age thirty-two.

Given that the previous four majors, starting with the 2002 PGA, had been won by first-time major winners—Rich Beem, Weir, Jim Furyk, and Ben Curtis—that wasn't a unique situation. What made the story unusual was the combined number of PGA Tour wins for the four contenders: *zero*. Not one of them had ever won on the tour. Clark was the youngest at twenty-seven; Micheel the oldest at thirty-four.

The hot players early on remained Clark and Micheel. Clark birdied three of the first four holes to draw even with Campbell at three under. Micheel gave back his birdie at number two when he found the right rough and had to punch out, even though he hit an iron off the tee. That led to a bogey. He settled down to par the third and fourth and the difficult fifth. All players in contention on a Sunday at Oak Hill breathe a sigh of relief when the fifth hole is behind them.

The fifth may be the golf course's most famous hole. It has a creek running down the right side of the fairway, and in 1989, seemingly in control of the U.S. Open on Sunday, Tom Kite had found that creek, which led to a triple-bogey seven that knocked him out of the lead and allowed Curtis Strange to win his second straight Open.

Micheel was thrilled to make a par there and run to the sixth tee, where he promptly hit a near-perfect six-iron to within four feet to set up his second birdie. Campbell also hit six-iron but missed the green left, chipped to 12 feet, and missed the par putt. Micheel was now back to five under and was leading Clark by two and Campbell by three. A few holes ahead, Cejka had made the turn in one-under-par 34 to get to even par for the championship.

Once again, Micheel's two-shot lead was short-lived. His next two drives were ugly. He found the deep rough on the right at the seventh, leading to a bogey and the trees on the left at the eighth, which also led to a bogey.

CBS's Lanny Wadkins observed that the two quick swings on the tee had "come out of nowhere," but Micheel hadn't driven the ball all that well on Saturday, finding five of fourteen fairways. On seven and eight, though, he had no play except to pitch out and make certain he didn't turn a bogey into a big number. Campbell also bogeyed the seventh and appeared to be heading south. As the two men walked to the ninth tee, Micheel and Clark were tied at three under, with Campbell—three over on the day—two shots back.

Clark shot 32 on the front nine and was playing the best golf of the day. He was a South African who had gone to college at North Carolina State and had made it to the tour in 2001 after finishing third on the Nationwide Tour money list in 2000. His rookie season had lasted three tournaments because of a wrist injury, but he had come back in 2002 to make more than $632,000 and finish 107th on the money list. He was a little guy—5 foot 7 and 150 pounds—who was known for consistently hitting fairways and greens, although he was not a big hitter. When he was putting well, he was extremely dangerous, because he did not miss many greens.

If you were going to place a bet on the four players in contention at that moment, Clark would have looked awfully good. On a tough windy golf course, he had made four birdies and one bogey on the front nine and was consistently finding the fairway off the tee. But as he prepared to hit his tee shot on the 10th, Wadkins—a past PGA champion himself—noticed something.

"He's changed his preshot routine," Wadkins said. "I think this is the first sign we've seen all day of nerves from Tim Clark."

Almost on cue, Clark's drive sailed right and found a fairway bunker. It was better off there than in the rough, and Clark managed to get his second shot just on the green, although it was a good 100 feet from the flagstick. His putt from there went eight feet past the hole.

"This putt will tell us a lot about his nerves," Wadkins said, as Clark lined up the par putt. Clark had used a long putter from his college days with mixed success, and this putt never touched the hole. Bogey.

Meanwhile, Micheel had caught the kind of break a player needs to win a major championship. His drive at the ninth started left and was trying to fade back to the fairway. It hit in the high rough and, instead of burying, took a big hop and scooted onto the fairway. Even from there, making par wasn't easy. From 136 yards, Micheel hit a dead pull way left of the flag with a nine-iron, and his 60-foot birdie putt rolled 12 feet below the hole. Just when it looked like he was going to make a third straight bogey, he drilled the putt for par.

Clark then made another mistake. After a brilliant five-wood to 15 feet on the 237-yard par-three 12th, he three-putted. Once again a CBS announcer was prescient. As Clark stood, seemingly forever, over his three-foot par putt, Peter Oosterhuis said, "He almost stands over these too long."

Yup. Clark yipped the putt left, and Micheel's lead was two again. When Clark made a third straight bogey, and Micheel parred 11 and 12, Micheel seemed to be in control once again, now leading Campbell by two and Clark and Cejka by three.

There is, however, no such thing as a safe lead on the back nine at a major on Sunday, unless you are Tiger Woods and are up by five. Or ten. Clark and Campbell both birdied the par-five 13th, and Micheel did not. Now, with five holes to go, they were lined up this way—Micheel: three under; Campbell: two under; Clark: one under; Cejka: even par.

The CBS guys wondered if Cejka could post even par if that might not be good enough to win. Micheel changed that thinking with perhaps his best shot of the week at the 14th. The hole is one of those Donald Ross masterpieces, a tiny 323-yard par-four that may tempt players into trying to drive the green but is fraught with danger if a mistake is made off the tee.

Campbell, up first after his first birdie of the day, took a driver and pushed it just enough to find a bunker right of the green. Not a bad spot to be in, especially compared with some others. Micheel, refusing to try to run out the clock (impossible in golf, obviously), also took a driver. He hit a gorgeous fade that stopped on the right corner of the green, 45 feet from the hole. Nonetheless, he had a crack at an eagle or a two-putt birdie.

"That shot pumped me up a lot," Micheel said later. "I hadn't been driving the ball that well for a while, and I knew I was taking a chance when I pulled the driver, but I thought it was the time to take a chance."

Campbell actually left his bunker shot in the rough, trying to punch the ball out rather than playing a standard bunker shot. He then hit a good shot out of the high grass to six feet but missed the putt for par.

Micheel, wanting to be sure he didn't let his downhill putt wander too far past the hole, left it 10 feet short. A three-putt par would definitely be a downer. But, as he had done all week when he had to, he came up with a great putt, the ball diving straight into the hole. He was back to four under for the tournament and suddenly led Campbell and Clark by three, with four holes to go.

Prosperity, however, was not Micheel's friend on this particular Sunday. After taking so long to choose a club on the 189-yard 15th hole that he actually apologized to Campbell for the delay, he hit a seven-iron. The ball found the left corner of the green, leaving him a tricky, hard-breaking 45-foot putt. Campbell hit six-iron and was 35 feet below the hole.

Once again, Micheel left himself with some work to do when his birdie putt slid 10 feet below the hole. Given the way he had been putting, that didn't seem too daunting. Plus, even if he missed, he would still lead by two with three to play.

Except that Campbell proceeded to drill his birdie putt—the first long putt he had made all day—and Micheel's putt got a good deal longer. He put his first truly bad stroke of the day on the ball, leaving it short and left. Bogey. Two-shot swing. In golf vernacular the score was now Micheel 3, Campbell 2, Clark 1. Cejka was about to finish at even-par 280. Chances were that would not be good enough. But the ballgame was back on.

The 16th was the last real birdie hole on the golf course. It was 439 yards but was a straightforward hole that was playing straight downwind. Statistically it was the second easiest hole on the course, playing at 3.96 strokes per player on the day. Clark had just birdied it to get back to one under.

Campbell's drive found the left rough, and Micheel's the right rough. They both drew decent lies, but Micheel had a much better angle with the pin back left. Campbell found the front of the green with a pitching wedge but was 60 feet short. Micheel also hit a hard pitching wedge, and his ball skidded to a halt 20 feet below the flag. Campbell cozied his birdie putt close to the hole and tapped in safely for a par. Micheel stalked his putt for a good long while before settling over it. His putting stroke, missing a hole earlier, came back. The ball went straight into the hole. Now the score was 4–2–1.

Micheel understood the situation clearly. A CBS graphic showed that Ben Curtis's win a month earlier at Royal St. George's had made him the seventh man in history to make his first tournament victory a major championship. The first player to accomplish that feat had been Jack Nicklaus at the 1962 U.S. Open. Of course Curtis had taken it a step further, becoming the first man since Francis Ouimet to win the first major he had ever played in. Micheel, playing in his third, wasn't that far from Curtis.

On the 17th tee, Micheel took a deep breath, much as he had done on the first tee, to calm himself. This time, though, it didn't help. His drive sailed left into the deep rough. Seeing an opening, Campbell hit his best drive of the day, crushing it way down the fairway. Length was key on the 17th since the hole was 495 yards long. That was one reason why Billy Andrade had said that Micheel's closing bogeys on 17 and 18 on Saturday were almost like pars.

Micheel had little chance to make a par after his drive. He was forced to punch out of the rough and wedged safely to 30 feet. From there he two-putted for bogey. Campbell had a birdie chance, hitting a seven-iron to 25 feet, but his putt went wide and he tapped in for par.

One hole to go. Clark had missed a 15-foot birdie putt at 18 to finish at 279 — one under par. Micheel had a one-shot lead on Campbell, and he knew he had to stay out of the deep rough off the 18th tee, especially after Campbell's tee shot found the right side of the fairway, bouncing from the first cut into the short grass.

Micheel had been thinking that the golf tournament was going to come down to himself and Campbell since the 15th green. "I knew Tim was close and that Cejka was in at even, but I just thought it was going to be Chad or me," he said. "I didn't feel like it was match play until those last three holes. Then I did."

The 18th was the hardest hole on the golf course. For the day the field had averaged 4.50 strokes per man on the hole. There had been only five birdies among the 68 players who had completed the hole. Micheel just wanted to make par and force Campbell to make a birdie to tie him.

He liked the way his drive felt coming off the club, but his heart almost stopped when he saw the ball heading in the direction of the left rough. The ball hit the ground in the first cut, about a foot from the deep rough, and bounced *right,* stopping in the first cut with a good lie.

"I could see the ball from the tee after it stopped," Micheel said. "That was all I wanted. I knew if I could see it, I had to have a reasonable lie. That was a huge relief."

By now Stephanie Micheel was walking inside the ropes because it had become impossible to see from outside, and PGA officials had invited her and Pam Campbell inside so they could see and for safety's sake, especially given Stephanie's pregnancy. Seeing Shaun's ball in a safe spot, Stephanie walked with Pam to an area behind the green so they could watch their husbands hit their second shots.

"I was a mess by then," Stephanie said. "It had been such an up-and-down day, and all I could do was watch. Sometimes it's just very hard to do that."

Micheel and Campbell walked to their balls, which were identical distances from the green—each man had 174 yards to the flag according to their caddies. When his caddy, Bob Szczesny gave him the yardage, Micheel smiled. "I had 174 yards to the flag from the other side of the fairway in almost the same wind on Friday," he said. "I had no doubt that seven-iron was the right club."

There was some question about who should hit first. Micheel, knowing what he wanted to hit, had his seven-iron out of the bag and was ready to play, so—almost by default—he hit first. Campbell didn't seem to mind. Wadkins thought Micheel had made a smart move being ready to hit first.

"It wasn't smart," Micheel said. "I wish I could make that claim. I was just ready to hit my shot. I felt very good about it. The lie was good, the club was comfortable."

Almost as soon as the ball was in the air, Micheel heard Szczesny's voice. "Be right!" he yelled.

When a player or caddy says that, it isn't a reference to direction but to distance. Szczesny could see that Micheel had hit the ball perfectly, and it was headed right at the pin. The question was the distance.

"I was really surprised when I heard Bob's voice," Micheel said. "In all the time [three years] we had worked together, I don't think he had ever once put his mouth on my ball."

That's player-speak for a caddy "talking" to a ball when it is in the air.

The ball landed short and right of the flag and began rolling directly at the hole as the crowd's roar got louder and louder. "This might go in!" Nantz screamed as the ball kept rolling.

It finally stopped two inches—that's two *inches*—from the hole.

The 18th green at Oak Hill is 45 feet above the fairway. From where Micheel was standing, he could see only the top of the flag, and when the ball landed there was no way of knowing how close it might be to the hole. Standing there, Micheel could hear the roar building, and he knew he had hit a good shot, perhaps a very good one. He shook his fist, figuring at that moment that he was close enough to guarantee a par but having no idea that he had just won the championship—barring a Campbell hole out from the other side of the fairway.

"I knew from the crowd reaction that it was good, but I had no idea how good," he said. "I turned to the CBS cameraman standing there and said to him, 'How close is it?' but he didn't answer me."

Up ahead in the fairway, CBS's David Feherty, who had walked all 18 holes with Micheel and Campbell, was frantically trying to get Micheel's attention to tell him where the ball had ended up. "He told me later he was standing there holding his fingers two inches apart," Micheel said. "I didn't see him."

Campbell couldn't see the ball either, but he knew it had to be close judging by the crowd reaction. "I figured he had stuffed it from what we were hearing," he said. "I didn't know it was literally a kick in, but I knew he'd probably hit the shot of his life."

Campbell's second shot was an excellent one. It bounced right and stopped 15 feet away. It was one of the best second shots of the day at 18. It just wasn't close to being the best shot in his twosome.

When the ball was in the air, Stephanie Micheel was standing in a spot where she didn't have a clear look at the flag. As the crowd's roar grew louder, she walked forward and shrieked in joy and shock when she saw where the ball had stopped. She turned around and saw Pam Campbell standing there.

"I was so happy, but then I saw Pam, and I had no idea what to say at that moment," she said. "She was great. She put out her hand and said, 'Congratulations.' Then other people came up to me, and I didn't see her again after that."

Inside the clubhouse, Billy Andrade, who had been paired with Els on Sunday and had shot 74 to finish in a tie for 10th, had joined his family after signing his scorecard and cleaning out his locker. Jody, his wife, their two children, and Jody's sister Betsy had flown in from Atlanta to watch him play the final round.

"Because we had such a big group, we didn't go into the player-family dining area," Andrade said. "I think they may have been breaking it down by then anyway. So we went into the members dining area to get something to eat. I had seen Shaun and Chad walking off the 18th tee, and I knew the situation.

"I wanted to watch the end. By then I was pulling for Shaun, in part because I'd played with him Saturday but also because I'd been so impressed by him. He was one of those guys you could tell right away 'got it.' He was just a consummate pro and a gentleman. I really liked him right away. It wasn't anything against Chad; I just wanted to see him win.

"I had just put some food on my plate and was about to go sit down near a TV set when the place just exploded. I mean exploded. I turned around, and I saw the ball rolling right next to the hole. I just couldn't believe it. The moment of his life, he hit the shot of his life. It was the kind of moment we all dream about."

Halfway up the hill, hearing the ovation building but still not knowing where the ball was, Micheel began running. When he got to the top of the hill and the front of the green, he was stunned. "I had thought it might be three, four feet," he said. "But then I looked and I saw where it was and it hit me that I'd won. I had actually won. The place was going crazy, people cheering and shouting. I'd never heard anything like that — not for me anyway — in my life.

"Then I saw Steph on the other side of the green, and I can honestly say it was the happiest, most perfect moment of my life. I simply couldn't believe it had all happened that way.

"I turned to Bob and said, 'Think I should just go up there and knock it in left-handed?' I was joking, but he looked at me and said, 'No.' I realized how big a moment it was for him too."

Instead of tapping in left-handed, Micheel marked his ball so Campbell could putt before bedlam broke out when he tapped in. Campbell two-putted for par, giving him second place alone, a shot ahead of Clark and two ahead of Cejka.

Micheel tapped in, took one more deep breath to take in all

that had happened, and found Campbell to shake his hand. After the handshakes on the green, Stephanie came out to hug her husband. Micheel gave her a hug and a kiss and then realized there was another member of the family he wanted to kiss too. So, he bent down and kissed Stephanie's stomach, thus including Dade—who would be born on November 20—in the celebration.

It was just about as sweet a moment as anyone had witnessed in golf in a long, long time.

16

Life Begins Anew

IT ALL BEGAN TO hit Shaun Micheel when he walked into the scoring trailer. No round of tournament golf is officially complete until a player signs his scorecard. Since a player's official card is kept by the other player in his twosome, it is incumbent on a player to be absolutely certain that he checks the card carefully.

Anyone who knows anything about golf history knows there are sad stories about players failing to check their cards carefully enough and signing for incorrect scores. Once a player signs his card, the score he signs for is his official score. If he mistakenly signs for a lower score, he is disqualified. If he signs for a higher score, that becomes his score.

The most famous wrong-score incident was the Masters in 1968. In that instance, Tommy Aaron, who would go on to win the Masters five years later, was keeping Roberto De Vicenzo's scorecard. On the 17th hole, De Vicenzo made a birdie three and finished the day tied with Bob Goalby, meaning the two men would play off (in those days 18 holes on Monday) for the title.

Except that Aaron had written down a four for De Vicenzo on the 17th hole, and De Vicenzo didn't catch the mistake. He signed the card and officially finished one shot behind Goalby. Ironically, it was Goalby who never completely got over what had happened. For years he felt as though he was not treated as a true Masters champion, which was unfortunate since he had nothing to do with what had happened.

Nowadays players have plenty of backup and checkpoints to make sure nothing like that can happen. They keep their own scorecards unofficially, and there is a walking scorer with each group who records each score hole-by-hole and inputs it into the computer scoring system. Most players will check their own card, then ask the walking scorer to read them their scores hole-by-hole, then they will finally check all of that against the official card.

As soon as Micheel sat down and began going through his card, he was almost overcome by the thought that he was going to sign for a wrong score. He went through the card he had kept, the walking scorer's card (read to him from the computer), and Campbell's card. He reread the scores to himself and then read each number aloud to confirm that the numbers on the card kept by Campbell were consistent with what everyone else had. Then he sat down and wrote out his scores hole-by-hole on a blank scorecard and compared them to what was on his official card to be absolutely certain he had it right.

Finally, cautiously, he signed the card. When it was done, he sat back in his chair completely drained and exhausted. "I swear that was more nerve-racking than hitting the seven-iron on 18," Micheel said. "The guy taking the scores drew a smiley face around my score and wrote down next to it, 'First place.' That was when I started breathing again."

Having signed his card correctly, he was fitted by CBS with an interrupted feedback (IFB) earpiece, because the network was hoping to hook him up with his parents before going off the air. That never happened, in part because Micheel had taken so long to sign his card. Still wearing the IFB that would never be used, he was escorted back to the 18th green, which had now been taken over by the suits of the PGA of America, all eager for their moment on camera during the awards ceremony. M. G. Orender, the president of the PGA, was so intent on making sure his official spiel got on the air—"On behalf of the twenty-eight thousand golf professionals who make up the PGA of America and work to grow the game of golf,..."—that Micheel almost false-started on several occasions, reaching for the trophy thinking Orender was finished. Not quite.

Finally, they handed Micheel the trophy, and he happily kissed it.

Throughout the telecast, Jim Nantz had referenced the fact that Micheel was planning to take the following week off so that he and Stephanie could look for a bigger house to accommodate Dade's impending arrival. "They may have to find one with room for a trophy room too," Nantz said on several occasions.

"That Wanamaker Trophy would take up a lot of space," Lanny Wadkins added at one point.

Not exactly. The Wanamaker Trophy never leaves the possession of the PGA of America, much like the Wimbledon trophies, which are handed out on center court, then instantly taken away from the champions and returned to their case once the new names have been engraved on them. Like Furyk and Curtis, Micheel would have the option of having a smaller (90 percent) version of the trophy made for his trophy room at a cost of about $40,000.

After the ceremony, Micheel went through his postround media paces and returned to the clubhouse for a toast from the Oak Hill members and the PGA of America (fortunately, all twenty-eight thousand men and women who work to grow the game were not present). Then he and Stephanie had to retrieve their luggage from their courtesy car because they were turning it in, a decent trade since the PGA had a chauffered limousine ready to take its place.

"It was a little bit eerie when we went to the car," Micheel said. "It was probably ten o'clock—at least—by then, and the lot was completely empty except for our car, which was parked at the far end because I'd been the last one to get there, being in the last group. It felt like we had parked the car about a year earlier, not nine or ten hours earlier."

Everything was piled into the limo, and Shaun and Stephanie and a friend from Memphis who had flown in to fly them home joined them. As soon as they were in the car, it occurred to Shaun and Stephanie that neither one of them had eaten since before the round had started. "We were starving," Shaun said. "It was 10:30 on Sunday night. There weren't a lot of options. And I knew room service at the hotel would be closed when we got back."

They found a Wendy's, and the limo driver went through the drive-through window. "How he maneuvered that thing around those turns and through the lane and got the food, I'll never know," Micheel said, laughing. "I do think it was the best-tasting meal I've ever had."

There were still quite a few people in the hotel lobby when they got back, and everyone began to clap when the Micheels walked in. People in the bar heard what was going on and came pouring out to join in.

"That was another really cool moment," Micheel said. "It all felt so great that night. It still hadn't occurred to me how much my life was going to change. Looking back now, it was a little bit like what my dad said after I made it through Q-School in '93, that I had jumped higher than I expected to jump and the landing might be hard. All I'd wanted to do was win a tournament. The thought of how winning a major would affect my life had never crossed my mind."

All their plans had changed. Because he was now the PGA champion, Micheel had qualified for the World Golf Championship event the following week in Akron. That meant the house hunting would have to be postponed. They flew home on

Monday—Micheel's friend let him fly the plane most of the way—and did laundry.

"I'd been away for most of four weeks," Micheel said. "It actually felt good to do something mundane and normal."

But there wasn't much mundane and normal about the next few days. While Micheel was doing the laundry, his cell phone rang. It was Paul Stanley, the lead guitarist for the rock group KISS. Micheel had been a KISS fan since boyhood and had met members of the band once during a tournament in Greensboro. He had become friendly with some of the band members, and since the band's manager was a big golf fan, they had exchanged numbers.

Stanley wanted to know if Micheel wanted to come to their concert in Columbus on Tuesday night. Since Micheel was going to be a couple of hours down the road in Akron, he said absolutely. When the folks at PGA Tour Productions, who were trying to line up a show segment with Micheel, found out, they asked if they could film Micheel hanging out with the band. Sure, come on ahead, was the response.

In a matter of forty-eight hours Micheel had gone from being the 169th-ranked golfer in the world to a major champion hanging out backstage with the members of his all-time favorite band.

He played reasonably well in Akron, finishing tied for 23rd. Three of the four newly minted major champions finished within a shot of one another: Micheel and Weir both shot 281 (one over par), and Ben Curtis ended up one stroke in back of them, a pretty good performance considering he spent Saturday evening getting married. Jim Furyk, who almost never finished out of the top 10 any week, tied for sixth.

It was in Akron that the changes in Micheel's life began to hit him. His agent, Richard Gralitzer, had flown in to talk about all the new opportunities that were suddenly showing up on his radar. He was as much a friend as he was an agent, an accountant by trade who also handled Micheel's business for him. Until the seven-iron landed on the 18th green at Oak Hill, that hadn't been too difficult a job. Now, Gralitzer's life had changed too.

"We were in my car talking about everything that was going on, and all of a sudden Richard started to lose it," Micheel said. "He's a guy with a family who had never traveled much as my representative because, to be honest, there wasn't much need for it. Now, all of a sudden, people want a meeting here one week, there another week, and his phone won't stop ringing. He just said, 'Shaun, I honestly don't know if I can do this. It may just be too much to handle.'"

"I felt bad for him because I knew he wanted to do the right thing and do what was best for me. But I don't think he ever expected to be in this situation—representing someone who had won a major championship. It occurred to me in the car that my life had changed and the lives of a lot of other people had changed because of what happened at Oak Hill. Up until then, I'd been vaguely aware of it, but I was kind of joyriding.

"You know, hang out with KISS—cool. Have people want to talk to you in the media room—great. Sign more autographs than ever—fine. But this was different. This was sort of real life starting to kick in. I mean, the fact that people now wanted to pay me to do a lot more things was, obviously, a good thing. But it began to occur to me that it wasn't quite as simple as it might have looked when I was watching other guys go through it."

One guy who was going through it but on a different level was Furyk. He had already been considered an elite player before he won the U.S. Open, but he remembered what it had been like to come close to winning majors early in his career, even though he hadn't won one then.

"I know this sounds strange, but I almost felt sorry for Ben

[Curtis] and Shaun," Furyk said. "I mean, that's such a huge jump from never having won, especially for Ben as a rookie, to being a major champion. It's like trying to jump up ten steps on a ladder by skipping the first nine. I can only imagine how overwhelming it was for them."

Ben and Candace did hold their wedding as planned on August 23 in spite of all the "opportunities" IMG had to turn down on their behalf as a result. But Ben's new notoriety forced them to make changes. Everyone who was invited was sent a note asking them to please bring their invitations because they thought crashers were not only possible but likely—especially paparazzi.

On the way from the church to the reception, Candace looked up and saw a local news helicopter hovering above them. "We had to have the limo go around the block to a back entrance so we could avoid the photographers," she said. "A month earlier, no one had heard of Ben. Now it seemed as if everyone wanted a piece of him. It was really hard. We're two quiet kids from the Midwest. We aren't stars. We just wanted to enjoy the day with our friends."

In the meantime, IMG had convinced Curtis that he should try to play on both the PGA Tour and the European Tour in 2004. As a British Open winner, he was exempt on both tours, and European tournaments were allowed to pay appearance fees. Sure, it would mean a lot of travel, but Curtis could now afford to fly first class, and seeing Europe would be fun.

"It wasn't a decision that was all bad," Curtis said. "I think Candace and I did enjoy a lot of the traveling and the sightseeing. We didn't have kids yet, so it was fun. But it probably wasn't very good for my golf."

All four major winners were adapting to new lives as 2003 wound down and, for the most part, enjoying themselves. Each had had the best year of his life on the golf course, thanks in large part to his major victory.

Furyk finished the year fourth on the PGA Tour money list with more than $5.1 million in earnings. He won again—at the Buick Open—in July to, he felt, kind of back up his Open win. That victory was his ninth on the PGA Tour and put him in a position, at age thirty-three, where thinking he could rack up the kind of numbers that would make him a candidate for the Hall of Fame someday was certainly not unreasonable.

Weir finished one spot behind Furyk on the money list, winning just under $5 million. He didn't win again after the Masters, but adding a tie for third at the Open and a tie for seventh at the PGA made him a legitimate candidate for Player of the Year. He would have been a lock winner if he had been able to catch Micheel on the last day of the PGA.

The voters went instead with—surprise—Tiger Woods, who won five times in spite of playing (for him) poorly in the majors. One year after going 1, 1, T-28, 2 in the four majors, Woods went T-15, T-20, T-4, T-39. In truth, Woods probably would have traded his year for Weir's year in an instant, because one of Weir's three wins was a major. But the voters went with quantity—and the Woods name—over quality and gave Woods the award for a fifth straight year.

Curtis finished 46th on the money list with $1.4 million, $1.1 million of that coming from the British Open. He had always had a reputation as a player who was very good when at his best, and there was no better example of that than the week at Royal St. George's.

Micheel won a little more than $1.8 million for the year and finished 32nd on the money list, by far his highest finish ever. For him, the fall was truly a joyride because he didn't have to sweat out making enough money to keep his card for the next year. All four players were exempt through 2008 thanks to their major victories. (Once upon a time, the exemption for winning a major had been ten years, but the tour had cut it in half because a lot of players believed that major winners sometimes lost their incentive when given such a long exemption.)

All four gathered in Hawaii in early December for an event called the "Grand Slam of Golf." It was a 36-hole event put on by the PGA of America for the four major champions each year. Of course in 2001 Woods had won three of the majors, and in 2002 he had won two of them. A points system based on performance in the majors by nonwinners determines the other participants in years like that.

The Grand Slam was held on the island of Kauai, Hawaii, at a resort golf course. Furyk, who owned a home on Maui, brought his family. Weir did too. Ben and Candace Curtis came, but Micheel came without Stephanie. Dade had been born two weeks earlier, and it was too early for Stephanie and the baby to travel.

"I really had mixed feelings about being there," Micheel said. "We were in this gorgeous place, and I had a spectacular room. When I walked in, I called Stephanie and, without thinking, started telling her how beautiful it all was. She said, 'You know, I really don't want to hear how beautiful it is there.'

"It hit me that she was missing out on something really cool, and I wished she could have been there. The timing just didn't work out."

Furyk won the event easily, beating Weir by eight shots, Micheel by 10, and Curtis by 11. No one was terribly concerned about the quality of their golf that week. It was all just another reward for what each had accomplished earlier in the year. For Furyk, there was one other piece of good news: when they gave him the trophy, no one told him that he had to have it engraved himself.

It was the perfect end—or close to it—to what had felt like a perfect year for all four men. Their futures had never seemed brighter.

"All I could think at the end of that year was 'I can't wait for next year,'" Weir remembered. "I really wanted to see if I could do it again. When you've done it once and had that feeling, you really want it again. I had every reason to believe I was capable of doing it again. I'm sure all four of us felt that way."

17

Still Champions

IT WAS A WARM September night in Atlanta, the humidity still hanging in the air even after the sun had set. Shaun Micheel stood outside a downtown steak house looking relaxed in blue jeans, checking in at home with Stephanie to see how the kids were doing. He would have some dinner, then get to bed at a reasonable hour because he had an early tee time in the morning.

The 2009 Tour Championship was being played a few miles east of downtown Atlanta, at East Lake Golf Course, a wonderful old layout that had once been a favorite haunt of Bobby Jones. Throughout the old-style, rebuilt clubhouse were pictures and photos of Jones during his heyday as the world's greatest player in the 1920s.

The closest Micheel would be to East Lake during the Tour Championship had come earlier in the day when his plane had flown almost directly over the golf course as it landed at Harts-field International Airport. Down below, the top-30 players in the FedEx Cup points standings for the year were playing the first round of the Tour Championship on a course soggied by torrential rainstorms earlier in the week.

Micheel had played in sixteen tournaments in '09 and had earned $257,590. That put him in 169th place on the FedEx points list, meaning he was nowhere close to making the newly

invented (as of 2007) playoffs that the top 125 point/money winners qualified for. He was also in no position even to compete for
a spot among the thirty players who made the Tour Championship—the last of the four tournaments that the tour was now
calling "the playoffs."

There were some pretty good reasons for Micheel's limited
play and—by tour standards—limited earnings for the year. To
begin with, he hadn't played in his first tournament until March,
because he was rehabbing after major shoulder surgery the previous June. He had held off on the surgery repeatedly, hoping the
pain in his shoulder would subside. It hadn't, though, and by the
time spring rolled around, other players could literally hear his shoulder snap, crackle, and pop when he swung the golf club. He hung
on until the tour came to Memphis, gritting his teeth and missing
the cut by one shot, then had the surgery on June 10.

"Looking back, I wasn't very smart," Micheel said on that
warm night in Atlanta. "I kept playing when I really couldn't play.
Every tournament I played, I was giving up a tournament that I
could play in when I was healthy after the surgery."

Once injuries shut a player down for the year, the tour gives
him a medical extension whenever he returns, which allows him
to, in essence, combine two years into one year. Micheel had
played in sixteen tournaments before shutting down in 2008 and
had earned $157,828, making only six cuts. At year's end, Martin
Laird had finished 125th on the money list, earning $857,752,
making him the last player off the money list to be fully exempt.
So when Micheel returned in 2009, he was allotted thirteen
tournaments—since when healthy in 2007 he had played in a
total of twenty-nine—to make up the difference between Laird's
money and the money he had made before his surgery in order to
remain fully exempt.

"The timing couldn't have been worse," Micheel said, shaking
his head. "I'm going into the last year of the exemption I got [five

years] for winning the PGA. I asked the tour if I could just roll that year over to 2009 if I didn't play. The answer was no. It was also the last year I was exempt into the Masters, the [U.S.] Open, and the British [Open]. I wanted to play in them. But I missed the cut at the Masters and couldn't play in the other two. Then, when I did come back, I could feel the clock ticking. Thirteen tournaments to make enough money, then twelve, then eleven."

The comeback actually began well. On a sparkling Thursday morning in Palm Beach, Micheel teed it up at the Honda Classic. He had joked with friends that he couldn't understand why his return to the tour hadn't received quite as much publicity as Tiger Woods's return from knee surgery the week before in Tucson.

"I think Golf Channel is doing a special on my comeback too," he said, laughing. "It's going to air at three o'clock in the morning on New Year's Eve."

He was touched by the number of players who went out of their way to welcome him back but a little bit surprised when several said, "Shaun, where've you been? We haven't seen you for a while."

"Okay, I'm not exactly Tiger Woods," Micheel said. "But all the golf publications did mention that I was having shoulder surgery when I had it done and that I'd be out for the rest of the year." He shook his head. "I guess it proves the old adage out here about life on tour: if you shoot 75, half the guys are happy and the other half wish you'd shot 76."

Micheel's first competitive round of golf in nine months began as well as he could possibly have hoped. He walked onto the first tee shortly after eight o'clock in the morning along with Joe Ogilvie and Jonathan Byrd. "Two guys I really like," he said later. "A great first-day-back pairing for me because I knew I'd be relaxed playing with them. I didn't want to be in one of the glamour groups. I wasn't ready for that."

Even with two players he was comfortable with and no more

than a dozen people watching (Stephanie among them), Micheel could feel his heart pounding as he was introduced. "I think I was more nervous right there than on the first tee on Sunday at the PGA," he said. "I just had no idea what was going to happen or what kind of golf I was going to play."

His opening tee shot faded into a fairway bunker, but from there he hit a gorgeous six-iron to six feet and made the putt for birdie. That got a lot of the butterflies out. Then he birdied the next two holes and was actually at the top of the leaderboard less than an hour into the beginning of his comeback.

"You know, if you make 72 straight birdies you're going to win the tournament by about 66 shots," Ogilvie joked as they walked onto the fourth tee. "You're making this look way too easy."

Of course it was never going to be that easy. Micheel managed to hang on to shoot an even-par 70 that day, making a nice up and down from a back bunker on 18. He shot 71 the next day, but made the cut—PGA National, where the Honda is held, is one of the tour's tougher courses—at one over par. The weekend was routine: nothing great happened; nothing horrible happened. Ogilvie's call that 72 straight birdies would win the tournament by 66 shots proved spot-on—Y. E. Yang, who would go on to make a major name for himself later in the year, was the winner at nine under par. Micheel finished in a tie for 52nd place at four over par.

"It's a start," Micheel said. "There were times last year both before and after the surgery when I questioned whether I even wanted to play golf again. I felt worn out, tired—tired really of not playing well—and I was getting ready to turn forty [January '09]. I just thought to myself, 'I'm a college graduate; I'm a pretty smart guy. There must be something else I can do.'

"I even started to write a book. I sat down when I was on vacation with my family right after the surgery and tried writing for a few days. Then I looked at what I'd written and thought, 'Why would anyone want to read this?' Then a few days later, I started thinking, 'Your life's been pretty interesting; maybe you should give it another shot?' But I didn't. I've just been all over the map.

"I know I do love golf, and I love competing. So this is where I belong. The question now is, can I stay out here? Time will tell I guess."

Micheel paused and leaned back in his chair. "One thing I can tell you for sure," he said. "That day at Oak Hill, the feeling I had walking up on the 18th green and seeing my ball right next to the cup, feels like it was about a million years ago."

THE SAME COULD BE said, for varying reasons, about all eight men who either won major championships in 2003 or came achingly close.

None of them has won a major since that year. Jim Furyk twice had chances to win a second U.S. Open title. In 2006 at Winged Foot, he had a five-foot par putt at the 18th hole that ultimately would have landed him in a playoff with Geoff Ogilvy had he made it. He looked at the putt from every possible angle, stepped up to it, backed off (as he always did in his routine), stepped up again, and then backed off again.

"I just couldn't get comfortable over it," Furyk said later. "I didn't feel as if I had the line. I kept looking at it, trying to be absolutely sure I had it right and never felt as if I did. As it turns out, I was right. I never did figure it out."

The putt slid past the hole, and Furyk could do nothing but watch in frustration while Colin Montgomerie and Phil Mickelson both imploded with double bogeys on the 18th hole, leaving Ogilvy one shot ahead of all three of them. The difference, as it turned out, was Ogilvy's ability to par the final hole.

A year later, at Oakmont, Furyk was again in position to win. He walked onto the 17th tee tied for the lead with Angel Cabrera, one shot ahead of Tiger Woods. Two pars would almost certainly get him into a playoff. But there was no scoreboard on the 17th tee, and Furyk thought he was a shot behind Cabrera. He knew his best birdie chance was the short par-four 17th, so he pulled his driver and tried to reach the green. The ball sailed left into a bunker, leaving Furyk with a nearly impossible shot. He ended up making bogey and again missed playing off by one shot, finishing in a tie for second with Woods, behind Cabrera.

"I can honestly say that if I hadn't won in '03, those two losses would have been completely devastating," Furyk said. "They still hurt because you only get so many chances to win majors in your career, but they didn't hurt quite as much because when I walked into my house, the '03 trophy [Furyk did have a replica made after finishing his engraving chores] was still there. I would like to win again before I'm done, but it does take some pressure off knowing they can't take that one away, regardless of what I do or don't do in the future."

The other player in the group who had a serious chance to win a major was Chad Campbell. Undeterred by his loss to Micheel at Oak Hill, Campbell had gone on to win his first PGA Tour event later that year. The Tour Championship was a good tournament to win, not a major but an impressive victory over an elite field nonetheless. He won again (Bay Hill) in 2004 and added victories in 2006 and 2007. In his quiet way, he had become one of the tour's better players.

He even did a commercial that emphasized his quiet nature. In it, Campbell looks into the camera and says, "They say if you're good, you don't need to talk about it." After a pause and a smile he adds, "Maybe that's why I don't talk that much."

Still, the major that his fellow players had predicted for him in 2003 had eluded him. He led the Masters after 36 holes in 2006, then finished tied for third, as Phil Mickelson (who had finally won his first major in '04 at Augusta) blew everyone away on Sunday to win his second green jacket.

Three years later, Campbell had an even better chance at the Masters. He opened the tournament with a 65 to take the lead and still had the lead at nine-under-par 135 after 36 holes. He dropped back to third after 54 holes but trailed the leaders — Cabrera, who had been largely invisible since his win at the '07 Open, and Kenny Perry — by just two shots.

After 16 holes on Sunday, it was Perry's tournament to win. He led both Cabrera and Campbell (who had shot a final-round 69) by two shots. But he made nervous bogeys on 17 and 18 to fall into a three-way tie with Cabrera and Campbell.

In a rare concession to television, the Masters had slightly altered its playoff format beginning in 2005. Instead of going to the tenth tee — the way Weir and Mattiace had in 2003 — the players returned to the 18th tee. TV has always preferred an 18th-hole finish to tournaments, and some regular tour events just keep sending the players back to replay the 18th until someone wins. The Lords of Augusta wouldn't go quite that far. They started the playoff on the 18th, but if it didn't end there, the players then moved over to the 10th tee.

Playing the 18th, Cabrera pushed his drive into the trees that had brought Len Mattiace grief six years earlier; like Mattiace, he had no choice but to punch out. Perry found the fairway on the left side, but his second shot landed in the left bunker. Campbell, having driven the ball perfectly down the right side, appeared to have a clear advantage as he stood over a seven-iron for his second shot. But his nerves came into play, the ball fading into the right bunker.

With no one on the green in regulation, Cabrera hit a wedge to six feet. Perry, who hadn't hit a green since birdieing the 16th in regulation, hit a perfect bunker shot to inside a foot, giving him a kick-in for par. Campbell hit a good bunker shot too, leaving himself four feet. Cabrera made his par putt, and Campbell then had to make *his* par putt to stay alive. He missed.

Cabrera and Perry moved onto the 10th, where Perry hit his second shot to almost the same spot Mattiace had hit his second shot three years earlier, leaving him with a similarly almost impossible up and down. When he bogeyed the hole and Cabrera parred it, Cabrera had his second major title.

By then, Campbell was wrapping up his postround conversation with the media. "In a way, this one hurts more than the PGA," he said. "At least at the PGA I played the 18th hole well, gave myself a shot at a birdie. Shaun [Micheel] just hit a great shot there. Here, I feel like I did it to myself. It's disappointing."

Other than Furyk, Micheel had come closest to a repeat major victory, finishing second at the PGA at Medinah in 2006, although he never had a real chance to win. Someone named Woods beat him by five shots and beat everyone else by more than that.

"I was the winner in the mortal division that week," Micheel said, laughing. "I really felt as if I played just about as well as I did at Oak Hill. I made the exact same number of birdies [21]. It was just that Tiger was being Tiger that week. When he plays like that, no one beats him. It reminded me that I was fortunate that he was a nonfactor in '03 when he was going through his swing change."

Woods had failed to win a major in 2004 too, stretching his winless streak to ten by the end of that year. If anything, he played worse in 2004 than he had in 2003. He won only one tournament (the match play) and, for the first time since 1998, he didn't win the Player of the Year title; Vijay Singh did. The major champions in '04 were a bit more glamorous than in '03: Mickelson finally had his breakthrough at the Masters (catching Ernie Els down the stretch); Retief Goosen won his second U.S. Open title in four years at Shinnecock, outdueling Mickelson down the stretch; Todd Hamilton, who did fit the unknown mold, beat Els in a playoff at the British Open; and Singh won his third major title, winning a playoff from Justin Leonard and Chris DiMarco to take the PGA.

Woods started to become Woods again when he beat DiMarco (a hard-luck player in majors if there has ever been one) in the first Masters playoff that began at number 18 (Woods won it with a birdie after bogeying the hole minutes earlier). He then went on to win five of the next thirteen majors to up his total to fourteen prior to undergoing knee surgery in 2008. He also finished second in four majors during that stretch. That meant that after going zero for ten from the middle of 2002 through the end of 2004, with one second-place finish (at the '02 PGA before he really began overhauling his swing), Woods went six for fourteen and was in the top two ten times in fourteen majors. His other four finishes were a tie for fourth at the '05 PGA, a tie for third at the '06 Masters, a missed cut at the U.S. Open in '06 (his first tournament back after his father's death), and a tie for 12th at the '07 British Open.

That consistency meant one thing: players constantly had to be looking over their shoulders for Woods, and it had not been that way in '03 and '04. "It was definitely a period in time when the rest of us had an opportunity," Mike Weir said, smiling. "I'm just happy when I had the chance, I was able to take it. Because there's no guarantee for any of us that a chance like that is going to come again."

Which is why looking back on 2003 is so difficult for the four runners-up: Mattiace, Leaney, Bjorn, and Campbell. Of the four, the only one still playing at a consistently high level is Campbell. The other three are still searching for the magic, or near magic, that each found six years ago. It is easier said than done.

"When you know you've been good enough to get to that level, it's much tougher to accept not being there," Mattiace said quietly one day in 2009. "That's why, even though it's been six years, it's still tough for me to talk about Augusta. In a lot of ways, it was the absolute highlight of my golf career. But bringing back the memories, conjuring that Sunday up again in my mind, is very, very hard."

He paused and looked off into the distance. "It's just all so... personal," he finally said. "Maybe someday, it won't feel quite like that."

Maybe someday. But not quite yet.

18

Dealing with It All

As 2004 BEGAN, FEW golfers in the world felt better about their games than Mike Weir did. He'd had a remarkable 2003 and would arrive at Augusta in April as the defending champion, a role he cherished. He was thirty-three and, he believed, starting into the peak years of his career.

After the Masters victory and his huge year financially — on and off the golf course — he and Bricia talked about building a new house or buying one. But they liked where they were, so instead they settled for some renovations to give themselves a little more space. Mike had passed up a number of off-season opportunities that would have involved going overseas to play for big appearance fees.

"I was already making a lot of money," he said. "I just didn't see any reason to chase anymore, especially when it meant being away from my family. I didn't make any real lifestyle changes other than to fly privately more often. Usually when I did that, it was to give myself extra time with the kids — either leaving a little bit later for a tournament or trying to get home Sunday night when I couldn't do it flying commercially. I felt like I had things pretty well under control, to tell you the truth."

The year began well. After not playing up to his expectations in his first two tournaments — finishing tied for only 41st in defense of his title at the Bob Hope—Weir got on a roll not unlike the one he had been on for most of '03. He finished tied for fifth in Phoenix, tied for fourth at Pebble Beach, and then successfully defended the title he had won a year earlier in Los Angeles.

But, as Greg Norman often says, there's a reason why golf is a four-letter word. When the tour shifted from the West Coast to the East Coast, Weir felt as if he had left his swing and his putting stroke out West. He missed the cut at the Players Championship and then finished tied for 45th in Atlanta, the week before the Masters.

"I didn't arrive in Augusta brimming with confidence," Weir said. "I felt like I needed to find something in my swing before Thursday. I was defending my title, and I wanted to play well. So, I did what I normally do when I feel that way: I went to the range and worked."

He was out there late Tuesday afternoon, hitting ball after ball, while caddy Brennan Little and teacher Mike Wilson watched. "I completely lost track of the time," Weir said. "All of a sudden, I noticed the range was getting pretty empty, and I looked at my watch and it was 6:30. I thought 'Oh my God. I'm hosting the Champions Dinner in thirty minutes, and I'm pouring sweat.'

"I ran into the clubhouse and up to the champions locker room. I got out of my clothes and headed into the shower. There was just one problem: there's only one shower up there, and Tom Watson was in it. Arnold Palmer and Jack Nicklaus were sitting there waiting their turn. I couldn't exactly ask those guys to let me cut in front of them."

Weir managed to get showered and to the dinner just in time to greet his guests. It was one of the more memorable nights of his life. "Just to look around that room and see all those guys and realize I was part of their club now and for the rest of my life, it gave me chills," he said. "The storytelling that goes on in there is unbelievable.

"Sam Snead had died two years earlier, so a lot of the guys told some of the stories that Sam would always tell. They were price-less—also not repeatable in polite company."

As it turned out, the dinner was the highlight of the week for Weir. He continued to fight his swing on Thursday and shot 79–71 to miss the cut by one shot. "It was a huge letdown," he said. "It wasn't as if I went in there thinking, 'I'm going to win this thing again,' especially given that I didn't feel all that good about my game at that moment. I was just terrible on Thursday. I was tight, nervous, as if I had to prove myself somehow. Friday I finally loosened up and played better, but it was too little, too late. To not play the weekend hurt. Plus, I had to stick around until Sunday to present the green jacket. When you miss a cut, any cut, the last thing you want to do is hang around while everyone else is playing and you're not."

He didn't let up on his search for his swing or his putting stroke after Augusta, and, as always seemed to be the case, he eventu-ally found what he was looking for. He played well at the U.S. Open at Shinnecock, finishing tied for fourth, and had a solid British Open at Troon, finishing tied for ninth. That gave him five top-10 finishes in seven majors, a good run for any player not named Tiger Woods.

Through it all, Weir was trying to adapt to his new life as a Masters champion. Even though he had no trouble saying no to overseas temptations, Weir had to say yes to extra days on the road his sponsors wanted to add to his schedule, because he was now being paid a lot more money by them than in the past.

"A lot of little things added up fast," he said. "There were extra days for the sponsors, which meant more days away from home, and sometimes meant that my schedule on a playing week was more hectic. If I can plan ahead, I'm fine. But I was getting a lot of 'Mike, have you got five minutes,' when I was on the range. You don't want to say no to guys and act like you're big-timing them, especially guys you know, but it's never five minutes.

"When I got to the British Open, someone told me that a lot of the guys in the Canadian media, who had covered me long before I won the Masters, were upset because they thought I was blowing them off. I talked to all of them, and they said I hadn't been returning phone messages that they had left at my office.

"I'm not sure what was happening, whether the people who represented me just started deciding on their own what messages to pass on and what messages not to pass on, but I hadn't been getting messages. I was upset about it, and I told the guys I would get it straightened out, which I did. But I'm sure they thought I was the bad guy in all of it, and it upset me, because I'd always had a very good relationship with all of them."

Six weeks after the British, Weir had a chance to win the tournament that, next to the four majors, is the one he would most like to win: the Canadian Open. "It's definitely my fifth major," he said. "Every year up there, I feel tremendous pressure, because I know how badly people want me to win."

Bricia Weir could feel her husband's tension too. "On the one hand, it's really wonderful that people up there care so much about how he plays and enjoy his successes," she said. "On the other hand, I know he feels like he's carrying the hopes of the entire country, because there are times when that's exactly how it feels.

"When we're home in Salt Lake, Mike gets recognized some of the time when we're out. But in Canada, it seems as if everyone recognizes him. When he's up there, for him it's a lot like it must be like for Tiger everywhere. It's as if he's Mr. Canada."

Even when Weir was not playing, there were moments that made Bricia nervous. One afternoon when Mike was home, someone rang the doorbell. Living in a gated community, the Weirs didn't often have unexpected guests. Mike answered the door, and standing there was a man with a Masters flag in his hand, wanting Mike to sign it for him.

"He was flying through Salt Lake and had a three-hour layover," Bricia said. "He knew Mike wasn't playing that week, and he figured out where we lived, got someone to get him through the gate, and then asked people which house was ours. He was a perfectly nice guy, but it was kind of weird. It bothered me that it was that easy for someone to find our front door like that."

Weir took off the week prior to Canada in 2004 to go home and work with Wilson on his swing and his short game. Although he had played pretty well in the important summer events, he still wasn't thrilled with his swing. He arrived in Toronto feeling better about it and proceeded to play better than he ever had before in his "home" event.

By the time Sunday rolled around, Weir found himself battling Vijay Singh for the lead. The crowds were massive and roared every time Weir took the club back. "It was amazing," he said. "They just so wanted to see a Canadian win up there."

It had been fifty years since Pat Fletcher had won the tournament, and no Canadian had won since then. Even George Knudson, arguably the best player Canada had produced prior to Weir, never won in his home country. Now, with Weir battling Singh, the tension grew at every hole.

When Weir birdied the eighth hole to take a one-shot lead, the place was going crazy. Moments later, as Weir walked down the path from the ninth green to the tenth tee, an overzealous fan reached out to give his shoulder a good-luck squeeze and caught him just as he had gone past.

"The security guys were in front and in back of me," Weir said. "We needed a lot of security to get from the greens to the tees. This guy was to the side of me, and he reached across the ropes and, trying to grab my shoulder, kind of pulled me backward. I turned to try to get loose, and my spikes caught. I felt this shooting pain in my shoulder, but I just kept going.

"I didn't feel much pain after that first moment. I had a lot of adrenaline going, so I really didn't think much about it other than to wonder what in the world the guy was thinking doing something like that. It was annoying but nothing more."

Weir played well on the back nine and had a great chance to win. He three-putted the 16th hole after trying too hard to make a 15-foot downhill birdie putt but still had a one-shot lead coming to 18. He needed to make a six-foot par putt to win—and missed it by an inch. "That one hurt because I thought I'd hit a perfect putt," Weir said. "When it came off the putter, I thought I'd won. It didn't feel a lot different than the one I made at 18 at Augusta—except it didn't go in."

After missing a five-foot birdie putt on the second playoff hole that would have given him the victory, he ended up losing the playoff to Singh on the third hole. Even Singh, who rarely shows any emotion or feelings, understood how disappointing the loss was for Weir. When the two men shook hands, he said softly, "I'm really sorry."

So was Weir, who had been convinced he was destined to win. As disappointing as the loss was, the worst was yet to come. Over the next few days and weeks, it became apparent that the jerk who had jerked his shoulder had done some damage.

"It hurt, but it wasn't as if the pain was overwhelming," Weir said. "I could still play, could still swing the club. But without knowing it, I was compensating, changing my swing to deal with the pain. I should have gotten it looked at a lot sooner than I did, but I was thinking I needed to be a man and play through it."

There were moments when he was able to do that. A final-round 67 at Pebble Beach early in '05 allowed him to finish second, four shots behind Phil Mickelson. He played solidly at

Augusta, making up for the missed cut in '04 by finishing tied for fifth. But nothing was easy. When he played well, it was usually because he was "short-gaming it to death," getting up and down all over the place to score better than he was hitting the ball.

He was missing cuts too, something he rarely did. By year's end, he had missed nine cuts, only four fewer than he had missed in the previous four years combined.

He reached a nadir at the British Open, the tournament he had probably most looked forward to that year because it was his first chance to play at St. Andrews. Knowing that Jack Nicklaus was planning to make it his last competitive event, Weir had called Nicklaus in the spring to ask if he could play a practice round with him over there. Nicklaus had told him he would arrange everything, and they would play on Tuesday.

Which they did: Nicklaus, Tom Watson, Kenny Perry, and Weir. The crowds as they worked their way around the Old Course felt like Sunday at a major. Everyone wanted to see Nicklaus and Watson together. Perry and Weir were pretty much along for the ride, but they loved every second of it.

"When we got to 18, we took pictures on the Swilcan Bridge. Then when we got near the green, Kenny and I just stayed back so Jack and Tom could walk on the green together," Weir said. "It was just incredible. I could see they both had tears in their eyes, and I know Kenny and I did too. It was magical."

The only down part of the day was Weir's play. "Jack and I played against Tom and Kenny," Weir said. "The only reason the match was even close was because Jack held us in there. It was discouraging having to be carried by a sixty-five-year-old man, even if it was Jack Nicklaus.

"When we finished, though, I was inspired. Mike [Wilson] and I went to the range and worked, and I was convinced I was going to play well. Then I went out and missed the cut by a mile."

Weir shot 76–75 and never had a chance to play the last two

304 • JOHN FEINSTEIN

days, the cut coming at 146. It was the sixth time in seven tournaments since the Masters that he had failed to make the weekend.
The only exception had been the U.S. Open, where he tied for
42nd place. Weir had steam coming out of his ears after he signed
his scorecard. Lorne Rubinstein, who wrote for the Toronto *Globe
and Mail* and had known Weir his entire pro career, was waiting
for him. Weir was in no mood to talk to anyone, but he wasn't
going to say no to Rubinstein.

Rubinstein asked the usual questions, and Weir gave the usual
answers about his disappointing play. Then Rubinstein threw out
a comment in the form of a question that stunned Weir.

"There are some people who think you aren't trying as hard,
working as hard, practicing as much as you used to," he said. "You
think there's anything to that?"

Weir likes Rubinstein and respects his understanding of golf.
But he was really angered by the comment. "You think I don't
work hard enough?" he said, his voice as cold as ice. "Follow me
around for a while, then tell me what you think. I really can't
believe you'd say that after all the years you've known me. That's
not who I am, and you know it."

With that, he stalked away as angry as he could remember
being in a long time. He spent most of the evening thinking about
what could possibly be wrong with his golf game. He thought
blaming it on the shoulder pain was excuse making. It had to be
something else. He finally called Mike Wilson on the phone and
asked him if they could meet on the range early the next morning.

"I wanted to get out early so I wouldn't be in the way of the
guys still in the tournament when they got there to warm up,"
Weir said. "But I didn't want to fly home in the mood I was in. A
lot of my family was over, so I was going to stay until Sunday anyway. I thought working with Mike would help."

It didn't. Wilson kept making suggestions, Weir kept hitting
balls all over the empty range, and finally Weir couldn't take it

anymore. "I just told Mike to leave the range, to leave me alone out there," he said. "I didn't want to talk to anyone, listen to anyone. I just wanted to be by myself and hit some balls. He left, and I stayed there and kept beating balls until guys started to show up. It didn't get any better, so I just got out of there."

He spent the afternoon with his family, then flew home. He finally went to have someone look at the shoulder. There was nothing major wrong, nothing that needed surgery, but there was soreness that had been caused by the shoulder being wrenched that day in Canada. Someone recommended a chiropractor in Salt Lake City, and Weir began getting treatments. He could feel the difference almost right away.

He finished the year 56th on the money list—most of which came from Pebble Beach and Augusta—only the second time he had been out of the top 20 since his rookie year on tour. Still, he was somewhat hopeful because his shoulder felt better. He believed he had bottomed out at the British. He certainly hoped that was the case.

"I had struggled in 2002 because I was making swing changes and routine changes that turned out not to be a great idea," Weir said. "But that year, only a few people noticed. I was 'Mike Weir, nice player.' When you're 'Mike Weir, Masters champion,' it's completely different. Everyone wants to know why you aren't playing as well as you did when you were winning the Masters.

"If you say your shoulder hurts, you sound like you're making excuses. In '02 there were a lot of weeks when I'd miss a cut or not play well, and not a single person would ask me about it. In '05 anytime I didn't play well, there were a bunch of people asking 'What's wrong?' Your instinct is to say, 'If I knew what was wrong, I would have fixed it already.' But that's not the right thing to say. I understood why they were asking the questions. It's a whole new world when you win a major. You have to take the good with the bad."

He smiled. "Of course it's like anything else. It takes you a while to figure that out."

By fall 2006, he still didn't feel comfortable with his swing or his game. "It seemed to come and go," he said. "Some weeks were pretty good; other weeks weren't so good. My short game was still good enough that I could compete some of the time, but I knew my swing hadn't been the same since I'd hurt my shoulder. Mike and I tried everything, and nothing seemed to work."

He managed a third-place finish at Pebble Beach and tied for sixth at the U.S. Open and was sixth at the PGA Championship. To the outside world, Weir was playing solid golf, if not the kind of golf he had played in 2003. He was making lots of money, but he hadn't won since his successful defense in Los Angeles at the start of 2004.

"One thing that happens after you reach a certain level is that it isn't about the money anymore," he said. "Early on, how much money I made week to week and year to year really mattered. But at this point in my life, honestly, it doesn't. I was very lucky to make as much money as I did, especially after the Masters win.

"We don't have an exorbitant lifestyle. We're still in the same house as before. Don't get me wrong, I'm happy that I have the chance to make the money I make and that my family lives very comfortably. But the work I put into the game, the time I put into it, the time I'm away from my family to try to compete, has nothing to do with the money. Winning—playing as well as I possibly can—that's what I'm out here for."

Weir tried taking the Vijay Singh approach to fix his game—pounding range balls for hours and hours. "About the only thing that happened," he said, smiling, "is that my short game suffered because I wasn't paying enough attention to it. After a while out there, I'd lose focus. Vijay is about the only guy I know who can just go out there and pound balls for hours and make it worthwhile. It just didn't work for me."

During the summer of 2006, while playing his regular Tuesday practice rounds with Dean Wilson, his old college teammate at Brigham Young, Weir began talking to Wilson about the "stack-and-tilt" golf swing. The stack-and-tilt was becoming a much-talked-about swing theory on tour, and Wilson had started working with Andy Plummer and Mike Bennett, the two men who were teaching it. Wilson was very enthusiastic about the changes in his golf swing and had just won on tour—at the International—for the first time in his career.

"Dean was clearly a lot more confident with his swing," Weir said. "Mike [Wilson] and I had been searching for a while and hadn't come up with anything. I finally decided it was worth at least hearing what Andy and Mike had to say."

Weir hadn't qualified for the Tour Championship in fall 2006, but American Express had asked him to fly into Atlanta that week to be involved in a commercial that he and several other players were to appear in. It was one of those trips Weir dreaded—extra time on the road when he wasn't playing—so he decided to make it more than a trip to do a commercial. Through Wilson, he tracked down Plummer and Bennett and asked if they might have time to meet with him in Atlanta.

They met in the clubhouse at East Lake Golf Club, in the small players' dining room next to the locker room area. Plummer and Bennett first showed Weir what the stack-and-tilt looked like on their computer and explained to him that a lot of great players used the stack-and-tilt concept, Hogan and Nicklaus among them, without ever calling it stack-and-tilt. The essence of the theory was simple: less movement in the swing. There was more detail than that, but Weir quickly grasped that they were talking about a basic feature of almost any golf swing: keeping the head directly above the ball.

"We talked for a while and then went out on the range and hit some balls," Weir said. "I picked up what they were trying to get

me to do pretty quickly, and I liked it. I flew home the next day
and called Mike to tell him about the session and that I'd decided
to work with these guys at least for a while.

"It was one of the toughest phone calls I've ever made. Mike
and I had worked together for ten years, and I had made huge
progress working with him. I'd gone from a guy who wasn't on the
tour to a guy who won the Masters. It was difficult, painful in
fact. But it was something I really felt I had to do at that moment.
I couldn't keep doing what I was doing.

"I told him, and I was being honest, that I didn't think it was
his fault. Maybe after ten years, I just wasn't listening anymore or
I wasn't hearing him anymore. Regardless, I felt as if I was beating my head against the wall, and I was tired of fighting my swing,
which I'd been doing for two years. He was great about it. But it
was still really hard."

Soon after the session in Atlanta, Weir played in an event
called the Champions Challenge, which Johnny Miller puts on
annually in Salt Lake City. Nicklaus was there playing with his
son Michael as his partner. Standing on the range, Weir asked
Nicklaus if there was any one thing that Jack Grout, his longtime
teacher, had emphasized with him through the years.

"Jack said absolutely. That every year when they would start
out, [Grout] would take his head and hold it absolutely still so he
couldn't move it even if he wanted to move it. He wanted him
centered over the ball so he couldn't shift his weight too much
and so his left shoulder stayed over the ball.

"It was exactly what Mike and Andy had been talking to me
about. To be honest, I couldn't really handle all those swing
thoughts, so I just focused on one thing: keeping my head centered and unmoving over the ball."

Weir spent most of the next few months working on his new
swing to prepare for the start of the 2007 season. In past years
when he went home to Salt Lake, he had been happy to put his

clubs away until just before he began his new season, when he would usually go to Palm Springs to spend some time with Wilson.

Now, he found an indoor facility where he could go and hit balls when the weather was cold. "It was called Mulligans," he said. "I thought that was appropriate."

The initial returns on the new swing were mixed. Weir didn't have a top-20 finish until the Masters, where he finished tied for 20th. Things began to pick up during the summer—a tie for eighth at Tiger Woods's new event held at Congressional Country Club, a future U.S. Open venue, and a tie for eighth at the British Open.

The turning point, though, came at the Presidents Cup. Weir was a captain's pick for the International Team since he had not finished in the top 10 in the point standings for the team. Gary Player picked Weir, in part because of his past experience, but largely because the event was being played at Royal Montreal Golf Club, and it made sense to have the most famous Canadian golfer in history on the team.

The U.S. won with ease, but that didn't dim the enthusiasm of the Canadian fans, especially in Weir's matches. Looking to add a little drama to the final day, Player matched Weir against Woods, figuring that would add spice to at least one of the twelve singles matches.

"I saw a comment in the paper that morning from Peter Thomson saying that matching me with Tiger was like feeding a lamb to a lion," Weir said. "Peter was my captain in '99 when I beat Phil [Mickelson] four and three in the singles. I remember thinking, 'I thought Peter knew me better than that.'"

The lamb beat the lion one-up that day, with seemingly all of Canada going crazy on every shot. Whether it mattered that the matches were already decided is hard to say (the U.S. won 19½ to 14½), but there was no doubt that Weir and Woods were throwing everything they had at each other.

When the two men shook hands, Woods smiled at Weir and said, "Great playing. I can't wait till we do this again. I'll kick your ass."

Weir took the comment as a compliment, which it was. Woods went on to tell the media he had played as hard as he could—Woods always plays as hard as he can—and that Weir had deserved the victory.

"It's funny how much attention you get when you beat Tiger anywhere, anytime," Weir said. "Doing it head-to-head was such a big deal to people. I mean, it was a big deal, I knew that. But when I beat Phil the way I did in '99, it hardly caused a ripple, and I was essentially a nobody at the time. Beating Tiger, even though they'd won the matches, was huge, especially to Canadians. To be able to give them something when we were getting hammered that way made me feel good. It was definitely a confidence boost for me."

A month later, playing at the Fry's Electronics Open in Scottsdale, Weir got his first win in almost four years. He held off Sean O'Hair and Mark Hensby, two rising young players, down the stretch, shooting 68 on Sunday, to hold up a trophy for the first time since February 2004.

"The last day was a tough windy day after we'd had absolute calm for three days," Weir remembered. "On 17 I had a six-footer I had to make with the wind blowing like crazy. Then on 18, I put my second shot in the left bunker and came out to eight feet. Had to make it or play off. It was actually a little bit like the putt I had on the 18th at Augusta. When I knocked it in, it was the best feeling I'd had since that day—including the win over Tiger.

"I played well for four days, not one. I'd had tournaments in which I'd have one good round or two, but you need four if you're going to win. I held up under pressure the way I did back in '03. I know there were people who doubted if I would win again, and I know there are people now who don't think I can win a major again.

"That's fine. I've had doubters all my life. I had people tell me I should play right-handed and people tell me I was too small or didn't hit it far enough to make it to the tour, much less win on the tour.

"I know now that ups and down are part of playing golf; even Tiger has his down days and—for him—down years. I've had both too. I turn forty next year [2010], and I still believe I have lots of good golf left in me. I like my golf swing, and I think through the years I've figured out how to deal with being someone who is always going to have to plan time in my schedule for people.

"That may sound like something that's simple, but, for me anyway, it hasn't always been that way. Especially when I'm not playing as well as I'd like to play."

In 2008, Weir won more than $3 million and finished in the top 10—including a second at one of the new "playoff" events behind Vijay Singh—in five of his last six tournaments. The next year wasn't quite as good—more than $2.2 million, again with a second and a third but no victories.

"The good news is I'm playing consistently solid golf," Weir said. "I still want to get better. More than anything, I'd like to feel that way I felt that Sunday at Augusta again. There's just no feeling quite like it."

BEN CURTIS PROBABLY WOULDN'T have minded if people had asked him what was wrong with his golf game in the two years after he became the first man since Francis Ouimet to win the very first major championship he played in.

Asking what was wrong would have at least implied that people believed him to be a better player than his results indicated. The questions didn't come very often.

"I think a lot of people had decided I was a fluke," he said. "I kept hearing I was a one-shot wonder."

Candace heard it too, frequently, while walking the golf course with her husband. Sometimes she sensed people whispering, other times she heard them talking out loud. "It was always something like, 'Can you believe this guy won the British Open?'" she said. "It was very hurtful to hear. I knew it wasn't true, but right at that moment I couldn't prove it."

Although he dismissed IMG's suggestion that he change his wedding date, Curtis did allow the company to talk him into trying to play two tours in 2004. Almost no one can pull that off, and those who do seemingly succeed doing it—Ernie Els, Sergio Garcia—usually end up tiring themselves out in the process, even if they play well. Players even have a term for those who spend a lot of time flying from continent to continent in the pursuit of money: being "IMG'ed."

Curtis was clearly being IMG'ed in 2004 and 2005. In his rookie year, he had only played in twenty-one tournaments on the PGA Tour, in large part because he didn't get into quite a few events the first half of the year, and then cut his schedule back the second half of the year after winning the British, in part to play overseas, in part to get married and go on his honeymoon.

There was absolutely no reason for him not to play a full schedule the next two years since he had access to any tournament he wanted to play in after his win at Royal St. George's. In 2004, though, he only played in twenty tournaments because he played in Europe seven times. The continental shuttling showed up in his play: he won a total of $500,818 on the PGA Tour, making just nine cuts. He had one top-10 finish, a tie for eighth at the Memorial. He didn't do nearly as well overseas. His best finish was a tie for 42nd at the Deutsche Bank Invitational in Germany.

A year later he cut back on the European travel, making only four trips to play overseas, and added four events to his U.S. schedule. But he still overtraveled. He improved to $594,000 in earnings and 129th on the money list, but that was hardly the level of play he was looking to achieve.

"I lost my confidence for a while," he said. "I probably traveled too much, especially in '04, but it was the kind of opportunity it was hard to say no to because you don't know if it's ever going to happen to you again. Still, it did get disheartening at times. I didn't think my win at the British was a fluke, but I know there were people who did."

Looking back now, Candace often wonders if having the chance to play so much affected Ben's game. After being unsure about whether they could afford to buy a house in Ohio, the newlyweds bought one there and a second house in Orlando after the win at the British. For a golfer, the Florida house seemed to make sense: having a winter home to go to when the weather turned cold so that year-round practice was easy and sensible.

"Except I don't think it helped him," Candace said. "Ben has always been a 'put the clubs up for the winter' guy. That's what he did all his life. I think it helped keep him fresh. When he started playing again after a break, he was fresh and excited to play."

Not long after their children were born, the Curtises had to decide where they would live when the children were old enough to start school. The decision turned out to be easy: Ohio. "It's home," Ben said. "And I like winter. Growing up there worked out all right for me, so why not for them?"

In the fall of 2004, Curtis was invited to play in the Dunhill Cup, which is played at St. Andrews. He was invited in part because he was a recent British Open champion, and in part because IMG runs the event. On the way over, he and Candace and his parents flew into London and took a drive to Royal St.

George's, since his parents hadn't seen the place where he'd had his moment of glory.

"I knew there was a spot in the clubhouse where they had a plaque with the names of the players who had won the Open at St. George's," Curtis said. "I wanted my parents and Candace to see it, so, after we'd walked around a little, we asked someone if they could direct us to the room where the plaque was located.

"The guy we asked was happy to tell us where it was, but there was one problem: they didn't allow women inside the clubhouse. I had to go and see the club secretary and explain the situation. He finally agreed to make an exception — just the one time — although he asked me if we could please not stay very long inside.

"So we went inside, looked, and left." Curtis smiled. "They're probably still talking about it over there."

After the lost years in 2004 and 2005, Curtis decided to limit any play outside the U.S. to a July trip for the Open Championship and perhaps one other trip in the fall for something like the Dunhill Cup. The new schedule worked. Curtis played in twenty-six events on the PGA Tour and won twice. Coming off two years in which he had finished in the top 10 a grand total of three times, the improvement was more than noticeable.

His first victory since the British Open came sixty-four tour events and almost three years after St. George's. The circumstances were slightly different. Playing in a tournament whose demise had already been announced — the Booz Allen Classic outside Washington — Curtis won going away, leading from wire-to-wire. But the tournament was jinxed. Rain pelted the course all weekend. The golf course was so saturated that the leaders couldn't finish until Tuesday. By then, the access roads were in such bad shape that no spectators were allowed to come watch the finish.

After winning for the first time with thousands watching from the massive grandstands at St. George's, Curtis won for the second time in front of about a dozen tour officials and volunteers.

"It was almost eerie because it was so empty, and it felt like we'd been playing the tournament for about a month," Curtis said. "I really played well [winning by five shots], but we were there for so long, I almost didn't feel as if I'd won. I felt more like I'd survived."

Ironically, his second win that year was in another doomed tournament — the 84 Lumber Classic in Pennsylvania. This time, though, he managed to win on Sunday in front of actual spectators, beating Charles Howell III down the stretch. That victory helped push Curtis's earnings for the year to $2,256,326 and got him into the Tour Championship (top 30 money winners) for the first time. Most important, it quieted a lot of the talk about his "fluke" win in 2003.

"It felt good to prove to myself that I wasn't a one-time wonder," he said. "I don't think I ever completely lost confidence in myself, but I did wonder at times if I was going to find what I'd had that one week. Knowing I had it was a nice feeling."

The same was true for Candace. "Ben's such a gentle person; he'd never let his frustration show that much," she said. "If he'd had the years he had in '04 and '05 without winning the British, he'd have been just another young player trying to find himself. But he wasn't. He was a major champion, and people kept saying he'd fallen apart because he couldn't handle the fame or the pressure. I was the one who had to try to pick up the pieces. I finally told Ben, 'You just worry about golf. I'll worry about everything else.' That seemed to work for both of us."

Candace missed the win at 84 Lumber because she was about to give birth to Liam. A little more than a year later Addison came along, giving the Curtises a boy and a girl and giving Ben all the more reason not to overtravel. His play slipped slightly in '07, but he bounced back in '08. Although he didn't win again, he had his most consistent year ever on tour. He finished second in Charlotte, seventh at the British Open, and second at the PGA Championship.

He led the PGA after 54 holes and still had a chance to win when he came to the 17th hole on Sunday. Trailing Padraig Harrington by one shot at that point, he hit a five-iron that went straight at the flag but took a big hop into the deep rough behind the green. "I was probably just a little too pumped up at that point," he said later.

From there, he made bogey, and Harrington won by two shots. Still, that performance clinched a spot for Curtis on the Ryder Cup team, and he played solidly in the U.S. victory—its first win over Europe since 1999. He capped the year a week later by finishing fifth at the Tour Championship and ended up in 17th place on the money list, his best year yet on tour.

"People forget how young the guy is because he was only twenty-six when he won the British," Zach Johnson said at the end of '08. "He's got a world of talent, and he's still getting better.

"I know firsthand now [having won the Masters in '07] how differently people look at you when you've won a major. There are guys on tour right around Ben's age who have won a couple times and made good money who are considered up-and-comers. Ben would be in that same class if he hadn't won the British. Instead, you hear people say, 'Will he ever win another one?' First of all, he might; he's definitely good enough. Second, if he doesn't, how many players do you think would trade their wins for his major? It's a long list, believe me."

Sergio Garcia and Adam Scott would undoubtedly trade victory lists with Curtis. Both were turning thirty in 2010 [Garcia in January, Scott in July] while Curtis would turn thirty-three. Garcia had seven wins on tour; Scott, six. Each is considered one of the tour's biggest stars, perhaps only a rung below players like Phil

Mickelson, Ernie Els, Padraig Harrington, and Vijay Singh. Tiger Woods, even after the humiliating revelations about his personal life at the end of 2009, remains in another stratosphere as a player.

Garcia has been achingly close to winning majors; Scott has never come close. You can bet serious money either would trade any or all of his wins for Curtis's three, particularly since one of those three is the British Open.

And yet, Curtis remains in the shadows, the quiet kid from Ohio who put himself in the same sentence—a short one—with Francis Ouimet during a hot week in the south of England in July 2003.

"I would never ever change what happened that week," Curtis said with a smile. "It was magical and unforgettable, and I love my life. I only wish I'd known some of the things then that I know now. But that's the way things go. You learn as you go. I had to learn a lot in a hurry. It hasn't always been easy, but I think I came through it all right. I took some falls, had some bumps and some bruises, but I'm okay."

He smiled. "No permanent damage done. At least I don't think so."

19

Whatever Happened to . . . ?

It was one of those early-summer days in the Washington, D.C., area, where the only reasonable place to be is inside. It was hot and humid, there were thunderstorms in the forecast, and the idea of playing golf would appeal to almost no one.

And yet, the driving range at the Country Club of Woodmore was packed for as far as the eye could see. Woodmore is not one of the D.C. area's glamour clubs. It is several miles outside the Beltway on the outskirts of Prince George's County in Maryland.

But during the first week of June 2009, Woodmore was the site of the Melwood Prince George's County Open, a stop on the Nationwide Tour—golf's version of Triple-A baseball.

"A lot of us go through denial when we first find ourselves here," said Grant Waite, a past winner on the PGA Tour who was good enough to play in the big leagues regularly for ten years. "But after a while, you realize that you aren't on this tour because of bad luck or anyone being unfair. You're on this tour because it's where your game is at this moment. The goal, of course, is to get it back to where it's good enough to get back where you believe you belong."

While the Nationwide guys, including twenty-nine players who had won at some point in their lives on the PGA Tour, were playing at Woodmore for a total purse of $700,000, the big boys—or, more accurately, the rich boys—were playing at Jack Nicklaus's Memorial Tournament for a purse of $6 million, with $1,080,000 ($380,000 more than would be split up among all the players who made the cut at the Melwood) going to the winner. That winner would be Tiger Woods.

The driving range at Woodmore is about twenty-five miles from Congressional Country Club where the rich boys would be coming to play in four weeks. Twenty-five miles away by car, a lifetime away by lifestyle. The rich boys would be taking courtesy cars to and from the Ritz and the Four Seasons, host hotels for the AT&T National hosted by (and won by) Tiger Woods.

There were no courtesy cars to be found in the Woodmore parking lot. Many players on this tour drive their own vehicles from tournament to tournament. When they head home for the night while on the road, it is to reasonably priced hotels like a Courtyard Marriott, a Fairfield Inn, a Hampton Inn, a Country Inn and Suites.

On this humid Thursday, tucked quietly in amid the upcoming kids, the guys who have never made it and the guys, like Waite, who once lived the courtesy-car life, one could find Len Mattiace and Stephen Leaney.

Among the fans scattered around the golf course, there were some who knew the names, and others who would point and say, "Didn't he do something big once?" Or, "Why is his name so familiar?"

Six years after each finished second in a major championship, Mattiace and Leaney could only dream about perhaps someday playing in another major. For Mattiace, it had been four years since he had played in a major at all—he missed a cut at the 2005 U.S. Open, and he had played in only two majors since 2003: the 2004 Masters and the '05 Open. He had made the cut in all four majors in 2003, one of ten players to do so that year, but had not played a weekend since finishing tied for 51st at the 2003 PGA Championship.

"People talk a lot about what the difference is between first and second in a major," Leaney said. "I'm not sure the biggest difference isn't the five-year exemption."

A major champion is exempt for five years, not only to play on the tour but to all the majors. The runner-up usually makes enough money to lock up his tour exemption for the next year and is automatically invited back to that major the following year. But that's it. Leaney had played in all four majors in 2004 — his best finish a tie for 17th at the Masters, one spot out of qualifying to play there again in 2005 — but had played in two majors since then: the 2005 and 2007 PGA Championships. He had missed the cut in both. His last weekend appearance at a major had been the 2004 U.S. Open at Shinnecock, where he had finished tied for 40th.

Mattiace's career and life had changed forever during a family skiing trip to Vail late in 2003. A lot of golfers avoid skiing because of the potential for injury. Early in his career Phil Mickelson broke a leg while skiing and gave it up after that. But Mattiace had been a skier for years, and the trip was an annual family event.

Vail had just had about 18 inches of new snowfall the night before the Mattiaces arrived. "Lenny is a good skier, but he wasn't used to skiing in powder," his wife Kristen said. "He lost his balance and fell, and one of his binders didn't release the way they're supposed to when you fall. The ski got caught behind his other leg, and he snapped both ACLs [anterior cruciate ligaments], both MCLs [medial collateral ligaments], and a bone in his left knee."

He had to have surgery on both knees and then began what probably should have been at least a nine-month rehab program. For two months he was in a wheelchair, and when he began to rehab it was extremely difficult because he literally didn't have a leg to stand on.

"The other people at the rehab center nicknamed him Robo-Cop, because he clanked whenever he tried to move," Kristen said.

Mattiace could have easily sat out 2004 and been eligible for a full major-medical exemption from the tour in 2005. He asked the tour if, since he was exempt based on his victories in 2002 and his earnings in 2003, he could use his medical in 2005 but retain his last exempt year so that he would be exempt in 2006, regardless of how he played in 2005. No, the tour said, you can't defer a winner's exemption. There was also no deferring the 2004 Masters exemption he had earned with his second-place finish. If he didn't play in 2004, he would have to earn his way back in 2005.

"He really didn't want to miss the Masters," Kristen said. "Hindsight is twenty-twenty, but looking back now it's pretty clear he came back too fast."

To put it in perspective: Tiger Woods had ACL surgery on one knee in June 2008 and played his first tournament eight months later. Mattiace had surgery on *two* ACLs in December 2003 and was back on the golf course three months later.

"I'm not sure anyone has ever worked harder to get through rehab than Len did," Kristen said. "He was just absolutely determined to get better and to get back and to be ready for the Masters."

He did get back, returning to play at the Honda Classic in March. His knees still hurt enough that he had trouble getting in and out of bunkers without help from his caddy. He missed the cut badly (79–78) but kept grinding, missing another cut at Bay Hill before somehow shooting 69 in the second round at the Players Championship to make the cut. He went on to finish tied for 33rd. That gave him some confidence going into the Masters, which was what he was searching for in Florida, but he still missed the cut, shooting 76–75.

"He was okay dealing with the pain," Kristen said. "Len's tough. It's hard to tell when he's hurting either physically or emotionally. But without knowing it, he was making swing adjustments to compensate for the knees that he shouldn't have been making—it sent him into a tailspin for a good long while."

Mattiace ended up playing in twenty-five tournaments in 2004, making twelve cuts. His highest finish was a tie for 20th at the John Deere Invitational, and he earned $213,707 for his efforts for the entire year. A year later, trying to hang on to his playing privileges, Mattiace played in a staggering thirty-four tournaments. But he made only nine cuts and had *two* top-50 finishes (T-39 in Atlanta, T-12 at Westchester); he was 191st on the money list after making $209,630 for the year.

Nothing Mattiace tried seemed to stop the downward spiral. He still got into twenty-two tournaments the next year on his past champion's status and good-guy exemptions but made only six cuts and a little more than $66,000. A year later, the good-guy exemptions used up, he didn't make a single cut in ten events. When he made four cuts in 2008, that almost felt like a breakthrough.

By the end of that year, Mattiace had decided he had to change his comeback strategy. Waiting around to get into PGA Tour events and playing occasionally on the Nationwide Tour weren't getting it done for him. He felt healthy, felt as if he could play well again; he just needed a chance to do it. So, after playing better during a late-year trip to South Africa, Mattiace decided to play the Nationwide Tour full-time in 2009—he'd take the Grant Waite approach: if this is where my game is, this is where I should play.

"It was a very tough decision for him," Kristen said. "I know he believes he can still compete on the PGA Tour, and to have weeks where he knew he could get into a PGA Tour event and turn those spots down to play the Nationwide was going to be hard for him. But he made a commitment to give it a shot and see what would happen."

Mattiace actually began the year playing at Pebble Beach,

almost as a warm-up for the Nationwide, which didn't start until two weeks later. He got into Pebble Beach as a past champion (because four golf courses are used, 180 players get into the field), and he finished in a tie for 22nd place. That was his highest finish on tour since the tie for 12th in 2005 at Westchester.

Given that confidence boost, Mattiace headed off to Panama for the opening of the Nationwide Tour season. In order to increase the number of events on the tour, the Nationwide now opens the year with four overseas events—one in Panama, followed by two in New Zealand, and one in Australia. Having made the decision to play the Nationwide, Mattiace decided to play all four overseas events.

His start was encouraging. Coming off his solid play at Pebble Beach, he finished tied for sixth in Panama, earning $19,425 to start the year. But he couldn't keep up that pace. He missed three of his next six cuts, and his highest finish over the next nine weeks was a tie for 24th in Athens. Still, he arrived at Woodmore in reasonable position on the money list—45th place—with lots of golf still to be played.

"I think making the mental commitment to play on this tour is the hardest thing for anyone who has been on the PGA Tour for a while the way I have," Mattiace said. "But once I decided to do it, I've been okay. It's golf, I'm competing, and I really enjoy that. The only thing that's been tough has been spending time away from the family."

In fact, Woodmore was the beginning of a four-week stretch when he would be driving from tournament to tournament. Kristen and the kids had flown in to Washington to spend the week with him but were heading home after that.

The week at Woodmore turned out to be the kind every pro dreads. A thunderstorm swept through the area on Thursday afternoon with half the field still on the golf course, Mattiace among them. On Friday, no one hit a ball all day as the course was drenched by more rain. That meant the players who hadn't finished their first rounds had to tee it up at 7:30 on Saturday morning, complete their first rounds, then immediately head out to play their second rounds. Everyone who made the cut then had to play 36 holes in hot, humid conditions on Sunday.

Mattiace played well enough the first two rounds, shooting 70–70 to make the cut but ran out of gas the last two rounds, shooting 76–74 to finish in a tie for 65th place. The next morning he was in his car heading for Knoxville, hoping for better things.

While the memories of Augusta still remained too painful to recount in detail, Mattiace remained friendly and open to anyone he encountered—as long as the subject of conversation didn't turn to the 2003 Masters.

"The one thing he doesn't do is 'What if...,'" Kristen said. "I've never heard him say, 'Everything would be different if I'd parred 18' or anything like that. He's a guy who is very comfortable with himself. He can go off and hit balls alone for hours and be very happy. He's content. We're lucky he made the money he did so we aren't scrambling; we're comfortable.

"The other night we had Chinese food and Len's fortune cookie said, 'Relax and enjoy yourself.' I actually believe he's doing that right now. Would he like to play better? Of course he would. But his demeanor never seems to change. I'll go pick him up in the car after he plays, and when he gets in I have no idea if he shot 64 or 74. I still remember picking him up one afternoon in North Carolina a few years ago. It was a Friday and he'd played well on Thursday, so I asked what time he was playing the next day.

"He said, 'I'm not. I shot 78. I missed the cut.' I honestly didn't believe him at first, he was so calm about it. But he had. You can never tell if something is bothering him."

On the outside, anyway. On the inside, it is pretty clear that something still gnaws at him about that day at Augusta when he played the round of his life, a round he should remember proudly—and says he does. But the memory clearly isn't that simple or clear. He shot 65, one of the great Sunday rounds in Masters history.

But Mike Weir is the one who puts on the green jacket on the second Tuesday in April every year and has dinner with Nicklaus and Palmer and Woods and Watson and Player. It is almost as if Len Mattiace can hear their voices but can't quite make out what they're saying.

And whether he talks about it or not, the pain is still evident.

STEPHEN LEANEY'S SITUATION DURING that rainy, humid week in June was considerably different from Mattiace's. He had not dealt with a major injury or surgery after his Moment at the '03 U.S. Open, but he had dealt with a mystery illness that had made playing golf very difficult.

Things had gone well for him after his runner-up finish to Jim Furyk and his decision to move his family to Dallas so he could play the U.S. tour full-time. He hadn't done anything spectacular—his best finish during his first four years on the tour had been a third place at Hilton Head in 2007—but he had pieced together a solid, lucrative career when he finally made it to America after all the years of trying to get there.

He made more than $1.1 million in 2004, with two top-10 finishes and six in the top 25, including the tie for 17th at the Masters. That put him 68th on the money list. The next three years weren't as good, but he played well enough to keep his card comfortably and again went over $1 million in earnings in 2007.

Midway through 2008, Leaney began to feel tired and dizzy on the golf course. It made no sense. He was thirty-nine years old, in excellent shape, and all of a sudden he was having terrible trouble finishing his rounds without feeling exhausted. In addition, he felt unsteady as he stood over the golf ball. He went to the doctor and had all sorts of tests done. They couldn't find anything wrong. He kept playing but didn't feel better. Finally, after another round of tests, the doctors came back and said he had an inner-ear infection.

They told him he should shut down for a while, rest, take meds, and come back to play when he felt better. He had already played seventeen tournaments by the time the doctors told him to stop playing and had only made $157,963, well short of the $852,752 that he would need to finish in the top 125 on the money list. But at that point, Leaney wasn't worried about his standing on the money list—he was concerned about trying to get healthy.

"It's bad enough to not feel well, but when the doctors couldn't really tell me what was wrong, that made it worse because then there's no guarantee you're going to get better," he said. "When I stopped playing, I had no idea when I was going to feel well enough to play again."

The meds he was taking for the inner-ear infection didn't seem to help. Whenever he tried to play golf, even at home, he felt tired and unsteady. He was tested for diabetes. Negative. He went to see yet another doctor. More tests. This time the diagnosis was different: he had vertigo. At the very least, that might explain why he felt unsteady over the ball.

"They recommended I eliminate all dairy products from my diet," he said. "I stopped eating meat too. Right away, I started to feel better. It wasn't as if I was 100 percent in a week, but I definitely started to feel as if I was going in the right direction. It was a huge relief just to feel as if I was making some progress."

Leaney knew when he returned to the tour in 2009 that he would have just eleven tournaments to make almost $700,000. Given that he had been away from golf for almost nine months before he felt well enough to play, that was probably going to be a long shot.

"It's nice though that my major concern right now is my golf," he said, sitting out one of the rain delays at Woodmore. "I feel so much better. I just haven't been able to find my game again yet." He smiled. "I know it's in here somewhere."

Leaney had come back to the tour in Tampa in mid-March and, not surprisingly, missed the cut. He'd made the cut at Hilton Head (T-58) but hadn't made a cut since. He was playing at Woodmore because he had not been invited to play in the Memorial Tournament, and he thought it was important to keep playing.

"I'll play my eleven and see where I am," he said. "If I don't keep my card, I can go to Europe and play some events there. The important thing for me now is to figure out a way to play better. Having playing status doesn't matter very much if you can't play."

The idea of going back to Q-School, a place he hadn't been since 2002, didn't seem to frighten Leaney. "I'd rather not do it of course," he said. "But if it comes to that, it comes to that. I'm certainly not the first player who has faced this sort of thing."

He leaned back in his chair and smiled. "Just look around this room. There's no margin for error in this game."

Unlike Mattiace, Leaney has no ghosts chasing him from 2003. "Obviously, there are moments when I think about what it would have been like if I'd won," he said. "But Jim [Furyk] was so clearly the best player that week. I went into Sunday telling myself to try to win the tournament in large part because I was convinced if I played for second I'd probably end up 20th. You just can't have that 'hang on' mentality and succeed.

"There were a couple of moments where I might have cut the lead to two, and he made tough putts. On the one hand, you can say 'What if . . .' On the other, you can also say 'That's why he won. He was that good that week.' It's not as if I second-guess anything I did. I was second best, and for me that was a good showing.

"I'd love another crack at it, especially since I thought I held up pretty well that Sunday, being in the last group with all that pressure and so much riding on the outcome. Sometimes I think about that week and it seems so long ago, I wonder if it was really me. Other times it feels like it just happened.

"Right now, I just want to play good golf again. If I can do that, the rest will come. It always has in the past."

Leaney shot an opening round 76 at Woodmore, which meant that his second round 69 left him four shots outside the cut number. He went back to the PGA Tour to finish his eleven tournaments and made one more cut, finishing 50th in Milwaukee.

He played briefly in Europe but in October found himself playing in China, on something called the OneAsia tour, a start-up tour that consisted of players from China, South Korea, and Australia. He was, by far, the biggest name in the field. He was also a long, long way from Olympia Fields.

IF ANYONE CAN RELATE to the way Len Mattiace feels about the 2003 Masters, it is Thomas Bjorn. Of the four men who finished second in the 2003 majors (Bjorn actually tied for second at the British Open with Vijay Singh), no one had been closer to victory than Bjorn.

He was at the peak of his career, about to play on his third straight European Ryder Cup team. He had won nine times in international events, including his victory over Tiger Woods in Dubai in 2001. At age thirty-two, he appeared ready to take the next step and become one of the game's elite players.

For 14 holes on that Sunday at Royal St. George's, he was in control of his game and the championship. He stood on the 15th tee with a three-shot lead. Even after bogeying 15, he still led by two with three holes to play. And then came the 16th, a par-three that didn't really frighten anybody very much. But Bjorn's tee shot floated right of the flag and hopped into a bunker. From there, he had needed three swipes to get the ball onto the green.

It was so shocking to watch that Davis Love III, standing there with a 10-foot birdie putt, couldn't believe his eyes. "The thought that he might leave it in the bunker never crossed my mind," he said. "It wasn't necessarily an easy shot to get close, but as long as you made sure to fly it up onto the green, it shouldn't have given him any real trouble."

Except that it did. Bjorn was gracious in defeat, seeking Ben Curtis out to congratulate him and making no excuses for what had happened.

He continued to play well after the meltdown at St. George's but not as well. He won again, twice, on the European Tour and even finished tied for second at the 2005 PGA, one shot behind Phil Mickelson. But Bjorn was left off the 2006 Ryder Cup team by captain Ian Woosnam and was so critical of Woosnam for choosing Lee Westwood over him with his last captain's pick that eventually he had to apologize to Woosnam, especially after Westwood picked up four points in Europe's one-sided victory.

By 2009, Bjorn had dropped out of the top 100 in the world rankings, even though he was not yet forty years old. He entered the European qualifier for the U.S. Open but withdrew without ever teeing up. He did show for the British Open qualifier but failed to make the field for Turnberry. By year's end, he was 101st on the European money list — still exempt but a long way from where he had been in 2003.

And, like Mattiace, Bjorn just couldn't bring himself to talk about what had happened on those final holes or in that bunker at St. George's. Even when asked to answer questions by e-mail, he politely declined. When told about Bjorn not wanting to talk, one friend from the European Tour nodded his head in understanding.

"I'm not sure he'll ever be over it," he said. "People talk about [Jean] Van de Velde because he fell apart [with a triple-bogey 7 at Carnoustie] on the 18th hole. This was just as bad, at least as bad, it just happened on 16, and there's no picture of Thomas [as opposed to Van de Velde] standing in a berm with his pants rolled up to his knees.

"He knows he was the best player that week. But it doesn't matter — he didn't win. He's told people that sometimes when he goes into a bunker, he still sees demons. He's such a good guy. You have to feel for him."

Two people who have always felt bad for him are Ben Curtis, who walked off with the Claret Jug that day, and Love, the eyewitness to the crime.

"Obviously I didn't see it, and it played a big role in me winning and my whole life changing," Curtis said. "But how can you not feel for a guy when something like that happens to him? I thought he showed a lot of class coming over to congratulate me that day."

Love is more succinct: "I wouldn't wish something like that on my worst enemy. Even though it gave me a chance to win, I certainly wouldn't wish it on a guy like Thomas."

Bjorn's bunker debacle changed lives that day. Curtis and his family have had to live with the burden of being an out-of-nowhere major champion. Bjorn and his family have had to live with the burden of never being a major champion.

20

What Comes Next?

WHEN THE FOUR MAJOR champions for 2003 arrived on the island of Kauai for the Grand Slam of Golf, they were a bit awed by the show the PGA of America put on for them.

"Everything, I mean everything, was first class," Shaun Micheel said. "I remember walking into my hotel suite, looking around, and thinking, 'Wow, I have really arrived now.'"

Everyone brought family members. Since Dade was just two weeks old and too young for a plane trip, the baby and Stephanie Micheel didn't go, but Shaun brought his parents, his sister and her fiancé, and Sam Carmichael (his old college golf coach at Indiana) and his wife along with him. There were parties and dinners every night, and then—finally—the four players went out and played 36 holes on the Poipu course on the resort property.

Even though there was money at stake and the event was televised by TBS, this was just a step above hit-and-giggle golf. After all Ben Curtis, who finished last, walked away with a check for $100,000. Jim Furyk, who beat Mike Weir by eight shots to win (Micheel was two shots behind Weir, Curtis three back), won $400,000. Weir won $300,000, Micheel $200,000. Not exactly high-pressure work for the boys.

"In a way, though, I felt like we'd all earned it," Micheel said.

"After all, there is no event in golf that's tougher to get into than that one."

Certainly true. Tiger Woods, who would win the Player of the Year award, wasn't there. Neither was Phil Mickelson, who would finally break through and win his first major the following April.

None of the four players knew each other very well. Furyk and Weir had spent some time together since both had been tournament winners prior to winning their majors, and Micheel and Curtis, who had been nonwinners before the summer of '03, had a passing acquaintance with one another.

"Put it this way, I knew [Curtis] to say hello before he won the British," Micheel said.

That put him well ahead of Furyk and Weir. But even though they all had families around, the four players did spend some time together. The most talkative was Micheel, who tends to think out loud a lot. Furyk still remembers Micheel talking about his concerns about "living up" to the idea of being a major champion.

"He talked about it a couple times," Furyk said. "It was as if he felt he had skipped a step going from not winning a tournament to winning a major. In a sense, he had. So had Ben. When I won the Open, I felt prepared to deal with what came next because I'd had success beforehand. I'd won tournaments, I'd competed on Sunday in majors, I'd played on Ryder Cup teams. It was a natural step, one I very much wanted to make.

"I think for Shaun and Ben, it was a lot tougher because I doubt the thought of being a major champion seriously crossed their minds before they won. Then they woke up one morning, and it felt as if everyone wanted a piece of them. In a lot of ways, I felt sorry for both of them—not for winning but for what they had to deal with as a result of winning."

Although Curtis did struggle over the next two years, he was young enough and had an inner confidence that didn't let him get too down on himself, even when he heard the constant whispers that he had been a fluke. The two wins in 2006, the near win at the PGA in 2008, and the spot on that year's Ryder Cup team did a good deal to quiet all the talk.

"When you looked at him, you could always see he had a ton of talent," Furyk said. "The question was, could he find it again after all the distractions that came with winning the British. The answer turned out to be yes."

Micheel continued to play well in 2004, winning just under $1 million, although he didn't win again. But he wasn't happy with his play, wondered why he couldn't contend again, and began to beat himself up for not being a better player.

"I started hearing every single comment people made and taking them to heart," Micheel said. "I became really short tempered, which just wasn't a good way to be. It bothered me when I acted that way, but I did it anyway. It kept getting worse and my play kept getting worse."

Micheel's frustration crested during the opening round of the Honda Classic in March 2005. He felt tired and cranky even though it was a beautiful day in South Florida. "I still remember being on the eighth hole and thinking to myself, 'What am I doing here? I don't want to be here, playing golf right now.'

"I was less than two years removed from winning the PGA and all that came with it, and I didn't want to play golf? Something was wrong."

He ended up shooting 79 that day and withdrew from the tournament—a first for him. He had never withdrawn for any reason other than an injury. He played the next week at Bay Hill but shot another opening-day 79. This time he stuck around to shoot 74 Friday and missed the cut, but he felt as if his body was telling him that something was amiss.

It was. Testing showed that he had a testosterone deficiency, the good news being that it could be corrected by taking a pill a day to increase his testosterone level. His energy got better but his golf didn't, although he did finish the year on a positive note, with a tie for fifth place in Jackson, Mississippi. Still, he felt as if he needed some help with his swing and his confidence.

Often in the past he had gone to see Carmichael. Just prior to the PGA in 2003, Micheel had gone to see Carmichael, and he had made a suggestion about the way Micheel was chipping the ball. "I wasn't taking a divot," he said, laughing. "Simple thing, but I wasn't doing it. Once Sam made that correction, I began to get the ball up and down all over the place."

Now, though, he thought he needed someone who was a full-time teacher. As a past PGA champion, Micheel could have gone to almost anyone. Kenny Perry, one of his friends on tour, suggested he talk to Matt Cullen, whom he had been working with for several years. Cullen was young—only twenty-one at the time—but he was a good friend of Perry's son and had become fascinated with teaching the golf swing while in high school. Perry's game had clearly flourished since he had starting working with Cullen, so Micheel decided to give it a try.

"Matt saw things that needed correcting right away," Micheel said. "It wasn't like working with a twenty-one-year-old, because he was smart and mature and he had really studied the swing. Almost as soon as we started working together, I began to feel better about what I was doing."

Micheel's game steadily improved throughout the year, peaking, once again, at the PGA, which was held that August at Medinah Country Club outside Chicago. The course reminded Micheel of Oak Hill, and he played well all week. On a par-72 golf course, he finished the week at 275, 13 under par.

The only problem was that the nonmortal Tiger Woods had reappeared by then. Woods shot an otherworldly 18-under-par 270, beating Micheel by five shots and everyone else by six or more. "I looked at the tape when it was over," Micheel said. "He made a lot of long putts that last day, otherwise it might have at least been close. But that's why he's Tiger Woods. When he's on, he makes more long putts than anybody."

A few weeks after the PGA, Micheel finished seventh at the Deutsche Bank Championship and, thanks to the PGA finish, found himself back in the top 50 in the world. One of his rewards for that was an invitation to play in the World Match Play, the lucrative sixteen-player event held in London every September. As luck would have it, Woods had decided to play that year since there was a World Golf Championships event in Great Britain the next week, followed by the Ryder Cup the week after that at the Belfry, in the English Midlands. And who did Woods draw as his first-round opponent? Shaun Micheel.

"I was the 15th seed, which means you play the second seed in the first round," Micheel said. "I had just assumed since Tiger was ranked number one in the world, he would be the first seed. But the way they do it, the defending champion is always seeded number one, regardless of the rankings."

That meant Michael Campbell, who had won the event in 2005, was the top seed, and Woods was number two. The match-play event is one of the most grueling in golf: each match is 36 holes, meaning that the two finalists have played 108 holes over three days by the time they tee it up in the final. Of course, playing 108 holes was the least of Micheel's worries before he played Woods.

"Not long after we got to London, someone asked Stephanie if she was going to get a chance to shop or go sightseeing," Micheel said. "She laughed and said, 'Well, Shaun plays Tiger on Thursday, so we should have plenty of time on Friday.' I thought to myself, 'Even my own wife doesn't think I have a chance!'"

As it turned out Stephanie and everyone else underestimated Micheel. He beat Woods, four and three, closing him out on the 15th hole of the afternoon round. When the match was over, a local radio host conducted a live interview with both players.

"Tiger," he said. "There are those who will say we didn't see the best of you today."

To Micheel, the implication was clear: Woods had lost because he hadn't given 100 percent. Woods looked at the interviewer, eyes narrowed, and said, "Well, then I guess you don't know me very well."

"I liked that answer," Micheel said. "I thought [the interviewer] insulted us both, and I told him so later. If you know Tiger at all, he always tries. Was he at his very best that day—no. But I was pretty good. I made a lot of putts. I think I was nine under par for the two rounds when the match ended."

Micheel continued to make putts the next two days and reached the final. By then he was gassed and lost to Englishman Paul Casey, a rising young player. Still, the whole experience gave him another shot of confidence.

"At the end of that year, I felt as if I was back to where I was in 2003, or at least close to it," he said. "I liked working with Matt, I felt good, my putting had come back. I thought I was ready to do some good things, really good things, the next couple of years."

That was when he started to feel pain in his left shoulder. At first he didn't think too much about it, especially because he was still playing well. Every once in a while when he swung, he'd hear a little pop inside the shoulder, but it didn't hurt that much so he kept on playing, up through the first round at New Orleans in May, when he was paired with Boo Weekley.

"I can't remember what hole it was on, but I hit a shot and Boo gave me this funny look and said, 'Was that you?' I asked him what he meant. I really thought the popping was something only I could hear or feel. He said, 'It sounded like your shoulder made a popping sound when you swung.'"

Micheel continued to shrug it off, but when Cullen asked him during a session soon after New Orleans if he had been working with a different teacher, he knew something was seriously wrong.

"Without knowing it, I had changed my swing to deal with the pain," Micheel said. "I was coming up and out from the swing early in order to protect the shoulder. I had no idea until Matt asked me what was going on. At that point, I knew I had a problem."

He made the mistake of only getting an x-ray done rather than a more thorough MRI. The x-ray showed nothing. He still made almost $1 million for the year (down from a career high of $1.6 million in 2006) but started 2008 worried that he had a serious problem with his shoulder. He was playing in Charlotte with Zach Johnson, when Johnson turned to him and said, "Shaun, you've got to do something about that shoulder. It's so loud every time you swing, it's hurting me just to hear it."

Finally, Micheel went in to get an MRI, dreading the results. Sure enough, he had a torn labrum. The only way to get better, the doctor told him, was surgery.

"I kept putting it off, put it off for way too long," Micheel said. "When it first began to hurt in 2007, I didn't want to stop playing because I had just signed new contracts at the end of 2006. I'd gotten lucky that I'd played really well in what was basically a contract year. I didn't want to let my new sponsors down at that point. Then, in '08, it was my last year being exempt into all the majors, and I didn't want to miss that. It was pretty obvious by the Masters [where he missed the cut] that there wasn't much point in playing when I could barely swing the club."

The MRI confirmed that once and for all. Micheel played through Memphis, his hometown tournament—where he missed his 10th cut in 16 starts—and finally had the surgery on June 10.

As anyone who has ever had shoulder surgery can tell you, the first few weeks were miserable. He had to sleep on the couch, and almost any movement was painful. While he was going through rehab, he got more bad news: his mom had been diagnosed with cancer, and it was far enough along that the doctors were recommending against surgery. She began chemo treatments instead, which weren't pleasant.

"She's dealt with it remarkably well," Micheel said, not long after playing his first round on the comeback trail in March 2009. "She's really hung in there and not gotten down about it. All I can do is try to support her, along with my dad, the best I can right now."

He wasn't stunned when he didn't make enough money to keep his card when his thirteen medical exemption tournaments were over, though he did have one good chance in Reno for a high finish. What was a little disappointing was the negative response he got when he started to write tournament directors for sponsor exemptions. Early in the year, he'd gotten a no from Arnold Palmer's tournament (an invitational) at Bay Hill, but that was no surprise. "IMG runs the event," Micheel said. "If you aren't an IMG client, you probably aren't getting an exemption."

Jack Nicklaus did give him an exemption, in part because he remembered that Micheel had played hurt the previous year. "I remember seeing him, and he said, 'Shaun, why don't you withdraw? You're hurt.' I said, 'Mr. Nicklaus, I wouldn't ever pull out of your event.'"

But when summer rolled around, and Micheel had to start making plans to be a player whose only exemption was as a past tour champion (in that category, there's no difference between a major and a regular tour event in terms of priority), he began writing letters to tournament directors. After writing in June, he didn't hear back from the people in Greensboro until the week before the event (mid-August). Sorry, no room at the inn (or on the golf course), he was told. He ended up as the third alternate on his past champion's status but didn't get in. Turning Stone — no. Las Vegas — no.

"Look, I get it," Micheel said. "In this sport, it's what have you done for me lately. I've always thought I did a pretty good job with people when I was out here, but maybe people remember my temper. I've had some moments I'm not proud of, although I'd like to think they're the exception, not the rule. Still, it's kind of disappointing."

He went to play in Europe in the fall since he was still fully exempt on the European Tour. A major champion is exempt in Europe for ten years. He filled out an entry for Q-School and went back to second stage. He played well there and made the finals, but finished tied for 64th—six shots away from getting fully exempt status back, meaning he would begin 2010 as only a partially exempt player. "There are some days when I think I should just walk away and find something else to do with my life," he said. "I know I enjoyed the extra time at home with my kids after the surgery. I could get used to that very quickly.

"But golf is what I've done and what I've loved and what I've done well for as long as I can remember. I still think I'm capable of playing well again. I don't think I'm rationalizing when I say that the shoulder is what's put me in this situation. Before I got hurt, I had a great year in '06 and a pretty good year while I was already feeling the pain in '07.

"I should have stopped playing sooner than I did in '08. I cost myself a lot of chances to play fully exempt and healthy in '09. But there's really no point in second-guessing myself now. The question is, what do I want to do in 2010? I can go play in Europe, which is something I've enjoyed doing in the past, but that's going to mean extra travel and more time away from my family.

"Or I can get into as many tournaments as possible off my past champion's status, hope I have some luck getting sponsor exemptions, and play a few Nationwide events and a few European events so I'll stay sharp the weeks I'm not on the tour. That isn't exactly ideal, but I think I need to make a plan and then stick to it—whatever that plan might turn out to be.

"I've done a lot of thinking about my future these past few

months, really since I knew I had to have the surgery. My problem is I tend to overthink everything. Usually you'd think it would be good to think things through completely before you make a decision, but I think them through to the point of paralysis. I need to start to make decisions and take action."

He smiled. "I'm forty. If you look at a lot of other guys, there's no reason why I can't play well in my forties if I stay healthy. I still love the game, even though it frustrates me sometimes. I think it frustrates us all sometimes—even Tiger."

IT WAS TIGER WOODS'S frustration with his swing, even at a time when he was dominating the sport back in 2002, that helped something happen for Mike Weir, Jim Furyk, Ben Curtis, and Shaun Micheel in 2003.

That's not to say that Woods would have won all four majors that year if he hadn't decided to change his swing, but in all likelihood he would have been a bigger factor. He never played in the last group on any major weekend that year. He seriously contended once—at the British Open. None of the four winners had to play with him on Sunday, and three of them didn't even have to think about him.

As Furyk put it in describing how he felt on Father's Day morning: "The pressure came from having no excuses if I didn't win. I had the lead, I felt in control of my game, and Tiger was nowhere in sight. Realistically, I knew he wasn't going to go out and shoot 61 that day and catch me. It was all on me."

Furyk came through. So did the other three winners: Weir ramming home one clutch putt after another including the one on 18 to get into the playoff with Len Mattiace; Curtis making the 10-footer on 18 for par, which he thought he had to make to have a chance at a playoff; Micheel hitting one of the great shots in major championship history on the 18th hole at Oak Hill.

For each man, the change of life occurred in different ways. Furyk, the established star whom everyone was waiting to see win a major, had to take the smallest step up. He was, as he says, ready for it. Even so, Tabitha Furyk noticed a change in the way she and her husband were viewed on tour.

"There's a different level of respect," she said. "People look at you and know you're going to be around for a while because your husband has won a major. You're part of a much smaller club than the club of guys who have won tournaments. You notice it. People *do* look at you differently and, in some ways, treat you differently."

Mike Weir was also an established winner when he won the Masters, though he was not at Furyk's level. He was already a major celebrity in Canada but not in the United States. He still remembers returning to the tour in Charlotte a few weeks after his victory at Augusta and pulling open his locker upon arriving.

"There must have been fifty Masters flags put in there by other guys [players] that they wanted signed for charity events," Weir said. "I did a double take. At that moment I knew that my week-to-week life, even among my peers, was never going to be the same."

Even so, what Weir and Furyk went through in terms of change of life pales in comparison to Curtis and Micheel. Half the players on tour had no idea who Curtis was when he won. Players knew Micheel because he'd been on and off the tour for nine years, but he was considered a guy who'd had a good year if he didn't have to go back to Q-School. Prior to 2003, he had accomplished that feat twice in his career.

Since their victories, both Curtis and Micheel have heard many whispering that they were flukes. That's completely unfair. Pitching a no-hitter, one brilliant day in what is often an ordinary career, is a fluke. Upsetting Roger Federer can be a fluke — a bad day by the greatest tennis player ever or an especially brilliant one by the man pulling the upset. Leading a major championship for 18 holes or even 36 holes is often a fluke, a flash of brilliance by a player never heard from again. That may explain why Billy Andrade didn't take Micheel that seriously after 36 holes at Oak Hill.

But winning a major championship—72 holes of golf, the last 18 played under extraordinary pressure because of what is at stake—isn't a fluke. It may never happen again, but it isn't a fluke. Consider some other one-time major champions of the past thirty years: Lanny Wadkins, Fred Couples, Davis Love III, Tom Kite, Craig Stadler, Paul Azinger, and David Duval. Wadkins and Kite are in the Hall of Fame; Couples and Love will almost certainly get there. Consider also some players who have never won a major: Kenny Perry, Colin Montgomerie, Sergio Garcia, Adam Scott, Chip Beck, and John Cook—all outstanding players who have come close (except for Scott) and never crossed the finish line.

Not to mention Len Mattiace, Stephen Leaney, Thomas Bjorn, and Chad Campbell, all of whom are still waiting—seven years later—to take that final step and make themselves part of the golfing pantheon.

As Kite said when he finally won his major, the 1992 U.S. Open at age forty-two, "Now I know what the opening line of my obituary will say: 'U.S. Open champion.'"

As wonderful as that feeling is for anyone who wins a major, especially when it's a first-time win, there is no doubting the challenges that come with all those life changes. "I don't think you change," Curtis said. "But the way people look at you changes completely."

Furyk came through it all relatively unscathed, though he clearly chafes at not having added a second major, one that would almost surely clinch a Hall of Fame spot for him someday. Weir has had low moments but found a way back to the point where he too believes he can win again on one of golf's biggest stages.

Curtis and Micheel have bounced all over the map, wondering where their game got lost, finding it again, then seeing it slip away yet again. Even though they know that their victories weren't flukes—because they went through it—such suggestions still sting.

"I still remember walking on the range just before I was supposed to play at the Western [Open] a few years back," Micheel said. "A guy started yelling at me for an autograph. As I was walking, I said, like I always do [and as almost every player on tour does], 'I can't sign before I play; I'm happy to sign anything you've got afterward.'

"Most people understand when you say that. They know you've got a job to do and you're a few minutes from your tee time and you're trying to prepare. It's a little like asking a pitcher warming up in the bullpen before a baseball game to stop and sign autographs.

"This guy just ripped into me. 'Who do you think you are, Micheel? You got lucky one week in your life, and you're too good to sign autographs?' The guy got to me. I turned around and gave it back to him, which I shouldn't have. Looking back now, I realize I let him get to me. But hearing that bothered me." He smiled. "I guess you could say if his goal was to upset me, it worked."

Regardless of all that, all four players love the memories of their Moment. They will happily take the extra pressure, the demands on their time, the criticisms, and the frustrations in return for the way they felt on that one Sunday afternoon in their lives when everything they had worked for since they were kids reached the climax they had often dreamed about.

Weir can still remember what it felt like to make the tying putt at 18 and the look in his wife's eyes when he said, 'I did it,' moments later on Augusta's 10th green. Furyk can still feel the chill that ran through him as the tears overcame him walking onto the 18th green at Olympia Fields, and how it felt to hug his father soon after that. Curtis still hears Andy Sutton's voice saying, 'Ben, you've won the Open,' and remembers choking up while holding the Claret Jug and thinking about his grandfather.

And Micheel can still close his eyes and remember jogging up the hill to the 18th green at Oak Hill and seeing his golf ball sitting two inches from the flagstick.

"I can still hear the cheers ringing in my ears," he said, a smile creasing his face more than six years after it happened. "When you play golf all your life, you fantasize that moment in one form or another. You dream it, you hope for it, you act it out, but you know it may never happen.

"That day, it happened for me. I still get chills whenever I think about it. I doubt, regardless of what happens the rest of my career and the rest of my life, that will ever change."

Acknowledgments

THERE HAVE BEEN MOMENTS since I first began this book two years ago when I thought I would never finish.

In the summer of 2008 when I *thought* I was getting close to finishing the reporting, I got a call from Rocco Mediate, asking if I'd like to work with him on a book detailing his remarkable U.S. Open experience at Torrey Pines a few weeks earlier. I couldn't resist: Rocco was a friend, a good story, and a good storyteller. I said yes, did the book, and have no regrets. It landed on the *New York Times* bestseller list, which proves I was right: Rocco was a good story and a good storyteller.

I explained to the players I had been working with on *Moment of Glory* the reason for the delay, and they were all extremely patient. Not that the publication of this book was going to change their lives—winning a major championship or just missing winning one does that for you—but because they had already put in a good deal of time and effort into helping me with the book and were entitled to see it come to fruition.

Delay number two came late last June when I went to a doctor for a routine stress test and ended up undergoing septuple bypass surgery four days later. (Septuple is seven for those of you keeping score at home.) I think it's fair to say there is no such thing as good timing for something like that—although the fact that it probably saved my life would weigh in its favor—but this was especially inauspicious.

The PGA Tour was coming to Washington the same week I was to have the surgery, meaning I would have been able to wrap up the research with my final round of interviews without leaving my ZIP code. Instead, once I had recovered from the surgery, I had to go to Akron, Greensboro, and Atlanta to wrap up the research. Not to mention the fact that I wasn't exactly productive in the weeks after the surgery. (I did get to watch a lot of golf. I'm willing to bet serious money that I'm in a *very* small handful of people who watched every single minute of the John Deere Classic on TV this past July.)

I say all that by way of thanking everyone who helped me with the book for their extraordinary patience as I waded my way through to the finish line. The number of times I had to go back to Mike Weir, Jim Furyk, Ben Curtis, and Shaun Micheel to catch up and finish up is proof of what good guys they are. I'm also grateful to their wives; Bricia Weir, Tabitha Furyk, Candace Curtis, and Stephanie Micheel were also extremely helpful.

Thanks also to the runners-up, for whom this subject wasn't nearly as enjoyable to talk about, I'm sure. Stephen Leaney and Chad Campbell talked at length and in detail about their experience. As is apparent in the book, it was far more difficult for Len Mattiace and Thomas Bjorn. Len and I spent a good deal of time talking about *why* it was so difficult for him to relive the 2003 Masters. I'm grateful to him for hearing me out and giving me all he could and also to his wife, Kristen, for spending time with me. Thomas Bjorn simply didn't want to talk about or, I'm guessing, even think about Royal St. George's. I offered to talk by phone if that would be easier, or even e-mail. He politely refused. I was disappointed, but I certainly understand.

———

IT TAKES MANY, MANY people who play golf and work in golf to get me through a book like this. For this book I'm grateful to Davis Love III, Zach Johnson, Billy Andrade, Paul Goydos, Mike Furyk, Brennan Little, Andy Sutton, and Mike Cowen. Special thanks to Butch Harmon for his willingness to talk about his split with Tiger Woods — not one of his fondest memories, I'm sure. The number of people who helped me with much-needed background information, not to mention photos, at all of golf's various governing bodies is almost uncountable, but I'll give it a shot. At Augusta: Glenn Greenspan and his very young but very helpful successor, Steve Ethun. At the USGA: David Fay, Mike Butz, Mike Davis, Mary Lopuszynski, Craig Smith, David Fanucchi, and Peter Kowalski. At the European PGA Tour: Mitchell Platts and Kate Wright. At the PGA of America: Joe Steranka, the groovy Julius Mason, and Bob Denney. At the PGA Tour: Tim Finchem, Marty Caffey, Dave Lancer, Denise Taylor, Todd Budnick, James Cramer, John Bush, Joel Schuchmann, Chris Reimer, and Guy Scheipers.

Others connected to the tour who always deserve thanks: the one and only Henry Hughes and also the one and only Sid Wilson.

And, as always, the rules guys: Mark Russell (not to mention Laura and Alex), Jon Brendle, Slugger White, Steve Rintoul, and Mike Shea.

If the subjects of this book were patient, then what about my editor and my agent? Michael Pietsch at Little, Brown and Company is blessed with great patience, which is needed to be my editor. Esther Newberg, my agent for twenty-six books now, has no patience at all but somehow puts up with me. Thanks, as always, to their staffs: Vanessa Kehren, Eve Rabinovits, Heather Fain, Heather Rizzo, Marlena Bittner, Katherine Molina (emeritus), and Holly

Wilkinson (always emeritus) at Little, Brown; and Kari Stuart, John Delaney, and Liz Farrell at ICM.

Anyone who reads my books may well know the following names by heart: Keith and Barbie Drum; Jackson Diehl and Jean Halperin; Ed and Lois Brennan; David and Linda Maraniss; Lexie Verdon and Steve Barr; Jill and Holland Mickle; Bill and Jane Brill; Terry and Patti Hanson; blogmaster David Stewart; Bob and Anne DeStefano; Mary Carillo; Bud Collins and Anita Claussen; Doug and Beth Doughty; David Teel; Stan Kasten, John Dever, Eric Spitz (yes, Eric), Gary Cohen, Beth (Shumway) Brown; Beth Sherry-Downes; Bob Socci; Pete Van Poppel; Omar Nelson; Frank DaVinney; Chet Gladchuk; Eric Ruden; Scott Strasemeier; Billy Stone; Mike Werteen; Chris Day; Chris Knocke; Andrew Thompson; Phil Hoffmann; Joe Speed; Jack Hecker; Steve (Moose) Stirling; Bob Beretta; Jim and Tiffany Cantelupe; Derek and Christina Klein; Anthony and Kristen Noto; Pete Teeley; Bob Zurfluh; Vivian Thompson; Phil Hochberg; Al Hunt; Wayne Zell; Mike and David Sanders; Bob Whitmore; Tony Kornheiser; Mike Wilbon; Mark Maske; Ken Denlinger; Matt Rennie; Matt Vita; Jon DeNunzio; Kathy Orton; Camille Powell; Dan Steinberg; Chris Ryan; Harry Kantarian; Jim Rome; Travis Rodgers; Jason Stewart; Mike Purkey; Bob Edwards; Tom and Jane Goldman; Jake Pleet; Mike Gastineau; Mary Bromley; Kenny and Christina Lewis; Dick Hoops and Joanie (Mrs. Hoops) Weiss; Jim O'Connell; Bob and Eileen Ryan; Frank Hannigan; Jerry Tarde; Mike O'Malley; Larry Dorman; Jeff D'Alessio; Marsha Edwards; Jay and Natalie Edwards; Len and Gwyn Edwards-Dieterle; Chris Edwards and John Cutcher; Aunt Joan; and Neil Oxman, Bill Leahey, Andy North, Steve Bisciotti, Kevin Byrne, Dick Cass, Mike Muehr, Martha Brendle, Joe Durant, Gary (Grits) Crandall, Drew Miceli, Bob Low, Steve Flesch, Brian Henninger, and Tom and Hilary Watson.

Thanks also to Tom Stathakes, for taking a chance on a somewhat out-of-the-box writer to do Golf Channel commentaries, and to all those I worked with at TGC this year: Joe Riley, Kristi Setaro, Scott Rude, and Lori Sullivan. Thanks also to Joe Yasharoff, Larry Duvall, and Manda Gross at Comcast, D.C.

More of the usual suspects. Basketball people: Gary Williams, Mike Krzyzewski, Rick Barnes, Roy Williams, Brad and Seth Greenberg, Mike Brey, Jeff Jones, Billy Lange, Jim Crews, Karl Hobbs, Fran Dunphy, Jim Calhoun, Jim Boeheim (the klutz), Billy Donovan, Larry Shyatt, Tom Brennan, Tommy Amaker, Dave Odom, Jim Larranaga, Mack McCarthy, Pat Flannery, Emmette Davis, Ralph Willard, Tim Frank, and David Stern, our differences on the WNBA notwithstanding. Frank Sullivan always deserves his own sentence.

As you get older, you have more doctors in your life. Thanks as always to the orthopods: Eddie McDevitt, Bob Arciero, Dean Taylor, and Gus Mazzocca, and to the world's best trainer (ask the kids at Army), Tim Kelly. Thanks also to my doctors: Joe Vassallo, for insisting I get a stress test, and Steve Boyce, who managed to rip me open and put me back together again. "The good news for you," he told me, "is I do 500 of these a year." To which I replied, "I'm not all that concerned about the other 499."

Howard Garfinkel turned eighty this summer; may he be around to smoke and give me a hard time for at least another eighty years. Tom Konchalski is ageless and will always be the only honest man in the gym.

The swimmers who will inspire my comeback in 2010: Jeff Roddin (the newlywed), Jason Crist, Clay F. Britt (who broke the world record this past year by retiring for the hundredth time), Wally Dicks, Mark Pugliese, Paul Doremus, Danny Pick (who can *really* cook), Erik (Dr. Post) Osborne, John Craig, Doug Chestnut, Peter Ward, Penn Bates, Carole Kammel, Margot Pettijohn, Tom Denes, A. J. Block, Mary Dowling, and the still-missed Mike Fell.

The China Doll/Shanghai Village Gang: Aubre Jones, Rob Ades, Jack Kvancz, Joe McKeown (shivering in Chicago), Bob Campbell (MLB security honcho), Pete Dowling, Chris Wallace (who has moved so far right, he may be left soon), Arnie (the Horse) Heft, Stanley Copeland, Reid Collins, Harry Huang, George (sigh) Solomon, Ric McPherson, Geoff Kaplan, Jeff Gemunder, Joe Greenberg, and Murray Lieberman, who gets extra kudos for sending me to Dr. Vassallo when my doctor retired a couple of years back. Red, Zang, and Hymie will always be there in spirit.

The Rio Gang: Tate Armstrong, Mark Alarie, Clay (LB) Buckley, and Terry Chili.

The Feinstein advisory board: Drummer, Frank Mastrandrea, Wes Seeley, Dave Kindred, and Brill, who has already booked a plane ticket for Duke's next Bowl appearance.

And of course: the world's two best kids (not that I'm biased), Danny and Brigid; Bobby, Jennifer, Matthew, and Brian; Margaret, David, Ethan, and Ben; Marlynn and Cheryl; and last—but certainly not least—my wife, Christine.

The past couple of years have often been challenging, to put it mildly. I would not be here—literally or figuratively—without all of the people named above. It takes a village. At the very least.

Index

JOHN FEINSTEIN is the bestselling author of *Are You Kidding Me?* (with Rocco Mediate), *Living on the Black, Tales from Q School, Last Dance, Next Man Up, Let Me Tell You a Story* (with Red Auerbach), *Caddy for Life, Open, The Punch, The Last Amateurs, The Majors, A March to Madness, A Civil War, A Good Walk Spoiled, A Season on the Brink, A Season Inside, Forever's Team, Play Ball, Hard Courts,* and four sports mystery novels for young readers. He writes for the *Washington Post,* Washingtonpost.com, the *Sporting News,* and *Golf Digest,* and is a regular commentator on National Public Radio's *Morning Edition.* For more information about John Feinstein, please visit www.feinsteinonthebrink.com.